The Second Great Awakening and the Transcendentalists

Recent Titles in
Greenwood Guides to Historic Events, 1500–1900

The Dreyfus Affair
Leslie Derfler

The War of 1812
David S. Heidler and Jeanne T. Heidler

The Atlantic Slave Trade
Johannes Postma

Manifest Destiny
David S. Heidler and Jeanne T. Heidler

American Railroads in the Nineteenth Century
Augustus J. Veenendaal

Reconstruction
Claudine L. Ferrell

The Spanish-American War
Kenneth E. Hendrickson, Jr.

The American Revolution
Joseph C. Morton

The French Revolution
Linda S. Frey and Marsha L. Frey

The French and Indian War
Alfred A. Cave

The Lewis and Clark Expedition
Harry William Fritz

The Second Great Awakening and the Transcendentalists

BARRY HANKINS

Greenwood Guides to Historic Events, 1500–1900
Linda S. Frey and Marsha L. Frey, Series Editors

GREENWOOD PRESS
Westport, Connecticut • London

Library of Congress Cataloging-in-Publication Data

Hankins, Barry, 1956–
   The Second Great Awakening and the Transcendentalists / Barry Hankins.
      p. cm. — (Greenwood guides to historic events, 1500–1900, ISSN 1538–442X)
   Includes bibliographical references and index.
   ISBN 0–313–31848–4 (alk. paper)
   1. Second Great Awakening. 2. Transcendentalism (New England) 3. African
Americans—Religion—History. I. Title. II. Series.
BR525.H323   2004
277.3'081—dc22   2003026705

British Library Cataloguing in Publication Data is available.

Library of Congress Catalog Card Number: 2003026705
ISBN: 0–313–31848–4
ISSN: 1538–442X

First published in 2004

Greenwood Press, 88 Post Road West, Westport, CT 06881
An imprint of Greenwood Publishing Group, Inc.
www.greenwood.com

Printed in the United States of America

The paper used in this book complies with the
Permanent Paper Standard issued by the National
Information Standards Organization (Z39.48–1984).

10 9 8 7 6 5 4 3 2 1

This book is dedicated to Robert D. Linder.

CONTENTS

Photo essay follows page 108.

SERIES FOREWORD

American statesman Adlai Stevenson stated that "We can chart our future clearly and wisely only when we know the path which has led to the present." This series, Greenwood Guides to Historic Events, 1500–1900, is designed to illuminate that path by focusing on events from 1500 to 1900 that have shaped the world. The years 1500 to 1900 include what historians call the Early Modern Period (1500 to 1789, the onset of the French Revolution) and part of the modern period (1789 to 1900).

In 1500, an acceleration of key trends marked the beginnings of an interdependent world and the posing of seminal questions that changed the nature and terms of intellectual debate. The series closes with 1900, the inauguration of the twentieth century. This period witnessed profound economic, social, political, cultural, religious, and military changes. An industrial and technological revolution transformed the modes of production, marked the transition from a rural to an urban economy, and ultimately raised the standard of living. Social classes and distinctions shifted. The emergence of the territorial and later the national state altered man's relations with and view of political authority. The shattering of the religious unity of the Roman Catholic world in Europe marked the rise of a new pluralism. Military revolutions changed the nature of warfare. The books in this series emphasize the complexity and diversity of the human tapestry and include political, economic, social, intellectual, military, and cultural topics. Some of the authors focus on events in U.S. history such as the Salem Witchcraft Trials, the American Revolution, the abolitionist movement, and the Civil War. Others analyze European topics, such as the Reformation and Counter

Reformation and the French Revolution. Still others bridge cultures and
continents by examining the voyages of discovery, the Atlantic slave
trade, and the Age of Imperialism. Some focus on intellectual questions
that have shaped the modern world, such as Darwin's *Origin of Species* or
on turning points such as the Age of Romanticism. Others examine
defining economic, religious, or legal events or issues such as the building of the railroads, the Second Great Awakening, and abolitionism.
Heroes (e.g., Lewis and Clark), scientists (e.g., Darwin), military leaders
(e.g., Napoleon), poets (e.g., Byron), stride across its pages. Many of
these events were seminal in that they marked profound changes or
turning points. The Scientific Revolution, for example, changed the way
individuals viewed themselves and their world.

The authors, acknowledged experts in their fields, synthesize key
events, set developments within the larger historical context, and, most
important, present a well-balanced, well-written account that integrates
the most recent scholarship in the field.

The topics were chosen by an advisory board composed of historians, high school history teachers, and school librarians to support the
curriculum and meet student research needs. The volumes are designed
to serve as resources for student research and to provide clearly written
interpretations of topics central to the secondary school and lower-level
undergraduate history curriculum. Each author outlines a basic
chronology to guide the reader through often confusing events and a
historical overview to set those events within a narrative framework.
Three to five topical chapters underscore critical aspects of the event. In
the final chapter the author examines the impact and consequences of
the event. Biographical sketches furnish background on the lives and
contributions of the players who strut across this stage. Ten to fifteen
primary documents ranging from letters to diary entries, song lyrics,
proclamations, and posters, cast light on the event, provide material for
student essays, and stimulate a critical engagement with the sources.
Introductions identify the authors of the documents and the main
issues. In some cases a glossary of selected terms is provided as a guide
to the reader. Each work contains an annotated bibliography of recom-
mended books, articles, CD-ROMs, Internet sites, videos, and films that
set the materials within the historical debate.

These works will lead to a more sophisticated understanding of
the events and debates that have shaped the modern world and will

stimulate a more active engagement with the issues that still affect us. It has been a particularly enriching experience to work closely with such dedicated professionals. We have come to know and value even more highly the authors in this series and our editors at Greenwood, particularly Kevin Ohe. In many cases they have become more than colleagues; they have become friends. To them and to future historians we dedicate this series.

Linda S. Frey
University of Montana

Marsha L. Frey
Kansas State University

PREFACE

By any statistical measure, the United States remains at the outset of the twenty-first century the most religious industrialized nation on earth. More than 85 percent of Americans profess belief in God and nearly that number identify in some way with one of the myriad Christian denominations, which is not to mention the growing numbers of adherents to non-Christian faiths. More than half of Americans are formally members of a church, synagogue, or mosque, and weekly attendance at houses of worship is usually estimated at roughly 40 percent of the population. While the foundation for this level of religiosity can be traced back to the Puritans of the seventeenth century, two intense periods of religious revival profoundly shaped the tenor of American Christianity: The First Great Awakening of the 1730s and 1740s, and the Second Great Awakening of the first half of the nineteenth century. The latter, along with the development of an alternative and distinctly American way of being religious known as Transcendentalism, comprise the subject of this book.

There are many fine books on these movements, as the endnotes and bibliography will show. This volume is intended to condense and synthesize the best scholarship available and make the story of nineteenth-century revivalism and Transcendentalism accessible to general readers, especially to students working on term papers and other similar projects related to these subjects. The book starts with a general survey of the Second Great Awakening in chapter 1, and moves to an overview of Transcendentalism in chapter 2. The remaining four chapters are topical, seeking to show specific ways in which these religious impulses profoundly shaped American culture. Following these chapters are a series of mini-biographies of significant revivalist and Transcendentalist figures, a collection of excerpts from important primary documents, a glossary of selected terms, an annotated bibliography, and an index.

ACKNOWLEDGMENTS

The author would like to thank Baylor University for a sabbatical leave to write this book and for the support of the J. M. Dawson Institute of Church-State Studies and its director, Derek Davis, and the Baylor history department and its chair, James SoRelle. Lee Canipe and Marshall Johnston served as graduate assistants tracking down sources and documents while the project was in its research stage. Graduate assistant Randa Barton compiled the index. Series editor Marsha Frey's corrections and stylistic suggestions were invaluable, but any errors that remain are the author's. Greenwood Press editor Mike Hermann was also of great assistance, especially as the project entered the production phase.

CHRONOLOGY OF EVENTS

1706	Missionaries granted access to slaves with caveat that any conversions did not equal physical freedom
1729	Slave rebellion asserting that baptized slaves should be freed
1730s–1740s	First Great Awakening
1775–1783	American Revolution
1760	James McGready born in Pennsylvania
1780	Methodist conference issues statement condemning slavery
1786	McGready converts to the Presbyterian faith
1786–1797	Blacks grow to almost 25 percent of Methodist membership
1787	U.S. Constitution adopted
1789	John Leland proposes an antislavery resolution at the Baptist General Committee of Virginia
1790s	Appearance of black pastors in Virginia and the South
1790	First national census—94 percent of Americans live in the original 13 colonies
1791	First Amendment and Bill of Rights adopted
1792	Discrimination prompts black Methodists in Philadelphia to form the African Methodist Episcopal (A.M.E.) Church

1793–1813	Black membership in Baptist churches grows from 18,000 to 40,000
1797	Benevolence Empire begins, characterized by widespread social reforms
1798	McGready leads first stirrings of mass conversions in Kentucky
1899	Red River and Muddy River, Kentucky, revivals, led by McGready, William Hodges, John Rankin, and John and William McGee
1801	Barton Stone organizes Cane Ridge Revival with as many as 25,000 in attendance; acknowledged beginning of Second Great Awakening
1809	General Assembly of Presbyterians rules against Cumberland, Kentucky, Presbytery's practice of ordaining uneducated revival preachers
1812–1826	Various churches create missionizing social-action groups: Home and Foreign Mission Society, American Bible Society, American Tract Society
1816	A.M.E. officially splits from white Methodist denomination
1820	Census shows 25 percent of Americans live outside of the original 13 colonies
October 1821	Charles Grandison Finney's conversion
May 1822	Denmark Vesey plans slave revolt for mid-June; put down before it started and Vesey executed
1824	Charles Grandison Finney sent to western New York as a missionary
1824–1827	Finney leads revivals throughout New England
1826	Theodore Weld converted by Finney, becomes abolitionist alongside William Lloyd Garrison
1828	Virginia, like most of the South, rules that black congregations must have white representatives at the general assemblies, inspiring the creation of all-black denominations and assemblies
September 1830–March 1831	Finney holds Rochester, New York, revival—established him as an urban revivalist

1831 September– April	Finney invited to Boston to preach with Lyman Beecher and other conservative revivalists
August 21	Nat Turner leads bloodiest slave uprising to date
October 30	Turner apprehended and executed on November 11
1832	Stone and Alexander Campbell align and form the Disciples of Christ
1833	Massachusetts becomes the last state to end tax support for religion
1836	Finney moves to the Broadway Tabernacle in New York
	Finney invited by "Lane Rebels" to teach at Oberlin College; resigns his pastorate in New York and moves to Ohio
1836	Emerson's *Nature* published
September 19	First meeting in Boston of what would become the "Transcendentalists"
July 15, 1838	Emerson gives controversial commencement address at Harvard
1840s–1850s	Transcendentalists join abolitionist activism
1840	Liberty Party runs antislavery candidate for President, James Birney
1841	First communal Transcendentalist effort, Brook Farm, begins
June 1843	Bronson Alcott's Fruitlands opens
December 1843	Fruitlands experiment ends
1845	Finney defends women's praying and participating in assemblies
1847	End of Brook Farm community
1850s	Women's rights movement becomes linked with abolition movement
1850s	Republican Party formed with antislavery plank of platform
1850	Nearly 50 percent of Americans live outside of the territories of the original 13 colonies
1854	Thoreau's *Walden* published

1858	Revival of 1858
1860	Abraham Lincoln elected as Republican President
1869	Susan B. Anthony, Elizabeth Cady Stanton, and others organize National Woman Suffrage Association
1920	Nineteenth Amendment gives women the right to vote

CHAPTER 1

THE SECOND GREAT AWAKENING: AN OVERVIEW

In the early twenty-first century, with much of American culture seemingly beyond the reach of religious influence, it is sometimes forgotten the extent to which the nation was shaped by revivals in its formative period. The revival movement known as the First Great Awakening of the 1730s and 1740s has been called America's first national event, and there is wide agreement among historians that it helped meld the colonies into a national unit, setting the stage for the American Revolution (1775–1783). Likewise, the Second Great Awakening of the first half of the nineteenth century helped shape the new nation in powerful ways. This second wave of Christian revivals, largely the subject of this book, was surprising because it seemed to many that following the Revolution a very different kind of religion would become dominant in America—a religion based on reason and promoted by figures of the Enlightenment such as Thomas Jefferson. Sometimes called *deism*, this form of religion downplayed or dismissed traditional Christian ideas having to do with the supernatural and was thus quite at odds with revivalism. Enlightenment deism, in other words, held to the morality of the Old and New Testaments, while dismissing as myth such things as miracles, the deity of Christ, and his resurrection from the dead. For the deist, God was like a watchmaker who created the world, then stepped back and let it run on its own according to the laws of nature. Deists rejected the idea that God intervened in history through revivals or any other supernatural means. Moreover, they tended to emphasize the goodness of human beings and their natural capacity for understanding the world through the use of reason. This was opposed to the Puritan, or what is called the evangelical Protestant, idea that humans were fallen creatures greatly in need of God's grace. Evangelical Protestants taught that the Bible was the sole authority in matters of faith and that individuals needed a life-transforming, supernatural conversion that would lead to a holy life. During the quarter century after the Revolution almost all of the elite colleges, most of them in New England, switched from evangelical Protestantism to this new Enlightenment faith, prompting Lyman Beecher, one of the great Protestant preachers of the day, to complain that at Yale the students knew more about Rousseau and Voltaire than they did about Christ. Only Princeton remained evangelical.

In addition to the challenges posed by Enlightenment deism, the Revolution affected American Christianity in other ways as well, most of which were negative. For example, the war brought about the destruction of church property, meaning that many people had no place to worship regularly. Also, the fervent support many preachers gave to the Revolution alienated the people in their churches, many of whom were either opposed to the Revolution or unsure whether or not they should rebel against England. One preacher even turned over a church's songbooks to soldiers so they could rip out the pages and use the paper for musket wadding. One can only imagine how the elders of such a church might have felt if they were cool toward the Revolution in the first place. It is a well-known fact that Protestant preachers supported the war in much greater percentages than the people as a whole. Often this was because the preachers believed that the movement of God during the revivals of the First Great Awakening was the beginning of a larger work God intended to do in the world. They, quite naturally, tended to believe that the Revolution might be part of this larger work and so they easily fused patriotism and religious fervor.

One other factor that posed a challenge for religion during and after the Revolution was migration to the West. Prior to independence, the British had forbidden the colonists to move beyond the Appalachian Mountains, which was territory the colonists had helped take from the French during the French and Indian War (1754–1763). With that restriction gone after the Revolution, many Americans were poised for a foray into the new territory. The first national census of 1790 revealed that 94 percent of Americans lived in the original 13 states. By 1820, one-quarter lived beyond the line that had demarcated the western edge of the original 13, and by 1850 nearly one-half lived outside the original states. It is estimated that close to 800,000 people from New England alone immigrated to the west between 1790 and 1820. As people moved westward they left their churches and often their pastors behind. With few churches and pastors, church participation declined and ceased to be a habit for many who settled in the new western communities. As the virtual founder of American Methodism Francis Asbury wrote, "[W]hen I reflect that not one in a hundred came here to get religion, but rather to get plenty of good land, I think it will be well if some or many do not eventually lose their souls." Or, as Andrew Fulton, a missionary to Tennessee from the Seceder Presbyterian Church of Scotland, put it, "[In Nashville] and indeed almost all the newly formed towns in this western colony, there are few religious people."[1]

These factors made the years from about 1776 to 1800 a difficult period for traditional, evangelical Protestantism. Cognizant of the problems Protestant Christianity faced, a group of Presbyterian ministers met in 1798 to discuss what they perceived as religious decline, or declension, as it has been called. These educated elite ministers may have had an exaggerated view of declension because they overlooked the growth of the Methodists and Baptists among the common people—those viewed as rabble by the elites—and were alarmed by the growth of Catholicism, which they viewed as a threat to the Protestant consensus that would continue to exist through much of the nineteenth century. Among New England elites, especially in the Congregational Churches, Unitarianism was becoming popular, which appeared to orthodox ministers to be the appropriation of the Enlightenment rationalistic views that were threatening the faith. This more liberal brand of Christian faith was also moving into the frontier. Methodist preacher James Smith, itinerating near Lexington, recorded in 1795 that "the Universalists, joining with the Deists, had given Christianity a deadly stab hereabouts." About that same time David Barrow reported that "deists, nothingarians, and anythingarians" were predominant in Kentucky and were strengthened by the recent publication of Thomas Paine.[2] While these and the many other accounts of the threat of Enlightenment rationalism may have been exaggerated, there can be little doubt that the orthodox Protestant ministers of America were convinced in the 1790s that biblical Christianity was about to be replaced or snuffed out by deism. Preacher after preacher recorded the apparent threat in the most dire warnings imaginable.

Ignoring the Methodists and Baptists, dismissing the Unitarians, or fearing Catholics and deists, these Protestant ministers saw the declension of their own kind of religion everywhere they looked. They believed something had to be done, and clearly the government was not going to do anything about this decline. With the adoption of the U.S. Constitution in 1787, then the First Amendment and the rest of the Bill of Rights in 1791, the status of religion in the new republic was left to the people. With the exception of the prohibition against religious tests for office, there is no mention of religion in the body of the Constitution, and the First Amendment states explicitly that the federal government will not establish religion or prohibit the free exercise thereof. Some state governments continued for a time to use tax monies to support religion, but this practice would be phased out in all states by 1833, which meant that if the nation were going to remain religious, the impetus was going to have to come from private sources; government was not going to help. While combating Enlightenment deism in their own towns, eastern elite ministers were also concerned about the West, so they began to form missionary societies to take the gospel there. Understandably, in fundraising efforts leaders of these societies tended to emphasize how bad things were out west, which furthered the somewhat exaggerated view of declension.

On the heels of this religious decline, real and imagined, and in conjunction with government getting out of the business of promoting and supporting religion, America entered what has been called the Second Great Awakening. Although the practice of revival had been around for three-quarters of a century, in 1800 the word revival first came into use. Ministers chose it apparently because it conveyed the need to recapture the religious vitality of an earlier day. In this sense it was a term of rebuke for the decline of religion that had occurred. While there was not a continuous series of revivals, they did wax and wane, hot and cold, from 1800 until 1858, with the most intense period being the twenties and thirties. In other words, during the Early National period and leading up to the Civil War, waves of revivals were common occurrences every few years in various parts of the United States.

While the term *revival* was not common before 1800, the practice of what came to be called revivalism was fairly well established by the end of the eighteenth century. Revivalism is best defined as a preaching method, primarily within Protestantism, which is geared toward eliciting immediate conversions to the Christian faith. Typically, a revivalist preacher, either in a church or quite commonly in the open air of a field or city street corner, gathers an audience and preaches the need for salvation. The preacher, almost always a man in that time period, seeks to convince his listeners that they are wretched sinners in need of God's grace. While many such preachers emphasized sin and its resulting damnation, many others emphasized God's love and his desire to rescue souls from the threat of hell. This type of preaching began among Protestant preachers such as John Wesley, George Whitefield, and Theodore Freylinghhuysen during the mid-eighteenth-century Methodist revivals in England and the First Great Awakening in America. Just as the First Great Awakening shaped the end of the Colonial period of American history, the Second Awakening shaped the Early National period and even the rest of the nineteenth century and into the twentieth. As any late-night channel surfer knows, one can find revivalist preaching on television any day of the week even today.

In addition to individual conversion, the revivals engendered a series of reform movements that helped shape the political and social culture of the new nation, and they ensured that America would continue to be broadly Protestant until immigration in the late nineteenth century brought increasing numbers of Catholics and Jews to America's shores. In other words, the revivals of the Second Great Awakening stemmed the tide of declension and ensured that America's dominant religion would be evangelical Protestantism and not some form of Enlightenment deism.

While the largest, most intense, and memorable revivals early in the Second Great Awakening took place in the West, the first stirrings were actually on the eastern seaboard. This is understandable given that society was more stable there and churchgoing was still a habit. Revivals in America usually take place not so much among people who hear the gospel for the first time, but among those who have a basic understanding of the faith. Until at least the mid-twentieth century the vast majority of Americans had a working idea of the Christian faith whether they were believers or not. Revivals, therefore, often occurred among those who were raised in the faith but had not found it meaningful in their own lives.

One of these early stirrings took place at Yale University under the presidency of Timothy Dwight. Dwight was the grandson of the great preacher-theologian Jonathan Edwards, whose preaching was instrumental in the First Great Awakening and who became president of Princeton shortly before his untimely death in 1758. When Dwight arrived as president of Yale in 1797, he claimed he could find only two students who would admit belief in God. What Dwight meant, of course, was that the vast majority of students had ceased to believe in God as understood in the evangelical Protestant faith—that is, a God who was incarnate (made human) in Jesus Christ and worked supernaturally in the world. Most of Dwight's young charges had gone over to the deistic view of a God who created the natural order then stepped back to let it run according to Isaac Newton's laws of nature. Under Dwight's preaching in the Yale chapel services, a revival occurred among the students, resulting in about a third of them being converted by 1801. One of these converts became the noted American scientist Benjamin Silliman, who would later recall the Yale of his student days as "a little temple."

The revivals in New England were moderate by comparison to the West, and they were based on a modified Calvinist theology that was as simple as 1, 2, 3. Calvinism, in its purest form, stemmed from the great sixteenth-century French Protestant reformer John Calvin who spent most of his adult life in Geneva, Switzerland. Calvin and his followers, among whom were the Presbyterians, put great emphasis on God's sovereignty, which meant that it was God who decided to save sinners, not the sinners themselves who made the choice to be converted. Calvin and Calvinists even taught that some people were predestined to be saved while others were predestined to be damned. Again, it was God's sovereign choice. In its modified form Calvinism emphasized the following: (1) God's sovereignty, which meant that ultimately human destiny was in God's hands and that God was responsible for revival; (2) Human depravity, which meant that there was nothing people could do to make themselves right with God; and (3) Christ's atoning love, which meant that God, through Christ, wanted to save sinners from hell and damnation. While there were many conversions and rededications in New England, there were few emotional excesses. The Calvinist brand of revival, even its modified form, put much less emphasis on emotion than some other forms of the Christian faith.

The early western revivals of the Second Great Awakening were different in at least two respects. First, there was a much greater tendency to dispense with Calvinist theology altogether. In other words, preachers began to believe that people were responsible for their own destiny. If they wanted to be converted, they need not wait for a special movement of God. Rather, they could respond any time and any place. This led to the belief that human effort could actually make a revival more likely. Preachers attempted to create the circumstances in which people would make a free-will decision to follow Christ. Second, western revivals differed from the early eastern ones in that they were far more emotional. In fact, because of the diminished emphasis on Calvinist theology, preachers wanted to create an emotional atmosphere that would spur people to repentance for their sins. This was often done in open-air camp meetings where hundreds, and sometimes thousands, of people from farm communities would gather to hear several men preach the gospel over the course of several days. The first of these western camp meeting revivals took place at a place called Gasper River and the second at Cane Ridge, both in Kentucky. Together, these have been called The Great Revival.

The Great Revival

The Gasper River revival was led by a Scotch-Irish Presbyterian preacher named James McGready. Born probably in 1760 in Pennsylvania, McGready's family moved to Guilford County, North Carolina, when he was in his late teens. His faith and intellect were the stuff of good ministers, so his family sent him back to Pennsylvania to study with a Princeton-trained minister-tutor named John McMillan. McMillan taught boys in return for labor. They worked off their room and board. While studying with McMillan, McGready had his own conversion experience in 1786. It was not unusual in the eighteenth century for the conversion experience to come at the end of a long period of effort to live in accordance with Christian teaching, thus it was quite normal that McGready's own experience of conversion would come after he had already shown signs of pious Christian living.

Having been converted and trained under McMillan, McGready was licensed to preach in 1788. He then moved back to Guilford

County and preached there for about eight years. In North Carolina he developed his revivalistic preaching style and mentored several young preachers who would later, with McGready, have a significant influence on the beginnings of the Second Great Awakening in Kentucky. At the same time that he was winning converts and mentoring young preachers, however, McGready also incurred a good deal of opposition. Eventually, some of his own well-to-do parishioners were angered by his scathing critique of their ungodly ways. They threatened him, actually ransacking one of his church buildings and sending him a letter purportedly written in blood. McGready requested and received a transfer to a presbytery in Kentucky where some of his supporters had moved.

McGready left North Carolina in 1796 and moved to Kentucky where he began pastoring three congregations—Red River, Gasper River, and Muddy River—all in Logan County. This was an even more remote part of the frontier than McGready's childhood North Carolina and Pennsylvania, but Kentucky was growing fast as settlers moved there in droves. The state's population increased from roughly 73,000 in 1790 to more than 220,000 by 1800. Despite the best efforts of Baptists, Methodists, and Presbyterians, churches were not keeping pace with the growth. Kentucky was in many ways a secularized and sometimes lawless frontier. In his preaching, therefore, McGready vividly described hell, the ultimate consequence of an unconverted life, and he often posed the rhetorical question, "If I were converted, would I feel it and know it?"[3] But McGready was not the only one preaching for conversion. Five others, all trained in the same revival techniques and mentored by McGready back in North Carolina, were also in Kentucky, four of them in the Cumberland region. This influx of revivalist Presbyterian preachers and a youthful population recently removed from Virginia and North Carolina combined to produce the necessary chemistry for an outbreak of revival fervor.[4] During the summer of 1798 there were several stirrings that took place under McGready's preaching as people converted. The following summer, at Gasper River, a revival took place under McGready in which some fell to the ground, crying out that they were bound for hell. These summer revivals, though still small, were becoming something of a pattern, usually interrupted by the onset of winter.

In June 1800, the Red River congregation under McGready held a sacramental service to be assisted by two other ministers, William

Hodges and John Rankin, both McGready protégés. Also present were two preacher brothers, John and William McGee. William was Presbyterian and a McGready convert and student; John was Methodist. After McGready, Hodges, and Rankin had all spoken, William McGee went to the front of the room and slumped to a sitting position next to the pulpit. John McGee rose and began to speak, calling the congregation to repentance. As he spoke, he walked about the room where the people sat on log benches. One account of this meeting says that he was "shouting and exhorting with all possible energy and exctacy [sic]."[5] People fell to the floor, some of them children as young as 10. They cried out for God's mercy. While only 10 people were actually converted, McGready and others present believed they had seen an outpouring of God's spirit. McGready soon went to his Muddy River church and experienced a very similar outpouring. He then sent out notice for a sacramental service to be held at Gasper River in July.

With McGready's advance notice, and with word of the events at Red River and Muddy River circulating around the frontier, many people traveled as much as one hundred miles by wagon to attend the Gasper River service. This was approximately a four-day journey at that time. The Gasper River meeting was also scheduled to be a three-day affair, America's first revival camp meeting, and people came expecting to see the work of God. In all, approximately 45 people were converted, and those present saw what they believed was a mighty outpouring of the Holy Spirit. By the end of 1800, much of southwest Kentucky and parts of Tennessee were in the midst of revival. This would set the stage for "The Great Revival" at Cane Ridge the following summer.

Having heard of the Gasper River revival, Barton Stone (d. 1844) decided to organize a second camp meeting. Originally from Maryland, Stone had spent time in Guilford County, North Carolina, where he had become one of those young preachers mentored by McGready. In fact, some accounts have Stone converting under McGready's preaching there. Having entered the Presbyterian ministry, he took charge of congregations at Cane Ridge and Concord, both in Bourbon Country. He went over to Logan Country where McGready's revivals had taken place, observed what was happening, and desired nothing more than to see an extension of the revivals that had started there. He was not alone; other ministers also modeled their preaching after the Logan County revivals.

Stone announced a sacramental service for August 6, 1801. While he surely believed that people would come, neither he nor anyone else could possibly have been prepared for the response that ensued. Eyewitness accounts estimated that between 10,000 and 25,000 people came to Cane Ridge. At the time there were only a quarter-million people in all of Kentucky and only 1800 in Lexington, Kentucky's largest city. Technically this was a Presbyterian meeting, but there were many Baptists and Methodists present, including preachers from those denominations. Preaching stands were erected at several points across the camp-meeting field so that several preachers could speak at once to separate audiences. Hundreds were converted, either for the first time in their lives or as part of what Protestants often called a rededication.

James Finley, who would later become a Methodist minister, was one of those converted at Cane Ridge, and his story was not unusual. He was 21 years of age at the time, the wayward son of a Princeton-trained Presbyterian minister. He had drifted off to the frontier and taken to drinking, dancing, and assorted other activities, all considered serious sins in the Protestant faith of the time. He went to Cane Ridge merely to observe the excitement, being determined not be drawn in. He was also an educated young man, and the frontier emotionalism of revivals was not for him. As he watched hundreds of people shrieking and gyrating in spiritual agony, he was deeply moved and felt physically weak. He rushed first to the woods, then to a tavern, where he took a stiff drink to calm himself. He returned to the meeting and walked again among the people caught up in revival, feeling the weight of his own sins pressing on his conscience. After a nearly sleepless night in a haystack, the next day he headed for home. Along the way he stopped in a woods to pray and fell to the ground, unable to move. Neighbors found him, took him to a nearby home and put him to bed. When he awoke, he reported, he felt spiritual release and was able to continue his journey home with the assurance that his sins were forgiven. Finley's is just one of the more vivid and detailed accounts of conversion at Cane Ridge. Another account has Rachel Martin entering into what was called "catalepsy." She lay in bed for nine days without moving, speaking, or eating before gaining spiritual release and conversion.[6]

When the revival was completed, it was referred to widely as the greatest outpouring of the Holy Spirit since Pentecost in the first century, when St. Peter and the other apostles preached and saw thousands converted to the new faith. Stone himself, being a somewhat crude practitioner of Baconian science, wrote a treatise describing in systematic fashion some of the emotional gyrations that people experienced during the revival. In addition to Rachel Martin's catalepsy, he catalogued these as spiritual exercises: "the falling exercise, jerking exercise, dancing exercise, barking exercise, laughing exercise, running exercise, and singing exercise."[7] Such emotional responses have made it very difficult to evaluate the Cane Ridge revival, and many of these physical manifestations were viewed unfavorably even by contemporaries. Hardly anyone in that day or since can be objective about such things. As one might guess, those who opposed the revivals used the "barking exercise" to argue that these meetings were excessive. Accounts of that particular exercise described people in the throes of spiritual agony rocking back and forth, causing grunts and groans. The faster they rocked, the louder and more staccato the noise, until it eventually sounded like a bark. Critics also pointed out that along with the spiritual experiences were other more sensate and sensory excesses. Specifically, there was a good deal of alcohol consumed by those who came to the revivals more out of carnal than spiritual curiosity. Hucksters sold whisky from wagons on the outskirts of the encampment. Moreover, for those who attended primarily to be part of a good party, there were sexual liaisons, leading some to claim that more souls were conceived than saved. While revivals were almost always emotional affairs with crying, shouting, and sometimes falling, excesses such as barking and treeing the devil, often cited to discredit the revivals, were limited. With the possible exception of the early meetings, they never became regular features of the Second Great Awakening.

It is worth noting the extent to which Stone's and other accounts of the revivals show how easily Protestant Christianity could be harmonized with the Baconian science of that day. Baconian science puts a premium on plain observation of the facts of nature, then the categorization of those facts. Both in their systematic planning of revivals, and in their rudimentary scientific explanation of the revival's effects, Stone and others were blending the best of science with the best of religion. This was long before any popular notion that science and religion were in competition with each other.

Cane Ridge set off waves of revivals that would last for years, and this Great Revival is generally regarded as the beginning of the Second

Great Awakening. The revivals also led to schism (splits) in various denominations, however, especially among Presbyterians. In colonial America there had been at least two broad kinds of Presbyterians. In New England, they tended to be descendents of the Puritans with clergy educated at Princeton or Yale. They followed the Calvinistic Westminster Confession of Faith and put a high premium on an educated clergy and worship held in high decorum. In the South and on the frontier, Presbyterians were much more populist, that is non-elite. The preachers were trained at crude log colleges and often believed that too much learning actually hindered the plain gospel. In addition to these divisions, and in some ways as a result of them, Presbyterians had experienced near-schism during the First Great Awakening between those who supported revivals and those who believed they were excessive. Similar divisions would take place during the Second Awakening as well.

One of these schisms took place in the Cumberland Presbytery, which had been established in 1801 by the Kentucky Synod. A presbytery is a grouping of several churches in a particular geographical area, and a synod is often the governing body for a whole state. Congregations elect representatives to the presbytery, and the presbytery does the same for the synod. In conjunction with the revivals, the Cumberland Presbytery began to ordain uneducated revival preachers. These were usually bivocational—that is, they were farmers or mechanics who took up preaching as a second career while continuing to support themselves with their labor. Conservatives opposed these ordinations and tried to dissolve the Cumberland Presbytery. In 1809, the General Assembly (the ruling body for the whole nation) ruled against the Cumberland Presbytery. But, instead of discontinuing their practices, the Cumberland folks just seceded from the Kentucky synod. The Cumberland Presbytery then remained a separate entity until 1906.

A similar schism occurred when the Kentucky Synod planned to charge Stone and another revival preacher with heresy for their starkly non-Calvinist approach to religion. Instead of accepting the discipline of the synod, Stone and his associates formed their own Springfield Presbytery and began to call themselves merely Christians. This signified their belief that denominational structures were unbiblical and detrimental to the simple faith. They soon rejected denominational creeds, such as the Westminster Confession, claiming they would follow only the Bible, and they dispensed with all hierarchical structures

and opted for a purely congregational polity where the people themselves would choose their pastors and make all decisions in a democratic fashion. Having renounced the presbytery, synod, and general
assembly, Stone and his followers were no longer Presbyterians. In this
way, the revivals were in harmony with the movement of American
political culture as the nation became ever more democratic and populist, especially as it entered the Jacksonian Era, which lasted from
1828 or so until the 1840s. While some of Stone's associates would
eventually join a small sect of Christians called the Shakers, Stone himself continued to build his loosely structured movement until 1832
when he would merge with another frontier preacher and organizer
named Alexander Campbell. This Stone-Campbell merger would be the
beginning of the movement that has given us today's Disciples of
Christ, Independent Christian Churches, and Churches of Christ.
Unlike Stone, McGready remained Presbyterian, was hauled before
Transylvania Presbytery in 1809, where in his own words he humbled
himself in "due submission to the discipline of our church in every
point of view."[8]

While Presbyterians sometimes divided over the revivals, the center of gravity for the Second Great Awakening began to shift to the
Methodists and Baptists. The Methodists were ideally suited for revivals
for several reasons. First, their theology was Arminian, as opposed to
Calvinist. Named for seventeenth-century Dutch theologian Jacob
Arminius, Arminianism was free-will theology. That is, Arminians
believed that anyone could be saved by making a free-will decision to
follow Christ in conversion. People were not predestined to be either
saved or lost, as Calvinists believed. All could be saved if they merely
chose to be. In conjunction with this was the belief that certain techniques would enhance the likelihood that people would make such a
decision. Second, the Methodist organizational structure facilitated
revival. Preachers rode circuits of several churches for a few years, then
were transferred to another circuit. Circuit riding alleviated the problem of there being far more churches than ministers since each minister
could ride a circuit of several churches, and the frequent transfers kept
the preachers from developing their own following, something that
could lead to heresy or an independent movement, as happened with
Stone and the Presbyterians. Superintendents and bishops were responsible for overseeing unity of doctrine and organization. Moreover, the

circuit riders were populist—that is, they spoke the plain language of the people—and they were highly dedicated to their tasks, so much so that they often wore themselves out and died young, only to be replaced by younger preachers who had caught the Methodist vision at a revival camp meeting.

Baptists were also well suited to the frontier revivals because they were congregational from their very beginning in early seventeenth-century England. Also, whereas Methodist circuit riders were full-time preachers who covered several churches, Baptist preachers were often bivocational preacher-farmers. This was made possible by the congregational polity whereby individual congregations could ordain pastors without having to seek approval from a bishop or presbytery. Baptist churches could be formed anywhere and at any time. All it took was a group of Baptized believers to pronounce themselves a church, ordain one among them as the pastor, and proceed. Again, we see religious democracy and political democracy flourishing side-by-side and usually for the same reasons—a growing nation, with a burgeoning frontier, demanded and encouraged methods that gave voice to the people.

The Second Great Awakening in the East

The revivals would not stay on the frontier. They would move back east, but, as one church historian notes, first they would need a period of "probation and polishing" before they would be ready to penetrate the urban centers of the Atlantic seaboard.[9] Much of the probationary period would be led by Methodists who picked up the revival fervor that regular Presbyterians tended to lay aside. Bishop Francis Asbury, the most important individual in the rise of Methodism during the Early National period, reported several revivals during the first decade of the nineteenth century. In his *Journal* he wrote of reports he had received by late 1805 telling of several revivals where two hundred to five hundred were converted. In 1806, he wrote of a major revival in Maryland, in 1808 another in Ohio, then others in Georgia, South Carolina, and North Carolina, with yet more recorded for 1809. After 1804 the camp meeting technique for revival had become an almost uniquely Methodist phenomenon, as the Baptists and Presbyterians tended to shy away from the protracted tent gatherings.[10] While camp meetings became a normal part of Methodism, however, they were never recognized officially and were often considered a mark of Methodist extremism. There is no mention of them in the official documents of the denomination.

This probationary period of frontier revivalism also saw the rise of Baptist revivals. These were usually in conjunction with congregational and associational meetings. As mentioned above, Baptists are congregational in their polity. There is no hierarchical body that can dictate to an individual congregation what it must do. Rather, Baptist organization extends from the bottom up with congregations voluntarily joining together in associations. At monthly congregational meetings, the emphasis was often on calling members of that congregation into account for personal sins, most often drinking or sexual sins, dishonest business practices, and others. This rigorous type of discipline, with its community pressure, often led to confessions followed by repentance. Baptist revivals usually began at congregational or associational meetings, leading to many conversions and rededications. Then, in addition, there were organized revivals that would bring the congregations of an association together specifically for revival preaching.

As the Second Great Awakening moved into its second decade, it became a New England, as well as frontier, phenomenon. There, however, it would be quite different, primarily because New Englanders viewed the frontier revivals as crude and barbarous. In New England, the key figures promoting a more sophisticated and less emotional style of revivals were Lyman Beecher, Nathaniel Taylor, and Asahel Nettleton. One of the key methods of promoting revival was the pulpit exchange, when the trained and experienced pastor of one congregation would go to another congregation for a period of time. This was a version of temporary Methodist circuit riding or itinerancy but without the dangers of preachers who were loose cannons, so to speak. The positive effect of this method was that people heard new ideas from fresh voices and were likely to be stirred to repentance and rededication. It also made for wider exposure for the most gifted preachers, as they were the ones most in demand for pulpit exchanges. In other words, a congregation with a preacher of meager ability would be treated to a period where the members would sit under outstanding preaching from a visiting preacher.

This system worked as new converts joined churches and old members were reinvigorated. The next step was to translate this fervor into social action aimed at further Christianizing New England culture. Beecher organized men and women into missionary societies that took the gospel into New England's own frontier, and he and the other revival promoters also began voluntary benevolent societies. Among these were the Home and Foreign Mission Society (1812), the American Bible Society (1816), the African Colonization Society (1817), the American Tract Society (1826), and the American Temperance Society (1826). Reforms such as temperance, anti-dueling, and Sabbath observance were all given a major boost, and in some cases actually initiated, by the New England phase of the Second Great Awakening. Whereas the western revivals were taken over increasingly by Methodists and Baptists, in New England, under Beecher and others, they remained primarily under the auspices of the Congregational and Presbyterian churches.

In the 1820s, as the moderate form of revivals continued in New England, and after things had cooled considerably on the frontier, Charles Grandison Finney became the key figure of the Second Great Awakening and indeed the most prolific preacher of the entire period. In the midst of a career as a lawyer, Finney had a conversion experience after which he allegedly told a client, "I have a retainer from the Lord Jesus Christ to plead his cause, and I cannot plead yours."[11] This was his declaration that he would cease practicing law and become a preacher. Finney began his public ministry in 1824 in Jefferson County in the central part of western New York where he was sent as a missionary. He rejected Presbyterian Calvinism and began to preach in schoolhouses and in the open air, emphasizing that any and all could be saved. Over time he began to utilize his own fairly well-developed methods of revival that were known as the "new measures." These included advance advertisement for revival meetings, the anxious bench where those who were agonizing over the state of their souls could sit while they contemplated their condition, praying for people by name in public prayer meetings held in conjunction with his revivals, and permitting women to pray publicly in the presence of men, the latter a harbinger of Finney's progressive reform-mindedness that will be discussed in the chapters that follow.

From 1824 through 1827, Finney's revivals swept through northern New York toward the Hudson River and eventually to the border of New England. As this happened, there was a near repeat of the schism that had racked Presbyterianism on the frontier two decades earlier. The conservative Presbyterian leaders of the east were determined to keep Finney out of New England precisely because he seemed too much like the unruly preachers of the frontier. He was a threat to the moderate brand of revivalism that was working nicely in New England. Beecher and Nettleton were concerned that revivals be orthodox in their doctrine and orderly in their manifestation. Yet, because they genuinely desired true revival, they decided to meet with Finney to discuss the matter, hoping to convince Finney to conduct his revivals in accordance with their own more moderate methods. Instead, at this meeting, Finney convinced them of the value of what he was doing, so Nettleton and Beecher invited him to Boston to hold services. This launched Finney into national prominence, and he spent the next eight years holding revivals in the major urban centers of the East before settling into a career as a professor, then president, at Oberlin College in Ohio. Having been converted as a Presbyterian, Finney came more and more to resemble a Methodist as his career as a revivalist progressed, so much so that after 1836 when Finney took his revival teaching to Oberlin, it became increasingly difficult for the college's graduates to gain appointments in Presbyterian or Congregational churches.

Finney's meetings in the 1820s touched off another phase of revival intensity that swept back and forth across western New York for two decades. This region came to be called "the burned-over district," and from it sprung several new and unorthodox religious movements, including the American religion known as Mormonism. From that time to the present scholars of American religion have been fascinated by the apparent relationship between the burned-over phenomenon and religious experimentalism.[12]

Finney, therefore, was largely responsible for turning revivals from a frontier phenomenon to one that was quintessentially American and could be found anywhere. In short, the urbanization of revivalism set the stage for later revival preachers who would have national, and even international, reputations. Among these would be Dwight L. Moody in the late nineteenth century, Billy Sunday and Aimee Semple MacPherson in the 1920s, and, the most prolific preacher in the history of the Christian faith, Billy Graham in the second half of the twentieth and into the early twenty-first centuries. Those figures move us well beyond the parameters of this volume, but the important point here is the extent to which by the 1830s, revivals were a rather normal part of American culture and would remain so ever after. During the period of the Second Great Awakening itself, however, there was one more phenomenal outpouring worth mentioning in brief. It is the revival of 1858, which is often considered the end of this particular period of revival history.

The Revival of 1858

By some accounts the period from the mid-1840s to the mid-1850s was one of religious declension not unlike the period following the American Revolution. Churches seemed to stagnate as the attention of the American people moved from religion to more secular concerns. We should remember, however, that just as was the case in the years leading up to the beginning of the Second Great Awakening, spiritual declension is often more in the eye of the beholder than in reality. The mid-1840s saw the potato famine in Ireland, which led to a mass influx of Irish immigrants to America. Most of these newcomers were Catholic. It may well be that just as orthodox Protestants of the late-eighteenth and early nineteenth centuries disregarded Unitarianism as inauthentic religion and saw Catholicism as a threat, likewise many Protestants of the 1840s and 1850s would have seen an influx of Catholics as a challenge to Protestant America. Many, if not most, evangelical Protestants of that time, and many yet today, believe that Catholics are in need of conversion; this despite the fact that they are already Christian. While not dismissing the concept of declension altogether, we should consider the context in which such claims were made.

As was the case with the beginning of the Second Great Awakening, there seem to have been preliminary stirrings of revival prior to 1858 as well. These took place in 1857 in Lawrence and Pittsfield, Massachusetts; Pittsburgh, Pennsylvania; Beaufort and Columbia, South Carolina; and perhaps especially in Hamilton, Ontario. The latter experience was a revival that started in conjunction with the Methodist ministry of husband and wife Walter and Phoebe Palmer. Phoebe, especially, was a gifted speaker and winsome personality who exuded the love of God. It is worth noting that unlike the revivals early in the century, these stirrings took place in cities, and indeed the Revivals of 1858 would be a primarily urban phenomenon. Churches in all these locations saw many conversions, baptisms, and additions to their rolls. Still, they seem but a prelude to what would happen the following year, first in New York then in many other places as well.

In New York that autumn of 1857 there was an earnest business-man named Jeremiah Calvin Lanphier who had been appointed as a city missionary for the North Reformed Protestant Dutch Church. He decided to begin noon prayer meetings in a business district of the city. His first meeting took place on September 23 and consisted of merely five or six men. Over the course of the next several months Lanphier's noontime prayer meetings grew exponentially as many other similar meetings began across the city. By spring there were an estimated 50,000 people meeting at noon in various locations across the city. Prayer meetings were held in print shops, fire and police stations, theaters, and any number of other venues. A March 20, 1858 *New York Times* article reported: "We have seen in a business quarter of the city, in the busiest hours, assemblies of merchants, clerks and working men, to the number of 5,000, gathered day-after-day for simple and solemn worship. Similar assemblies we find in other portions of the City; a theatre is turned into a chapel; churches of all sects are opened and crowded by day and night [punctuation added]."[13]

This was the beginning of the Revival of 1858, and like those of the early century, it spread, first through upstate New York. There was not always a causal connection between what happened in New York City and elsewhere. In other words, it seemed that revivals in other cities began almost simultaneously with those in New York and among people with no knowledge of what was happening there. At other times there was a connection between New York and other revivals—for example, the revival in Philadelphia. George Stuart traveled to New York in autumn of 1857 and participated in the noon prayer meetings. Returning to Philly he began to encourage similar gatherings. These began in November 1857; by May there were prayer meetings of five to six thousand people being held in Jaynes Hall, which had been reconfigured to increase its capacity from three thousand. Even with this connection between the New York and Philadelphia revivals, one scholar believes that prayer meetings for revival began in churches two months before Stuart's visit to New York, raising the question as to whether Stuart's stay in New York was what actually brought the revival to Philly.

As the Philadelphia revival progressed, John Wanamaker persuaded the YMCA to purchase a large tent that could be taken to various parts of the city. Beginning in May 1858 and continuing for five months, the tent was used for revival services. During that period an estimated 150,000 people attended meetings in the "Union Tabernacle," as the tent came to be called.

The Revival of 1858 spread throughout the nation, leaving hardly a region untouched. As it did it seems to have been far less divisive than revivals early in the century, and the movement encountered far less opposition. Whereas Presbyterians often split over revivalism earlier, in 1858 even the liturgical and traditional Episcopalians and Lutherans experienced revival and welcomed its effects. The secular press was positive about this last outpouring of the Second Great Awakening. All the major city newspapers reported regularly on the revivals, usually noting the vast numbers of people being converted and the salutary effects those conversions produced. Press coverage became a major source of promotion that no doubt furthered the cause of revivalism. Such support may have been due in part to the fact that the Revival of 1858 had a degree of decency, decorum, and lack of excessive emotionalism. There were very few reports of the type of "exercises" that had marked the frontier revivals of the first decade of the century. This, in turn, may have been due in large part to the fact that the later revivals began in cities among business classes who were more highly educated than the frontiersmen of the early revivals and, frankly, more civilized. On the other hand, however, the wide acceptance of the Revival of 1858 shows how mainstream revivals had become in America. The nation was increasingly open to religious influence, especially that of evangelical Protestantism, as church attendance and membership grew. Quite simply, revivals were no longer associated with unruly frontier America; they had gained acceptance among many in the influential urban classes.

It is also worth noting that the British Isles experienced revivals in the late 1850s. In some cases, such as Ulster and Wales, there seems to have been a fairly strong connection to and influence from America. As was the case during the First Great Awakening of the 1730s and 1740s, America's religious landscape was part of a larger trans-Atlantic phenomenon. It was in America, however, where the revivals would have the longest lasting, most far-reaching effects. The chapters that follow will consider the ways the Second Great Awakening shaped America's democratic culture and inspired a wide range of social reforms. We will also consider a small but highly influential alternative way of being spiritual known as Transcendentalism. This movement, mostly among New England elites, helped shape America's literary culture in profound ways.

Notes

1. Quoted in John Boles, *The Great Revival: Beginnings of the Bible Belt* (Lexington: University Press of Kentucky, 1972), 17.
2. See ibid., 17–18.
3. Quoted in Bernard Weisberger, *They Gathered at the River: The Story of the Great Revivalists and Their Impact Upon Religion in America* (Boston: Little, Brown, 1958), 24.
4. Boles, 45–47.
5. Quoted in Weisberger, 25.
6. Ibid., 33–34.
7. See ibid., 34–36.
8. Quoted in ibid., 42.
9. Ibid., 50.
10. Boles, 89.
11. Quoted in Keith J. Hardman, *Charles Grandison Finney, 1792–1875: Revivalist and Reformer* (Syracuse, New York: Syracuse University Press, 1987), 43.
12. See Whitney Cross, *The Burned Over District* (New York: Harper and Row, 1950).
13. Quoted in Roy Fish, *When Heaven Touched Earth: The Awakening of 1858 and Its Effects* (Azle, Texas: Need of the Times Publishers, 1996), 44. See also Kathryn Long, *The Revival of 1857–58: Interpreting an American Religious Awakening* (New York: Oxford University Press, 1998).

CHAPTER 2

TRANSCENDENTALISM AS A NEW RELIGIOUS MOVEMENT

As the Second Great Awakening moved into its later stage, another profoundly religious movement developed in New England. Known as Transcendentalism, it could not have been more different from the Protestant revivals. Transcendentalists' views of God, humankind, nature, and salvation were quite unorthodox by the standards of early nineteenth-century Protestantism. Even Unitarians, who themselves were thought by traditional Protestants to be unorthodox, believed the Transcendentalists had moved outside of Christian orthodoxy. Transcendentalists, however, believed they had found the truth, or at least the proper path toward it.

Although it is hard to pinpoint just when Transcendentalism began, a plausible date is September 19, 1836, when George Ripley, a Unitarian minister at Purchase Street Church in Boston, called together his friends: Bronson Alcott, Orestes Brownson, Ralph Waldo Emerson, Frederic Hedge, Convers Francis, and James Freeman Clarke. Their specific task when assembled was to discuss the shortcomings of Unitarianism. One scholar of Transcendentalism has called the group "as nearly diverse a group of 'like individuals' as one could hope to find for a study."[1] Emerson was the leader, best writer, and most famous of the group. His book *Nature* would become a virtual manifesto for Transcendentalism. By contrast, Francis was relatively unknown. Ripley and Alcott advocated community and would later found communes, while Emerson and Hedge were solitary individualists. Clarke, Francis, Hedge, Emerson, and Ripley were Unitarian ministers, but Emerson and Ripley would soon be ex-ministers.[2] Francis was the oldest at 40, Clarke the youngest at 26, while the rest were in their thirties. All seven at the first meeting were published scholars and were influenced in varying degrees by Platonism, Puritanism, Romanticism, and Orientalism. Notably absent was Henry David Thoreau, who would later become, along with Emerson, one of the two most important Transcendentalists. At the time of this first gathering, Thoreau was only 19 years old.

That first meeting was not much more than a planning session at which the group decided to hold its first substantive discussion on October 3. The topic was "American Genius: The Causes Which Hinder Its Growth, Giving Us No First-Rate Productions." The group also decided on rules for discussion. Because they wanted complete openness, they decided that no person would be invited if his or her presence precluded discussion of any topic. Members called their group the "Symposium," and met four or five times a year for the next several years. Some people called the group "Hedge's club" because meetings were always scheduled when he could travel to Boston from his home in Maine. As with so many religious groups in American history— Quakers, Shakers, Mormons, and others—the Transcendentalists got their name from outsiders who were never part of the movement. No one knows for sure who coined the term Transcendentalist, but it had been in use in Britain since the early nineteenth century, coined apparently in an attempt to describe the thinking of European philosophers such as Immanuel Kant. In January 1837, a Harvard tutor of philosophy wrote a review of Emerson's *Nature* in which he criticized the new school of thinking and called it Transcendentalist.[3] As the meetings of Clarke, Francis, Hedge, Ripley, Emerson, and the others became well known in Boston, the public began to refer to the members collectively as the Transcendentalist Club, and the name stuck. Most Transcendentalists actually preferred the name New School or Disciples of Newness, while Brownson liked Eclecticism and Alcott preferred the original name, Symposium.

In addition to the founding seven, others who became regulars at the meetings were Thoreau, Sophia Ripley (George's wife), Caleb Stetson, Margaret Fuller, Elizabeth Peabody, and Theodore Parker. Parker was a Unitarian minister and one of America's most influential nineteenth-century preachers. In many ways he would succeed Emerson as the intellectual leader of Transcendentalism. Also associated with the group on

a less consistent basis were renowned American historian George Ban-
croft, abolitionist agitator Samuel J. May, Sophia Peabody, and her hus-
band-to-be, Nathaniel Hawthorne, a leading literary figure.[4]

Defining Transcendentalism is no easy task. Unitarianism influenced virtually all Transcendentalists. Unitarians modified Protestant
theology in many ways. Scholars often call them "liberals," which is
accurate because they liberalized or broadened theology. The orthodox
Calvinists and non-Calvinist revivalists discussed in Chapter 1 believed
that Unitarians were unorthodox, barely Christian, if at all, because
they rejected historic Christian doctrines such as the Trinity, the divinity of Christ, and the Calvinist doctrines of predestination and election.
In the early nineteenth-century Unitarians still retained a belief in miracles as verification of the truth of Christianity, and while they did not
believe that Christ was divine, co-equal, and co-eternal with God, they
did believe he was uniquely God's son. Even though they had dropped
much of what their ancestors had believed, Unitarians were still the
spiritual descendants of colonial Puritanism, and nearly all the original
members of the Transcendentalist Club were direct biological descendants of Puritans.

Essentially, the Congregational Churches of New England, which
at one time had been Puritan Calvinist, had become for the most part
Unitarian by the early nineteenth century. They retained from Puritanism the emphasis on moral living, duty, and the responsibility to
build a just society. Stripped of the revivalist emphasis on spiritual transformation and the need to be saved from one's sins by a supernatural
work of God's grace, Unitarianism was largely about living rightly; it was
this emphasis that rankled Transcendentalists. It was not that they
wanted to be liberated from living a moral life. Rather, the Transcendentalists wanted to move from the mundane and often glum emphasis on
living by moral rules, to a deeper sense of experience. The experience
they desired, as we shall see, was not an emotional revivalist conversion,
but rather a quiet individualistic experience of oneness with nature.
Words used to describe this type of experience were "enthusiastic, mystical, extravagant, impractical, ethereal, supernatural, vague, abstruse, or
lacking in common sense."[5] One scholar defines Transcendentalism as
"a warm and intuitional religious, aesthetic, philosophical and ethical
movement—the American tributary of European Romanticism—a theo-
retical and practical way of life and a literary expression within the tra-

dition of Idealism—a new humanism based upon ancient classical or Neo-Platonic supernaturalism and colored by Oriental mysticism."[6]

Words such as intuition, mysticism, humanism, and romanticism will be very important for understanding Transcendentalism, but instead of elaborating on abstractions, it will be more interesting to look at Emerson's thought and Thoreau's actions to see how the two leading Transcendentalists embodied this movement.

Emerson's *Nature* had just been published in 1836 when the Transcendentalist Club met for the first time. As one scholar puts it, in roughly one hundred pages Emerson said "nearly every important thing that [he] or any other American Transcendentalist would ever say."[7] Emerson believed that Nature was very much like God. For Transcendentalists, God was not a being, as orthodox and liberal Christians believed. Rather, God was a universal spirit, much as eastern religions, such as Hinduism, teach. Nature is the organ through which the universal spirit speaks to human beings. To know God (the universal spirit), therefore, one must be in harmony with nature. Emerson quoted an "Orphic Poet," which many believe was either Alcott or himself, as saying, "nature is not fixed but fluid. Spirit alters, moulds, makes it. . . . Every spirit builds itself a house, and beyond its house a world, and beyond its world a heaven. Know then that the world exists for you. . . . All that Adam had, all that Caesar could, you have and can do. . . . Build therefore your own world."[8] Emerson's treatise was in one sense a revision of the concepts of God and creation as taught in the Christian tradition, and, in another, a revolt against the empiricism of Enlightenment science. The Christian concept of God is that he is the creator of the universe, and, as such, is other-than the creation. There is an emphasis on cause and effect as God spoke and caused the universe to come into existence. Having been made in God's image, human beings are the ultimate of the created order, but they are not God and do not have God within them, at least not until the Spirit of God enters them in the act of salvation. Moreover, they will not become all they can be until they meet God face to face in his kingdom. All this suggested to Emerson and other Transcendentalists that God's creation in the past and the consummation of history in the future were more important than the present. They rebelled against this.

The natural world as understood by Enlightenment (modern) science was much the same as that of orthodox Christianity. As Newton taught, God created the world with natural laws that function consistently in an orderly process that can be studied and understood. The natural world is God's creation but not itself divine. Enlightenment thinkers saw nature as an object of study, and they used the scientific method to quantify knowledge, often explaining the universe much like a well-oiled machine. Christianity and Enlightenment Science had roughly the same conception of the universe, which should be no surprise given that the most important Enlightenment thinkers—Francis Bacon, René Descartes, Galileo, Isaac Newton, and John Locke—were all Christians of one sort or another. Even the Unitarians retained this basic conception of the universe, many of them having become Deists who believed that God created the world but then allowed it to run according to the laws of nature without interfering via miracles or other supernatural acts. Enlightenment thinkers and more conservative Christians differed slightly on how best to discover the truth. Enlightenment figures tended to believe that all truth was already embedded in nature and could be understood by the application of reason alone. Orthodox Christians agreed that truth was created by God, but they believed that one could know the truth through reason and revelation. There were some truths that God revealed in scripture or in the person of Christ that could not be discovered by reason. Still, the Enlightenment and orthodox Christianity agreed that nature was other-than God. One could find evidence for God in nature, but one could not find God himself there.

By contrast, Emerson believed that the natural world was the actual manifestation of God; nature was part of the universal spirit. As one twentieth-century scholar of Transcendentalism has put it, "The universe became a living book in which one could read the secrets of the soul."[9] Another has written, "For the Transcendentalists (and nineteenth-century Romantics generally) the organic metaphor replaced the mechanical. In place of the clockwork universe of the eighteenth-century Enlightenment they put a universe that was living, growing, and endlessly advancing from lower to higher forms."[10] Indeed, all Transcendentalists seemed to agree that "there was a divine energy immanent in nature and in man, giving them meaning, purpose, and direction."[11] Emerson came very close to pantheism, the belief that God was in everything. For him, individuals should not study nature as if it were an object, but experience it as if it were a living spirit. In this understanding a forest was a church where one walked as an act of worship; a mountain was a cathedral where one stood in awe of God; a canoe trip down a river could be an experience every bit as spiritual as the ecstasy of conversion at the Cane Ridge revival. Pastor and Transcendentalist thinker Theodore Parker wrote that "the fullness of the divine energy flows inexhaustibly into the crystal of the rock, the juices of the plant, the splendor of the stars, the life of the Bee and Behemoth," while Thoreau said, "The earth I trod on is not a dead inert mass. It is a body, has a spirit, is organic."[12] Of course, because human beings themselves were also part of nature, they also participated in the divine as they contemplated themselves and the world around them.

Alluding to his distaste for the rationalism of the Enlightenment, Emerson wrote in *Nature,* "[T]here are far more excellent qualities in the student than preciseness and infallibility; that a guess is often more fruitful than an indisputable affirmation, and that a dream may let us deeper into the secret of nature than a hundred concerted experiments."[13] A modern analogy might be that the truths of nature were everywhere, as if on a grand internet. Individuals needed only a computer to access those truths, and the computer was a combination of the intellect, the emotions, and the intuitions, in short, one's whole person. Moreover, the truths on this grand internet were more than information; they were alive and divine, more like spirit than facts. For the Enlightenment rationalist, the computer was the mind alone, and the information, inert data waiting to be quantified. For the Transcendentalist, one could never get at the whole truth using merely the scientific method. In the final chapter of *Nature,* Emerson wrote, "Empirical science is apt to cloud the sight, and by the very knowledge of functions and processes to bereave the student of the manly contemplation of the whole."[14] In contrast to Unitarians and even many orthodox Calvinists who were busy harmonizing the Christian faith with the rationalism of the Enlightenment, Transcendentalists were Romantics. Where rationalists believe that all truth can be apprehended through the use of human reason, Romantics believe that some truths can best be attained through intuition, emotion, and aesthetic sense. In reading a good poem, experiencing a summer rainstorm, or contemplating a beautiful waterfall, individuals were more likely to see and feel the truth than in conquering a Newtonian equation expressing the gravitational relationship of bodies in motion.

Largely on the basis of the reputation he achieved by publishing *Nature,* Emerson was invited to deliver the Phi Beta Kappa lectures at Harvard in 1837. His lecture later became a well-known essay entitled "The American Scholar." The great American jurist Oliver Wendell Holmes called it "our declaration of independence."[15] In the essay, Emerson urged his listeners to understand themselves by experiencing nature. While all Transcendentalists read widely and were authors in their own right, Emerson told the students to avoid becoming merely bookworms. Rather, they should become men of action. They should be free and brave, remembering that "the world is nothing, the man is all; in yourself is the law of all nature, and you know not yet how a globule of sap ascends; in yourself slumbers the who of Reason; it is for you to know all; it is for you to dare all."[16] Moreover, Emerson hoped that a generation of such men and women of action would produce a distinctly American form of intellectual life that would be more complete and holistic than what one could gain in a library alone.

After his "American Scholar" address, the students at Harvard Divinity School invited Emerson, who had been a Unitarian pastor of Boston's Second Street Church until he resigned in the early 1830s, to give the commencement address on July 15, 1838. In this address, given to divinity students studying for the Unitarian ministry, Emerson launched his most specific and severe criticism of Christianity. He claimed that "historical Christianity has fallen into the error that corrupts all attempts to communicate religion."[17] That error was to make Christ divine and to call human beings to subordinate their natures to Christ's. Rather than subordination to Christ, people should realize that they, too, are capable of divine inspiration. "[T]he assumption that the age of inspiration is past, that the Bible is closed; the fear of degrading the character of Jesus by representing him as a man; indicate with sufficient clearness the falsehood of our theology." He said that true Christianity was "a faith like Christ's in the infinitude of man."[18] For Emerson, the words of Plato, Mohammad, or Luther were just as inspired as those of Christ. All were capable of divine inspiration.

Local ministers were outraged, and Emerson was not invited back to Harvard for nearly 30 years. Some accused him of atheism and of naturalizing religion. These charges were particularly important for Unitarians because while they had rejected much of historic Christianity, they maintained that miracles attested to the truth of the faith. Miracles were supernatural evidence that Christ, while not necessarily divine himself, was uniquely chosen as an instrument of God's activity. The leading Unitarian theologian of the day, Andrew Norton, made just this point, arguing that in denying miracles, Emerson had denied the truth of Christianity. Moreover, the Unitarians recognized that such statements as Emerson's fueled the Calvinist critiques of Unitarianism. Calvinists could argue that once the Trinity, the divinity of Christ, and the authority of scripture were jettisoned, ideas like Emerson's were merely the next logical step. Princeton's Charles Hodge, one of the leading orthodox theologians of the nineteenth century, wrote, "If it was not for its profaneness, what could be more ludicrous than Mr. Emerson's Address?"[19] Emerson's emphasis on the divine potential in all human beings was a prelude to his famous essay "Self Reliance," published in 1841. There, he wrote, "No law can be sacred to me but that of my nature. . . . [T]he only right is what is after my constitution; the only wrong what is against it."[20]

Contrast this with the Calvinist belief, shared by non-Calvinist revivalists, that human beings were sinful by nature, in need of salvation, and that there was a universal moral law to which they should adhere. Unitarians had for the most part dropped Calvinism's emphasis on the sinful depravity of the individual, but even they believed there was a moral standard created by God and that everyone had a duty to abide by it. Emerson was actually instructing individuals to follow what was already within them and to recognize that the moral law "lay at the center of nature."[21] Because of his belief that nature was a manifestation of the universal spirit, what he would soon call the "Over-Soul," he held that nature had a moral component. Human beings were part of nature and, therefore, imbued with this spirit. People did not need to be taught what was right and wrong, then strive to do what was right. Rather, individuals needed to get in harmony with nature, intuit the divine, and follow their inner impulses to the good. This idea, of course, was highly controversial. While many Transcendentalists agreed with Emerson, even some of his supporters criticized this particular view. His own aunt questioned his sanity and called "Self Reliance" a "strange medley of atheism and false independence."[22]

If Emerson laid the intellectual foundation for Transcendentalism, Thoreau, more than anyone else, lived out its meaning. As a biographer has written, "[T]here is hardly a major principle of the movement that he did not espouse. And in the long run he held more closely to its fundamental principles than did any of the others. He was a true Transcendentalist to the end of his life."[23] Although Thoreau was 14 years younger than Emerson, the two became friends in 1837 after Thoreau's graduation from Harvard. Thoreau seemed to Emerson to be that perfect American scholar he had been looking for, thoughtful and well read but active as well. Where Emerson at times seemed to believe that individuals could practically reach perfection by following their own star, Thoreau maintained a better balance between the real and the ideal, between the good of which individuals are capable and the evil they might also commit. In his famous book *Walden,* Thoreau wrote, "I found in myself, and still find, an instinct toward a higher, or, as it is named, spiritual life, as do most men, and another toward a primitive rank and savage one, and I reverence them both. I love the wild not less than the good."[24]

Walden was published in 1854 and was based on Thoreau's two years alone at Walden Pond, where he built a 10-by-15-foot hut and moved in on July 4, 1845, a symbolic reference to freedom. Two miles south of Concord, Walden Pond is approximately three-quarters of a mile long and a half-mile wide. The property belonged to Emerson, who had purchased it to save the trees from loggers. Thoreau's immediate goal was to escape from society enough to concentrate on writing a book about a journey down the Merrimac River he and his brother had taken in 1839. He would live at Walden Pond for two years, two months, and two days, doing his own cultivating, planting, and harvesting and hiring out his skills in carpentry and surveying. He wanted to prove that if he simplified his life, limiting his desires, he could accomplish all necessary physical labor in much less time than the average person who worked for a living, then he would have most of his time left over for reading, thinking, and writing. Finding that he could support himself on about six weeks of labor per year, he wrote to a friend, "I am convinced, both by faith and experience, that to maintain one's self on this earth is not a hardship but a pastime, if we will live simply and wisely."[25] Of course, many neighbors pointed out that Thoreau thrived partly because his friends, including the Emersons, frequently invited him to dinner.

Walden was the result of lectures he wrote trying to explain to people why a Harvard graduate had left civilization to live in the woods.

For stylistic purposes he condensed his time at Walden Pond to one year and organized the book according to the seasons. Thoreau believed that the hectic pace of nineteenth-century America resulted in most people living "lives of quiet desperation," a phrase he coined in *Walden*.[26] His method for avoiding such a life progressed logically in four stages: (1) man was made to be free but is enslaved and even enslaves himself; (2) freedom comes through self-reliance that is made possible by simplifying one's life; (3) living in accordance with nature is the best way to health and happiness; and (4) truth is ultimate and should be valued above money, love, or fame.[27] The primary goal of life was to cultivate the inner person, but the quest for material possessions interfered with this effort. Materialism, Thoreau believed, enslaved.

Thoreau's praise for simple living put him on a collision course with American capitalism and industry. In an essay entitled "Life Without Principle," Thoreau wrote a biting critique of the burgeoning capitalistic and materialistic America. "I think that there is nothing, not even crime, more opposed to poetry, to philosophy, ay, to life itself, than this incessant business. . . . [T]he ways by which you may get money almost without exception lead downward. . . . There is no more fatal blunderer than he who consumes the greater part of his life getting his living. All great enterprises are self-supporting"[28] Freedom and knowledge of God were possible through experiencing nature in the here and now, not in amassing wealth or in putting off salvation to the future. "God himself culminates in the present moment, and will never be more divine in the lapse of all the ages. And we are enabled to apprehend at all what is sublime and noble only by the perpetual instilling and drenching of the reality that surrounds us."[29] In his time at Walden Pond and for the rest of his life Thoreau tried to live out his personal creed, holding that individuals should live simply and enjoy nature. For him, this was a spiritual quest; it was his religion.

Even as Transcendentalism was itself what today would be called a New Religious Movement (NRM), it was also a revolt against the institutional religion of the nineteenth century in both its conservative and liberal forms—i.e., revivalist Protestantism and Unitarianism. While Emerson held Jesus in lowest esteem, Thoreau was the most anticlerical of the Transcendentalists—that is, opposed to organized religion. He said he preferred the sound of cowbells to church bells on Sunday morning. Having once lectured in the basement of an orthodox church, he remarked, "and I trust helped to undermine it."[30] Remarking on the fact that churches were always the ugliest buildings in town, he said, "[I]t is the one in which human nature stoops the lowest and is most disgraced. Certainly, such temples as these shall ere long cease to deform the landscape."[31] Preaching was merely a baneful, doleful disruption to the quiet peace that Sunday should be.

Even while rebelling against institutional religion, Transcendentalism shared with the revivalists and Unitarians a strong reform impulse. On this point, Thoreau was indeed Emerson's man of action. Most Transcendentalists were reluctant to join voluntary organizations that attempted to change laws. Instead, they were individualistic social critics who hoped that if people adopted the Transcendental pursuit of the truth, they would become purveyors of justice. Thoreau, more than any other Transcendentalist, however, acted on his views, albeit individualistically. He not only spoke out against the Mexican War and the annexation of Texas and the Southwest in the 1840s, he even stopped paying taxes to support the war and landed in jail. He advocated individual passive resistance and through his famous essay "On Civil Disobedience" influenced twentieth-century reformers such as Mahatma Gandhi in India and Martin Luther King, Jr. Both adopted Thoreau's maxim, "[U]nder a government which imprisons any unjustly, the true place for a just man is also a prison."[32]

Emerson and Thoreau were both highly individualistic. Thoreau lived his life as a bachelor, part of it in virtual seclusion from society. Emerson married twice and had a family. Still, Emerson had a strong antisocial side, seeming to fear dependence on any other person. One scholar has paraphrased Emerson's recognition of the antisocial side of the movement this way: "The Transcendentalist was neither a good citizen nor a good member of society, and he didn't even like to vote. It was impossible for him to take seriously most 'causes' that people proposed for his consideration."[33] Transcendentalists tended to make even friendship so idealistic that it was virtually unattainable. Thoreau thought friendship was useful for conversation and debate but said that a favor from a friend could destroy this purely intellectual relationship. Because each individual was to be self-reliant, all associations, including friendship, ran the risk of compromising one's true individual nature. Emerson wrote in his essay "Friendship," "The condition which high friendship demands is ability to do without it." He advocated the simple exchange of letters as better than direct contact that might lead to "rash personal relations."[34] One time, Emerson and Margaret Fuller resorted to writing letters to each other even while she was staying at his house, Emerson's son Waldo carrying the letters back and forth. Emerson believed that friends were fine as long as one did not depend on them. Such views led renowned author Herman Melville to remark that when in trouble, Transcendentalists were obliged to turn to strangers rather than friends.[35]

Not all Transcendentalists, however, were so opposed to community. In fact, there were two attempts to form Transcendentalist communes. The nineteenth century saw many such attempts, sometimes utopian in nature. Often these communities revolted against the highly individualistic and acquisitive nature of the burgeoning industrial economy in America. Brook Farm was the most important Transcendentalist communal effort and was an example of a social reform community. George and Sophia Ripley formed a joint stock company in 1841, enlisted about 10 fellow investors, and purchased Brook Farm as a place where they and some of their friends would live out the Transcendentalist creed. Original members included both Nathaniel Hawthorne and his soon-to-be wife, Sophia Peabody. A total of 32 people would become members. Some who never joined visited often. Margaret Fuller, for example, used the community as a getaway spot to rest. While Thoreau's move to Walden Pond four years later would be a solitary attempt to reduce his own physical labor in order to ensure that he would have more time to think and write, the founders of Brook Farm believed that if they pooled their labor they could grow all the crops they would need while having much time for literary and scientific pursuits. In both instances a large part of the motivation was to free up time for pursuits of the mind and spirit.

Brook Farm was also an experiment in practical Christianity, where residents would live in peace and harmony, exhibiting to the world what a true community should look like. While some communes required austerity and asceticism, Brook Farm emphasized enjoyment and pleasure. There was music, dancing, card playing, charades, drama, costume parties, picnics, sledding, and skating.[36] In his own words, Ripley wanted "to combine the thinker and the worker, as far as possible, in the same individual; to guarantee the highest mental freedom, by providing all with labor, adapted to their tastes and talents, and securing to them the fruits of their industry; to do away with the necessity of menial services, by opening the benefits of education and the profits of labor to all."[37] Although communal, the emphasis was clearly on the personal growth of the individuals who lived at the farm.

Emerson would have nothing to do with this sort of communal enterprise. In addition to his disdain for dependent friendships, he preferred to live within the larger society as an example, and he feared that communal life would be too confining. To an invitation to join Brook Farm he replied, "I am in many respects suitably placed, in an agreeable neighborhood, in a town which I have many reasons to love, & which has respected my freedom so far that I presume it will indulge me farther if I need it."[38] He believed that the tight-knit communal effort might actually cut him off from many friends and associates. Likewise, Thoreau refused to lend his support, writing in his journal, "As for these communities, I think I had rather keep bachelor's hall in hell than go to board in heaven."[39] Many other Transcendentalists, however, supported Brook Farm at first, but some who were initially positive became disgruntled. Hawthorne concluded over time that some residents failed to shoulder their fair share of the labor, while Charles Lane, writing in the Transcendentalist journal the *Dial*, said that even though a commune of sorts, it was too individualistic to be a real community. He called it an association, not a community, an aggregate of persons devoid of spiritual unity.[40]

Eventually newspaper editor Horace Greeley and others pressured Brook Farm to become a Fourieristic community patterned after the French thinker Charles Fourier (1772–1837) who believed that the key to human progress was the rearrangement of economic relationships. Fourier devised an elaborate blueprint for the size and structure of each community, where agriculture and manufacturing would take place side by side. He believed that if economic relationships were reorganized, people could better live in harmony. Ironically, Fourier, as a product of the Enlightenment, believed that reason applied to nature in a scientific manner was the surest road to reform. Transcendentalists who adopted his ideas were often in revolt against Enlightenment rationalism, but in this instance they tended to believe they could use science for religious and spiritual ends. In other words, they, like Fourier, believed that a better-organized economy and society, one based on scientific study, would help deepen peoples' spiritual lives. Members of Brook Farm changed the founding document to reflect Fourieristic principles and built a large wooden meeting place, as was customary for such communities. The structure burned, pushing the backers to the brink of financial collapse. By 1847 Brook Farm had run its course.[41]

A second communal attempt in the Transcendentalist movement was Bronson Alcott's Fruitlands. He had not been part of the Brook Farm effort but had already been experimenting in the 1830s and 1840s with an agricultural lifestyle that he hoped would free him from dependency on others and from the selfishness he believed inherent in capitalist economics. Consistent with the Emersonian notion that all of nature in some way reflected the world spirit or Over Soul, Alcott believed that animals were "fellow beings" with humans. He therefore opposed all slaughter of animals for food or their domestication for labor. Even more extreme, he opposed all use of animal products— milk, cheese, butter, fish, and such—and even opposed tea, coffee, molasses, and rice because they were foreign. In addition to these spiritual ideas, Fruitlands also had a strong economic component, which came by way of the British co-founder Charles Lane. Lane and Alcott both wanted to limit and, if possible, eliminate economic activity altogether in order to achieve complete freedom, hence the elimination of foreign goods that would have to be purchased. Lane believed in the efficient production of essentials, which would leave ample free time. Of course, this efficiency was impossible to achieve because it took much more human labor to plant and harvest crops without the help of work animals. Once they realized this dilemma, Lane and Alcott compromised their principles and bought an ox and a cow.[42]

Essentially, the diet at Fruitlands was fruit and water, but fruit cultivation was difficult without fertilizer, which was banned because it was an animal product. Vegetables such as carrots, beets, and potatoes were likewise forbidden because they showed a lower nature by growing downward. As for apparel, cotton fabric was prohibited because of the slave labor used to produce it, while wool was forbidden because it came from sheep. Dress, therefore, consisted primarily of linen clothes and canvas shoes. This extreme experiment lasted only from June to December 1843. Wearing linen clothes incapable of warding off the cold, and undernourished by the extremely ascetic diet, members abandoned the idea as winter ensued.[43]

As different as the Fruitlands commune was from the revivals of the Second Great Awakening, Alcott's community bore many of the same conversionist ideals. Members converted to a completely new lifestyle, leaving behind their former worldly and sinful ways. They came out of society and lived holy lives. The differences between revivalist theology and Alcott's ideas were very real, especially in the Transcendentalist conception of God as the world spirit rather than the creator God of the Old and New Testaments. Still, notions of sin, salvation, and renewed life were common to both movements. As one scholar puts it, "Alcott simply took the idea of conversion to its literal conclusion when he envisioned a new society, outside entangling corruptions, built up by individual acts of self-renunciation and obedience to the spirit."[44] As we will see in later chapters, revivalists and Transcendentalists often entered the entangling corruptions of politics and reform in efforts to change the world. At Fruitlands and Brook Farm, however, Transcendentalists attempted to live out the opposite impulse of withdrawal from society.

The experiments at Brook Farm and Fruitlands notwithstanding, Transcendentalism was a highly individualistic movement. It is difficult to locate in the writings of key Transcendentalists any substantial justification for community. Emerson taught people to be completely self-reliant, and the entire movement pretty much attempted to adhere to this ideal. One way of understanding this emphasis on individualism is that community was so much a part of life in the nineteenth century that it could be taken for granted. In other words, Emerson, Thoreau, and the others could emphasize individualism, safe in the knowledge that no matter how heartily they pursued it, there would still be sufficient community to sustain social life. This was still pre-industrial (or at least early industrial) and pre-urban America, where most people lived on farms with large families to sustain them or in small towns where everyone not only knew everyone else in their generation but also knew their friends' parents and grandparents. The further one moved westward, the less true this was, as the move across the frontier resulted in a higher degree of rootlessness. On the eastern seaboard, however, where Transcendentalism thrived, "thick community," as social theorists today might call it, was still intact.

On the one hand, such community sustains and nurtures individuals, but on the other hand it can be confining and stifling. Transcendentalism was in some ways a revolt against these more negative attributes of community. It is interesting to ponder in the early twenty-first century, when America has experienced a century of rather thoroughgoing individualism, where individual rights usually trump all claims to community values, if Transcendentalists would still advocate the level of individualism they did in their own time. Many communitarian social theorists today, for example, point out the excesses of American individualism that often leave people with no language to express their social needs. People today have difficulty saying why they should choose one lifestyle over another, except to say that one makes them happier as an individual.[45] Transcendentalists extolled this type of individual freedom to follow one's own star, never contemplating what might happen to community spirit if everyone actually lived this way. They had the luxury of pursuing and advocating individual freedom with little worry that rampant individualism could be harmful to society.

The positive and uniquely American legacy of the Transcendentalists was individual freedom at the emotional and aesthetic levels. Just one generation before the Transcendentalists, the American Revolution had emphasized political freedom. Transcendentalists built on that idea, taking freedom in a deeper, more spiritual direction. They cared little for established institutions, believing that they constrained individuals too much. To reach its potential the human soul needed to be unchained. In emphasizing this sort of individual freedom, the Transcendentalists also rebelled against what they believed was the cold intellectualism of the Enlightenment and its connotation that reason alone was the true road to objective truth. They were religious romantics who believed that many truths were not susceptible to rational processes but had to be intuited within one's soul and experienced with one's emotions. However unorthodox by both the Protestant and Unitarian standards of their day, the Transcendentalists were still profoundly religious in a new and less structured way. Their minds as well as their souls were on fire with creative energy no less than were the minds and souls of those converted in the camp meeting revivals of the Second Great Awakening.

Notes

1. Catherine L. Albanese, *Corresponding Motion: Transcendental Religion and the New America* (Philadelphia: Temple University Press, 1977), xvii–xviii.
2. Albanese, xvii–xviii.

3. Dean Grodzins, *American Heretic: Theodore Parker and Transcendentalism* (Chapel Hill: The University of North Carolina Press, 2002), 103–4.

4. Donald N. Koster, *Transcendentalism in America* (Boston: Twayne Publishers, 1975), 13–14.

5. Ibid., 3.

6. Quoted in ibid., 2.

7. Quoted in ibid., 32.

8. Quoted in ibid., 35.

9. Albanese, xiii.

10. Paul F. Boller, Jr., *American Transcendentalism, 1830–1860* (New York: G. P. Putman's Sons, 1974), 66–67.

11. Ibid., 66.

12. Ibid., 67–68.

13. Albanese, 8.

14. Quoted in Koster, 35.

15. Quoted in Robert D. Richardson, Jr., *Emerson: The Mind on Fire* (Berkeley: University of California Press, 1995), 263.

16. Quoted in Koster, 36.

17. Quoted in ibid., 36.

18. Boller, 4–5.

19. Quoted in ibid., 10.

20. Quoted in Koster, 37.

21. Quoted in Albanese, 7.

22. Quoted in Koster, 38.

23. Walter Harding, *The Days of Henry David Thoreau: A Biography* (New York: Dover Publications, 1962), 63–64.

24. Quoted in Koster, 50.

25. Quoted in Harding, 187.

26. Henry David Thoreau, *Walden* (Boston: Ticknor and Fields, 1862), 10.

27. Koster, 52.

28. Quoted in ibid., 55–56.

29. Quoted in ibid., 53–54.

30. Quoted in Boller, 29.

31. Quoted in ibid., 29–30.

32. Quoted in Koster, 54.

33. Boller, 94.

34. Quoted in ibid., 93.

35. Ibid., 94.

36. Anne C. Rose, *Transcendentalism as a Social Movement, 1830–1850* (New Haven, Conn.: Yale University Press, 1981), 131.

37. Quoted in ibid., 105.

38. Quoted in ibid., 106.

39. Quoted in Koster, 19.

40. Ibid., 19.

41. Rose, 140–47.

42. Ibid., 122–24.

43. Koster, 21.

44. Rose, 118.

45. See, for example, Robert Bellah et al., *Habits of the Heart: Individualism and Community in American Life,* updated ed. (Berkeley: University of California Press, 1985).

CHAPTER 3

CHARLES FINNEY AND THE DEMOCRATIC EMPOWERMENT OF URBAN REVIVALS

As the Transcendentalist movement was beginning to take shape in and around Boston, the revivals of the Second Great Awakening were more and more becoming an urban phenomenon. At the center of this transition to the cities was the greatest figure of the revivals, Charles Grandison Finney, who one historian has ranked with Andrew Jackson, Abraham Lincoln, and Andrew Carnegie "as one of the most important public figures in nineteenth-century America."[1] In the 1820s and 1830s, Finney took the revival fires from small towns in upstate New York into the burgeoning new city of Rochester, then on to New York City, Philadelphia, and Boston. Just as revivals shaped much of the frontier in earlier decades, so too in the cities did they profoundly affect both the merchant and working classes. The revivals of the Second Great Awakening may have started in the rural West, but beginning in the 1830s, the cities became the "vital center" of American Protestantism.[2]

Finney converted to evangelical Protestant Christianity of a revivalist sort on October 10, 1821. At the time he was a 29-year-old bachelor who was in a relationship with Lydia Root Andrews whom he would shortly marry. In the year prior to his conversion he struggled spiritually, mostly, he wrote in retrospect, because he believed God was calling him to the ministry. He preferred instead to pursue a career as a schoolmaster or lawyer. Moreover, he cared little for preachers, viewing emotional Baptists as ranters and Calvinist preachers as intellectual prigs. Finally, he put his own ambitions and prejudices behind and surrendered. On a wooded hill not far from upstate Adams, New York, he knelt by himself and begged God for forgiveness, saying, "If I am ever converted, I will preach the gospel."[3]

Some men seem born for public life, whether it be politics, athletics, or religion. At 6'2" with an athletic build, Finney might well have been an athlete had he lived in the sports-crazed twentieth century. Perhaps the greatest revivalist of the early twentieth century, Billy Sunday, actually gave up a promising major league baseball career in the 1890s to become a preacher, and one wonders if Finney would have had similar opportunities had he lived in the era of college and professional sports. Although somewhat stern in his looks, he was nevertheless handsome, even " good-looking," as his image in the photo essay of this volume reveals. He also possessed something of a regal name. At the time of Finney's birth it was a fad with parents to name their children after aristocratic figures in English novels. Finney was named after the novel *Sir Charles Grandison,* written by Samuel Richardson just before Finney's birth in 1792. As one of his principal biographers points out, it would be like late-twentieth-century parents naming a child Bruce Springsteen Finney or Michael Jordan Finney.

Finney spent most of his childhood in Oneida County, New York. His parents, like so many New Englanders of their generation, had moved westward from Connecticut when Finney was about two years old. He returned to Connecticut on his own as a teenager and attended Warren Academy for two years. He considered going on to Yale, but one of his teachers urged him to continue educating himself. Because he was by that time older than most college students, and because he was such an advanced student, this teacher believed Yale would have been a waste of Finney's time.[4] While in his twenties he apparently taught school for a time, perhaps in New Jersey, then moved back to upstate Jefferson County, New York, where he began to clerk for an attorney and study law.

While once claiming in his *Memoirs* that he rarely heard preaching before his conversion, there is now strong evidence that he heard a variety of preachers in the places where he lived. In reporting that he had heard little preaching, he probably meant that he had heard little good or true preaching, meaning that much of what he heard he thought to be dry, dead, and spiritually un-edifying. Much like the revivalists who preceded him on the frontier, he came to believe that non-evangelistic preaching, that is preaching that was not aimed at immediate conversion, was not preaching at all. What Finney failed to account for in his *Memoirs* was the extent to which he was exposed to the Bible in his upbringing and the ways in which that prepared him for his own conversion. Like so many products and producers of the revivals of the Second Great Awakening, Finney believed that conversion was instantaneous and came virtually out of nowhere. While he would later come to believe that certain measures or methods could raise the likelihood of revivals, the events themselves were supernatural, where people were sinners one minute, then miraculously converted the next. He tended to underestimate how childhood might have put an individual on the road to conversion many years before the event actually happened. Finney's own conversion was most likely influenced by his upbringing, and while in one respect it took place in solitude on a lonely hill, it also occurred in conjunction with a revival that had begun in Adams the summer before his October conversion. One contemporary estimated that between 800 and 1,000 people were converted in Jefferson County. It was in that context that Finney began to agonize over the state of his own soul.

Finney's conversion resulted in an immediate career change. After candidly telling a client that he could not remain on retainer as an attorney because he was now on a retainer with the Lord, he made plans for the ministry. Still, more than two years elapsed between Finney's conversion and his commencement as a preacher. During that time he prepared himself, largely through self-study and tutorials with established ministers and his own Bible study. He was examined by a Presbyterian board in St. Lawrence, New York, on December 30, 1823, and subsequently licensed to preach by the Presbyterian denomination. He preached his first revivals from March to September 1824 in north Jefferson County in the towns of Antwerp and Evans Mills, and people responded in ways similar to the Great Revival at Cane Ridge more than two decades before. They writhed in agony over the state of their souls, fell from their seats, and lay prostrate on the floor. It is worth noting that while Finney would fast become the most prolific and successful preacher of the Second Great Awakening, at every step of the way he was part of religious and cultural forces that were already in motion before his conversion. Still, one can hardly overemphasize Finney's influence.

Along with his looks and athletic prowess, Finney had piercing eyes that he used to good effect. Just as Charles Whitefield of the First Great Awakening had a flair for the dramatic, and had even trained in the theaters of England, so too Finney had a mesmerizing effect on his listeners. For almost the entire first decade of his ministerial career he used no notes and did not even decide what his subject would be until he stepped up to the pulpit. He believed he needed to rely completely on the spirit of God to supply him with the words, and the results seemed to confirm that this was the best method. He combined the cold logic of a lawyer with the passion of a revivalist preacher, putting both his former and new career talents to good use.

A large part of Finney's success as well as his motivation to work hard and preach often is that he utilized an increasingly modified version of Calvinism. Orthodox Calvinism taught that revivals were a "surprising work of God," as the greatest American Calvinist, theologian Jonathan Edwards (d. 1758), liked to say. Old School Presbyterians did not believe that human agency had anything to do with conversion because God, in his sovereign will, chose people to be saved through his election and predestination. Finney, by contrast, increasingly adopted Arminian theology like that produced by the Great Revival of Cane Ridge and other camp meetings of the early Second Great Awakening. He believed that while God must call sinners, all people had within them the power to respond to that call. He believed that every person "has the power and liberty of choice."[5] This conviction directly challenged the Calvinist belief that only those whom God had predestined and elected would be saved. In Finney's way of thinking, if people had the power to choose God, it logically followed that their desire to make that choice could be manufactured, or at least bolstered, by good revivals. And, what were revivals? They were hard work and good methods. This sort of logic led Finney to believe that the harder he and others worked to bring about revivals, the more likely they were to occur. As he would write many years later in his *Lectures on Revivals*, a revival is the "purely philosophical result of the right use of constituted means. . . . A revival of religion is not a miracle." Finney's most recent biographer calls this "one of the most controversial sentences in American religious history."[6] How much more American could one be than in believing that even the work of God is largely the product of Yankee effort and ingenuity, not to mention individual choice. As for the more orthodox Calvinist theologians at Princeton and elsewhere, they would lose influence, and Finney and the other Arminian revivalists of the Second Great Awakening would be on the winning side of this American theological debate.

In addition to the efforts of evangelists to bring about revivals, the transition from rural to urban revivalism was also aided by developments as mundane as the Erie Canal. The canal played a major role in making New York City into the leading commercial center of the country, and Finney's proximity to the canal in western New York opened the way for his move to urban evangelism. Construction on the $7 million project began in 1817. The canal started at Lake Ontario at Buffalo and ran across the state through Rochester and Syracuse to the Hudson River at Albany. In all, it was 363 miles long with 83 locks. Because shipping was so much less expensive than transport by wagon, the canal significantly reduced the cost of industrial and agricultural products, helping businesses flourish. The mill towns along the canal very quickly became bustling centers of enterprise. At the end of January 1826, Finney preached to mill workers and mill owners in the small city of Utica. Mill workers were often women and young girls who were powerfully impressed by Finney's preaching. From Utica he moved to Auburn, west of Syracuse, in October. From Auburn he went to Troy, near the Massachusetts border. The Young Men's Missionary Society was trying to lure Finney to Albany for a revival campaign there, while another group that included a state Supreme Court judge, urged Finney to go to New York City.

When Finney began this move east, especially when he was near the Massachusetts border, two prominent preachers, Asahel Nettleton and Lyman Beecher, became concerned. Their chief complaint against Finney was not theological, as was the case with Princeton-type Calvinists, but methodological. They believed Finney's revival methods, sometimes called New Measures, were extreme. When critics heard reports of Finney's revivals, they often thought immediately of the Cane Ridge revival excesses from early in the century—groaning, falling, barking, and the like—and were determined to quell the fanaticism. A press war ensued as newspapers and religious periodicals began printing Nettleton's and Beecher's criticisms and Finney's responses. When accused of extreme methods, Finney lashed back, saying that the Nettleton-Beecher group was spiritually dead.

Beecher was a well-known preacher from Boston who became even more famous historically because of his children. His son, Henry Ward Beecher, would become one of the leading big-city pastors in America in the second half of the nineteenth century, while his daughter, Harriet Beecher Stowe, would write *Uncle Tom's Cabin*, the literary classic that Abraham Lincoln credited whimsically with setting off the Civil War. Beecher, Nettleton, and Finney, along with associates from both camps, decided eventually to hold a conference where they would discuss their differences. All were pro-revival and therefore hoped that some accommodation could be reached that would facilitate the movement. The conference was apparently Beecher's idea and took place in July 1827 in New Lebanon, New York. It was an attempt to reach an agreement between Finney's western New York brand of revivalism and the more reserved form supported by New Englanders such as Beecher and Nettleton. As advertised, the organizers wanted to hammer out a consensus "in regard to principles and measures in conducting and promoting revivals of religion."[7] The meeting lasted nine days and was filled with sharp debate and intense prayer. There were several motions made, modified, accepted, and rejected. The Beecher-Nettleton group was unsuccessful in portraying Finney as crude and lacking in respectability, but neither could Finney convince them that his way was necessarily the best. Still, it appears that Finney emerged victorious. As Beecher would later record in his reflections, he at first proclaimed his intention to fight to keep Finney out of Boston, but ended up welcoming him to the city.

Before going to Boston, Finney's eastern seaboard stops in the late 1820s would be Wilmington, Delaware, Philadelphia, and New York City. Philadelphia, with 100,000 people, was the largest city in the United States when Finney held his first revival there in the summer of 1828. When his wife Lydia gave birth to their first child during the Philadelphia revival, Finney took her and the baby back to her parents in western New York, then preached his way back to Philadelphia where he would remain for the rest of the year and into 1829. One of his stops on the way back to Philadelphia was New York. During this period Finney established himself as an urban revivalist, and from this time forward he would be welcomed in all the cities of the Northeast. He even served as a pastor in major downtown churches in New York on two different occasions. Still, the greatest Finney revival would take place back in western New York in the city of Rochester in 1831.

Although only one-tenth the size of Philadelphia, Rochester was America's fastest growing city in the 1820s. Having been a wilderness until 1812, it quickly became the first inland commercial center, essentially the first American city created by the commercialization of agriculture. The city stands at the junction of the Erie Canal and the Genesee River. The canal was largely responsible for Rochester's growth because it gave western New York farmers access to the markets of the east. Rochester turned farmers into businessmen. The city was also the perfect mill site. The Genesee River drops over two hundred feet in what is now downtown Rochester. These falls provided the necessary waterpower to drive the machinery of the flour mills. In 1818, the city sent about 26,000 barrels of flour to New York City; ten years later, 200,000; and by 1840, about 500,000 per year. The mills did not employ very many workers, but they paid cash to farmers for their grain, and the farmers went into the streets of Rochester to spend their money on the goods they needed. This commerce gave rise to a thriving network of shops where artisans crafted goods that were much cheaper than European imports. More than half the adult men in Rochester in the 1830s were skilled artisans. As a result of Finney's great revival in 1830–31, Rochester became something of a "shopkeeper's millennium."[8]

Finney's former rival and critic, Beecher, would call the Rochester revival "the greatest work of God, and the greatest revival of religion, that the world has ever seen."[9] This remark reminded many of Cane Ridge where observers called that revival the greatest work of God since Pentecost in the New Testament book of Acts, but this time revival took place in a burgeoning city. Only slightly less effusive were the words of a scholar in the 1970s who made a thorough study of Rochester and Finney's revival. He concluded, "The city holds a special place in the history of revivals, for Charles Finney's triumph there in 1830–31 was the most spectacular event within the national revival of that year. In short, Rochester was the most thoroughly evangelized of American cities."[10] Between September 1830 and March 1831, Finney preached several times each week and three times on Sundays while also attending countless prayer meetings. Women from the churches went door-to-door during the day, praying for people and urging them to attend the meetings. The city high school suspended classes to hold prayer meetings, and businessmen sometimes shut down their shops to attend. As one person recalled, "You could not go upon the streets and hear any conversation, except upon religion."[11] This revival was the beginning of the kind of the urban revivalism that would culminate in the great campaigns in New York City and elsewhere in the 1850s, at the end of the Second Great Awakening.

After preaching in places such as Philadelphia and New York in the late twenties, Finney was now a much more refined speaker who even used notes for his sermons. A Rochester journalist reported, "It did not sound like preaching, but like a lawyer arguing a case before a court and jury."[12] This revival, while one of the greatest in the Second Great Awakening, was marked by few excesses. As historian Whitney Cross put it, "No more impressive revival has occurred in American history. . . . But the exceptional feature was the phenomenal dignity of this awakening."[13] The people of Rochester were largely from New England rural stock, more like Finney himself than the people of the East, and everywhere he preached to overflow crowds of millers, merchants, master craftsmen, and county-seat lawyers. These were the churchgoing people who had populated Rochester from its beginning. Finney also preached in the small country towns around Rochester, thus connecting the city to its rural surroundings.[14] The revivals produced an interdenominational Protestant unity. As historian Paul Johnson put it, "The strengthening of family ties that attended the revival cannot be overestimated. But it was in prayer meetings and evening services that evangelism spilled outside old social channels, laying the basis for a transformed and united Protestant community."[15] Finney himself was so encouraged by the events in Rochester that he would extol, "[I]f they were united all over the world the Millennium might be brought about in three months."[16]

What the revivals did for Rochester was but a microcosm of what they did for all of America. The Second Great Awakening set the tone for evangelical Protestantism's hegemony that would last until the late nineteenth and early twentieth centuries when large numbers of Roman Catholic and Jewish immigrants began to challenge the Protestant consensus the Awakening forged. Moreover, Protestantism itself, in the years 1880 through 1920, would divide between evangelical-fundamentalists who attempted to retain the revivalism of Finney and his heirs, and theo-logical modernists (also called liberals) who wanted to harmonize Protes-tant theology with modern science, especially Darwinism.[17]

In 1831, after leaving Rochester, Finney went to Boston. He had waited so long because he was determined not to go until he believed that he had substantial backing from the orthodox Congregational min-isters of the city. Boston was a city where most of the formerly Calvinist Congregational churches had become Unitarian, from which the Tran-scendentalists would emerge just five years after Finney's visit. Boston, therefore, was a difficult place for Finney because both the Unitarians and many of the orthodox Calvinists were opposed to his brand of revivalism. Orthodox Calvinists, his usual foes, were by far the closest to him theologically, as they believed in the fundamental tenets of scrip-ture—the divinity of Christ, his death and resurrection, and the need for conversion. Ironically, while the Calvinists criticized Finney for believing that individuals had too much choice and freedom to respond to God, Unitarians were just the opposite. In an 1826 booklet entitled *A Bunker Hill Contest, A.D. 1826,* a Unitarian layman labeled Finney the high priest of ecclesiastical domination over the human mind. The tract vilified revivals as a conspiracy against "Free Inquiry, Bible Religion, Christian Freedom, and Civil Liberty."[18] Beecher and other orthodox ministers eventually agreed to invite Finney, who preached in Boston from September 1831 to April 1832. Beecher supported him but also worked to soften Finney's radicalism. The Boston revival was not nearly as successful as Rochester. While he preached to large crowds, some believed that there were not enough conversions to warrant calling Boston a real revival. Finney himself was not as energized as he had been during his other revivals and said at the end of his time there, "I had become fatigued."[19]

After Boston, Finney returned to New York to serve as pastor of the Chatham Street Chapel then at the Broadway Tabernacle. The first was a renovated theater, while the latter was built for Finney by wealthy benefactors who supported revivals. This was actually the second time Finney had served as a settled pastor in New York City. The first had been as founding preacher of Union Church in the fall of 1829. He stayed only nine months there before going back into itinerant revival-ism and shortly thereafter to Rochester. The idea behind the Chatham Street Chapel was to bring revival to a part of the inner city that was rife with crime and poverty. Chatham Street was part of New York's Five Points area, which was known for its vice and corruption. Beginning in the fall of 1832 Finney preached to middle and lower-income New Yorkers. He was thrilled that for the first time he was reaching the lower strata of society.[20] Most of his converts to this point had been artisans, shopkeepers, lawyers, and businessmen like those in Rochester. Reaching the lower classes touched a democratic nerve in Finney. This idea of taking the gospel to the troubled areas of the inner city was part of the reform emphasis of urban revivalism promoted by wealthy Christian businessmen. Indeed, these philanthropic businessmen inspired Finney and became his model for how those with means should live out their Christian commitment. He increasingly emphasized stewardship, the idea that individuals were not the owners of their wealth but merely the stewards of God's wealth and required to use it to better the world. Luke 16:2, "Give an account of thy stewardship," became the text of one of his important sermons. He called it a sin for a wealthy man to use his wealth "for his own private interest . . . or the aggrandizement of his family. . . . You have God's money in your hands. . . . The world is full of poverty, desolation, and death; hundreds of millions are perishing, body and soul; God calls you to exert yourself as his steward, for their salvation, to use all the property in your possession, so as to promote the greatest possible amount of happiness among your fellow-creatures."[21]

Finney's emphasis on the simpler lifestyle was different from that of the Transcendentalists, who saw simplicity as a key to personal growth and development as an individual. For Finney, simple living was a moral point having to do with duty and responsibility, part of the very emphasis Unitarians had retained from Calvinist Puritans and against which Transcendentalists revolted because they believed it too confining. Finney believed that once a person converted, he or she would be satisfied with fewer material possessions and would be freed from the need for extravagance. Moreover, God commanded Christians to be satisfied with few worldly things and to live sacrificially for others. Like all biblical Christians, both Catholic and Protestant, Finney believed that true freedom resulted from becoming, in the words of the Apostle Paul in the New Testament, a slave to Christ and his commands. The Transcendentalists, by contrast, saw freedom as the condition of being liberated from external authority so one could become self-reliant and follow one's own inner impulses.

Finney would remain in New York City until 1836 when he moved to the newly constructed Broadway Tabernacle in April. At about the same time a group of anti-slavery seminary students in Ohio persuaded him to move to Oberlin College as a professor. Known as the Lane Rebels, the students who helped found Oberlin had left Lane Seminary in Cincinnati, where Beecher had gone as president, because they believed Lane was too moderate on the slavery question. Finney had become increasingly identified with the immediatist antislavery movement while at Chatham Street Chapel. Immediatists advocated the immediate end to slavery with no compensation for slave owners. For a time Finney attempted to pastor part of the year at Broadway in New York and lecture part of the year at Oberlin in Ohio, but he found it too difficult to divide his time and energy this way and, therefore, resigned his pastorate in New York. He would spend the rest of his career as professor, then president, at Oberlin, pastoring a church in town and preaching revivals wherever and whenever he could. He was clearly the most important figure of the Second Great Awakening and one of the most influential individuals of the nineteenth century. Like any significant movement, the revivals were controversial and have been subjected to various interpretations.

An Analysis of Urban Revivalism

There are two dominant ways of interpreting the urban revivals of the Second Great Awakening. The first is the "social-control" school of interpretation. Paul Johnson's *A Shopkeeper's Millennium,* a study of Rochester at the time of Finney's revivals there in 1830 and 1831, is the classic work of the social-control school. Johnson challenges older interpreters who portrayed revivals as the antidote for individualism. Those holding this older view taught that as industrial capitalism flourished, many people became highly individualistic in their pursuit of wealth, moving wherever necessary to enhance their business opportunities. As a result, they shattered the norms and rhythms of life and lost touch with their communities. Revivals then eased the dislocation and disorientation that this process wrought. Johnson argues, however, that the people to whom Finney's revivals in Rochester appealed were not extreme individualists disconnected from community. Migration and entrance into the commercial world simply had not been a "norm-shattering" experience for them. Rather, Finney-converts were firmly entrenched in the kind of trade between city and country that actually produced and/or strengthened social relationships, including even family ties, as many businesses were affairs that included extended family members as partners. Those to whom the revivals most appealed were the least rootless and least disconnected in the city. "Insofar as there was a relationship between revival religion and mobility and its attendant social isolation, it was demonstrably negative," Johnson wrote in 1978.[22] In other words, the most settled and connected were the ones who were converted and joined the churches in the Finney revivals.

For Johnson, "the revival of 1830–31, more than any other event, marked the acceptance of an activist and millennialist evangelicalism as the faith of the northern middle class."[23] The effects of the revivals on the middle class were nearly revolutionary as far as lifestyle and daily morality were concerned. In 1825, the typical northern businessman, Johnson argues, "dominated his wife and children, worked irregular hours, consumed enormous amounts of alcohol, and seldom voted or went to church." Just 10 years later, however, "the same man went to church twice a week, treated his family with gentleness and love, drank nothing but water, worked steady hours and forced his employees to do the same, campaigned for the Whig Party, and spent his spare time convincing others that if they organized their lives in similar ways, the world would be perfect."[24] Instead of seeing the revivals as the religious response of the dislocated lower classes, Johnson believes that the revivals helped to create the bourgeois middle class.

This middle class, the social-control theory holds, promoted revivals among the lower working classes in an effort to control their behavior. Johnson writes, "When Charles Finney arrived [in Rochester] late in 1830, he found merchants and master workmen at the top of a city that they owned but could not control."[25] Proponents of this interpretation emphasize the role mill owners and other businessmen played in paying revival preachers to come to their mills to preach to the workers, believing that if workers were converted, their lives would be more stable. Destructive personal habits such as drinking and gambling would decline, then disappear; they would become better workers and more peaceful citizens. Revivals were a civilizing influence that made for docile but efficient laborers.

For the social-control theorist like Johnson, temperance was the best illustration of middle-class control of the behavior of workers. Temperance, the push for moderation or prohibition of the use of alcoholic beverages, was nearly nonexistent in 1825. Three years later, it was a middle-class obsession. Society's worst ills were suddenly attributed to alcohol. How did this happen? Johnson believes that it took place in the transition from home work to an industrial economy. In the former, workers and owners often labored together in a relaxed atmosphere that blurred the distinction between work and leisure and between working-man and owner. Drinking on the job was common, but it usually took place at the owner's discretion and even expense. When industrialization began, the workers and owners were separated not only at work but after hours as well. The bourgeois home of the owner became a place of refuge from commercial life, and the presence of his wife and daughters made drinking less likely. In other words, owners drank less. Workers, on the other hand, were now on their own after hours, and the drinking they did was no longer under the supervision of the owner. The middle-class owner was losing control of the leisure time of his workers. Whereas drinking had been "an ancient bond between classes," it became within a very short time, "an angry badge of working-class status." Johnson sees the temperance issue as dominating Rochester politics and society from the 1820s onward. "At every step," he writes, "it pitted a culturally independent working class against entrepreneurs who had dissolved the social relationships through which they had controlled others, but who continued to consider themselves the rightful protectors and governors of their city."[26] In other words, a large part of the motivation for temperance, as with middle-class support for the revivals generally, was the need to control workers who had only recently become independent in their social lives.

Johnson's book appeared in 1978, and the social-control interpretation was dominant briefly in the 1980s. The social-control interpretation drew a distinction between rural, camp-meeting revivalism on the one hand, and urban revivalism on the other. While the camp meetings reached the masses and were democratic, urban revivals were largely middle-class affairs. Recent scholarship has challenged this notion and portrayed the revivals as largely democratic wherever they appeared. Historian Nathan Hatch has argued persuasively that revivals were a populist and democratic experience. Before the Second Great Awakening, colonial American religion tended to be elitist and hierarchical— that is, people tended to defer to their preachers because they were learned men with college degrees, part of the elite of society. During the Second Great Awakening, however, American Christianity changed. Rather than preachers gaining respect because of their social and intellectual status, they now had to earn the right to be heard by appealing directly to the masses. The audience became sovereign in its decision as to which preachers would become religious authorities. Those who could move the masses succeeded, while those who could not speak the language of the people failed. It no longer mattered what college or seminary a preacher had attended or how impressive his theological degrees were. Revivalism was a populist movement that empowered the masses, rather than controlling common people, as the social-control school emphasizes.[27]

What was happening in American religion was also happening in politics. The Second Great Awakening took place partly in conjunction with age of Jackson (1828–1845), a time when politicians such as President Andrew Jackson (1829–1837) began to appeal directly to common people for support. Prior to Jackson's election in 1828, America's first six presidents had all been from aristocratic Virginia or the Adams family in Massachusetts. They were educated elites. Jackson was from rough and rural Tennessee and seemed to reflect the spirit of the people. After Jackson, political candidates tended to extol their common-man roots, even if they were in reality wealthy elites. It became a badge of authenticity to have been born in a log cabin. No one can be sure if revivalist religion made Jacksonian America possible or the influence ran the other way. Most likely, democratic religion and democratic politics influenced each other in what could be called a symbiotic relationship.

Whereas Johnson, who focused on Rochester, viewed middle-class revivals as a component of social control, another study by William Sutton, who focuses on Baltimore during roughly the same decade, interprets revivalist evangelical Protestantism as a movement that empowered workers.[28] Precisely 20 years after Johnson, Sutton rebutted the social-control thesis by arguing that a "producer tradition" with a core of populist evangelicals opposed the middle-class business owners, providing a critique of capitalist ambition.[29] Hatch's thesis on the democratic and populist thrust of revivals appeared in 1989, roughly midway between Johnson's and Sutton's books. By the time Sutton wrote, revivals were viewed as populist movements—that is, they appealed directly to the masses with a message of liberation and empowerment.

Sutton writes, "Both populist evangelicals and artisan producers were active agents in shaping American culture by demonstrating their unwillingness to submit to any illegitimate authority and by defining the moral limitations to be placed on industrial capitalist transformation."[30] In other words, rather than revivals being used by the middle, bourgeois class as a power to control the workers, the workers themselves, emboldened by revivals that taught that all were sinners in need of salvation, used biblical themes to check the power of their economic bosses. "[Evangelical artisans] provided an oppositional language and legacy to challenge the rising hegemony of laissez-faire economics and industrial capitalism."[31]

The moderate way in which a revivalism of empowerment was often delivered can be illustrated briefly by the career of Henry Slicer, a Methodist revivalist in Baltimore. Born around 1800 in Annapolis, he moved to Baltimore at 16 and was apprenticed to a chair maker. After he converted a short time later, his employer began giving him time off to train for the ministry. He was licensed to preach by the Methodists at age 20, then sent to western Virginia to a three-hundred-mile-long circuit of churches. Like so many of the Methodist preachers of the Second Great Awakening, he would ride his circuit of churches, preaching about 25 times a month. He returned to the Baltimore–Washington, D.C., area after two years and thereby escaped the fate of so many Methodist circuit riders who wore out and died young from exhaustion. He spent the rest of his life in Baltimore and Washington, serving for a time as chaplain to the U.S. Senate. Although Slicer had access to the elites of society, he kept close contact with his artisan, journeyman roots. In his own words, he preached "so that plain men can understand every sentence, and the arguments are so aptly put that no one can fail to feel their force."[32]

Slicer, of course, preached regularly about conversion, but he also preached order, self-discipline, consolation in times of disappointment, empowerment, and the dangers of wealth. His message was clearly for workers, artisans, and mill owners—in short, for all strata of economic life. He once said, "By bringing the rich man and poor together and associating them in public, the strong lines that exist in private life are softened, and, engaged in worshiping a common lord, different ranks meet as brothers."[33] One of Slicer's most oft-preached sermons was on the Old Testament theme of Jubilee. In the Jubilee tradition, all property was to revert to its original owner every fifty years to ensure against the accumulation of wealth. Slicer utilized this concept very moderately, softening the hard words of scripture against owners. Instead, he tended to lump all together as "Captives to Satan—Slaves to sin— Debtors to divine justice."[34] Sutton actually sees Slicer as an example of the moderate way in which some evangelicals responded to capitalism in Baltimore. Far more radical were the evangelical laymen who headed journeyman labor unions and took direct and forceful action against the business class. Even at their most accommodationist, revivalists such as Slicer tended to place a biblical check on the power of businessmen over their workers.

Whereas Johnson believed that the evangelical culture produced by revivals was promoted by the middle class and fostered in the working class as a means of controlling the latter, Sutton and most scholars today see the evangelical ethos making demands on all groups. To the extent that business owners and laborers saw themselves as distinct classes, which is itself contested now, journeymen used evangelical tenets to place demands for justice and fairness on those who employed them. "Traditional Protestant economic morality prohibited evangelical masters from ill treating or underpaying workers, just as it commanded evangelical workers to work diligently," writes Sutton.[35] In other words, the evangelical upsurge brought about by the revivals of the Second Great Awakening fostered equality where owners could expect their workers to stay sober on the job and work diligently for a fair day's wages, while workers could expect justice and fairness from their employers. The demands of both were taken directly from scripture, the authoritative basis for all evangelical Protestantism.

There is also another point that the social-control school misses. Middle-class owners who promoted revivals among their workers may have been motivated by a sincere desire to see their workers saved. Marxist and quasi-Marxist interpretations tend to see religion almost exclusively as a social tool, not a genuine category of human life. Religious historians, however, some Christian, some not, are more apt to take religious impulses as either basic to human nature or so ingrained in theology that adherents actually do attempt to live virtuous lives of commitment merely because they believe they should. There is little doubt that America was littered with revivalist preachers and committed laypeople who were highly motivated by the biblical command to spread the gospel. If one sees religion as a genuine category of human life, then it is not so hard to conceive of mill owners and other businessmen wanting to make a profit and do good at the same time. They may have wanted their employees to work hard so the business would thrive economically, but it is possible that at least some of them also wanted their workers to be saved and live godly lives so the workers themselves would be happy in this life and find heaven in the next. Certainly, some business owners used revivalism to control and manipulate their workers, much like southern evangelical preachers used biblical arguments to justify slavery. The point is that revivalist, evangelical Protestantism, which increased its cultural influence in America during the Second Great Awakening, could be used for social control or liberation and empowerment. On balance, recent scholarship suggests that the latter was more often the case. It is even likely that while many business owners engaged in a benign form of paternalism, converted owners were more likely than the unconverted to see their business practices as constrained by the "Golden Rule" and not merely by market forces.[36]

Notes

1. Quoted in Charles E. Hambrick-Stowe, *Charles G. Finney and the Spirit of American Evangelicalism* (Grand Rapids, Mich.: Eerdmans, 1996), xii. Hambrick-Stowe is here quoting one of the preeminent historians of American religion, Mark Noll. Unless otherwise noted, the material on Finney in this chapter comes from Hambrick-Stowe. Direct quotes and material from other sources on Finney will be footnoted.

2. Timothy Smith, *Revivalism and Social Reform: American Protestantism on the Eve of the Civil War* (Baltimore: Johns Hopkins University Press, 1980), 9. Smith's book was originally published in 1957.

3. Quoted in Hambrick-Stowe, 2.

4. Keith J. Hardman, *Charles Grandison Finney, 1792–1875: Revivalist and Reformer* (Syracuse, N.Y.: Syracuse University Press, 1987), 33.

5. Quoted in Hambrick-Stowe, 80.

6. Ibid., 156.

7. Quoted in ibid., 69.

8. Paul Johnson, *A Shopkeeper's Millennium: Society and Revivals in Rochester, New York, 1815–1837* (New York: Hill and Wang, 1978), 15–18.

9. Quoted in ibid., 5.

10. Ibid., 13.

11. Quoted in ibid., 95.

12. Quoted in Hardman, 201.

13. Whitney Cross,*The Burned-Over District: The Social and Intellectual History of Enthusiastic Religion in Western New York, 1800–1850* (New York: Harper and Row, 1965), 155.

14. Johnson, 36.

15. Ibid., 100.

16. Quoted in ibid., 109.

17. For a brief account of the Fundamentalist-Modernist Controversy and the development of religious pluralism in America see: George Marsden, *Religion and American Culture* (New York: Oxford University Press, 1990), chapters 4 and 5.

18. Quoted in Hambrick-Stowe, 55.

19. Quoted in ibid., 124.

20. Ibid., 140–41.

21. Quoted in ibid., 99.

22. Johnson, 35.

23. Ibid., 5.

24. Ibid., 8.

25. Ibid., 38.

26. Ibid., 60–61.

27. Nathan Hatch, *The Democratization of American Christianity* (New Haven, Conn.: Yale University Press, 1989).

28. William R. Sutton, *Journeymen for Jesus: Evangelical Artisans Confront Capitalism in Jacksonian Baltimore* (University Park: Pennsylvania State University Press, 1998).

29. Ibid., 7.

30. Ibid.

31. Ibid., 8.

32. Quoted in ibid., 247.

33. Quoted in ibid., 250.

34. Quoted in ibid., 251.

35. Ibid., 31.

36. Ibid., 244.

CHAPTER 4

REVIVALS AND THE DEVELOPMENT OF AFRICAN AMERICAN RELIGION IN AMERICA

One of the most significant and interesting events in American history is the conversion of African American slaves to Christianity. While this process of conversion started during the First Great Awakening, the Second greatly accelerated it. African Americans thus became one of the most thoroughly Christianized ethnic groups in America. The experience of African Americans was different from that of other groups for two reasons. First, they were brought to America against their will, and, second, they were not Christian when they arrived. Unlike all European groups except Jews, African slaves belonged to other religions before coming to America. While their conversion was in one sense thorough, the faith that developed among African Americans was not merely European Christianity among black people. Rather, the mixture of African cultural factors, religious practices, and indigenous traditions with the Christian faith produced a distinct type of Protestant Christianity, most of which developed in conjunction with the Second Great Awakening.

The African Heritage

Although not Christian, Africans in the seventeenth and eighteenth centuries had religious influences that prepared them quite well for their exposure to Christianity. African religions were for the most part tribal, with each different tribe holding some beliefs that were unique. Still, there were a variety of doctrines that most West Africans held in common, and these beliefs facilitated their acceptance of Christianity. Most Africans believed in a High God or Creator who was often associated with the sky. This god had little to do with the affairs of the world or with the lesser, active local gods and ancestor spirits. Some of the lesser gods were grouped into pantheons. For example, the sky pantheon consisted of lightening, thunder, and rainstorms, while the earth gods governed fertility and punished wickedness. Many Africans also believed in world-inhabiting spirits, some of which could become angry because of peoples' sins. Many of these spirits had to be appeased by tribe members observing certain taboos. If the taboos were violated, the spirits would become angry and exact punishment. In addition to these pantheons of gods there were various so-called cults or sects, which had their own priests who performed worship rites and sacrifices, presided over festivals, and served as skilled diviners (those who could tell the future or read certain signs) and herbalists (those who used herbs to tell the future or predict calamity). African religious beliefs were carried into practice through religious rituals that included drumming, dancing, and singing. During ceremonies Africans often anticipated being "mounted" by a spirit or a particular god. This simply meant that the god had joined the individual, taking possession of his or her spirit. The individual would then dance in spiritual ecstasy.

Ancestor spirits also played a significant role in African religions, usually forefathers who were held in high esteem for having founded a village or a clan. Africans were often more afraid of offending these dead ancestors than they were of angering the gods. Some of these forefathers had died years or even generations before, while others had only more recently passed away. The spirit of ancestors from the past could be manifested anew in the birth of family members. For example, when a young boy looked like his grandfather, it was believed that the grandfather's spirit actually inhabited the child. Frequently people met their dead ancestors in dreams, believing their grandparents had visited them to warn of some calamity.

Because of the nature of African religions, most slaves who were captured in Africa and transported across the Atlantic were accustomed to a world where gods and spirits were quite active. They saw the universe in personal and supernatural terms. Taken together, these religious beliefs prepared Africans for conversion to revivalist Christianity. As Albert Raboteau, one of the leading scholars of African American religion, has put it, "Thus the religious background of the slaves was a complex system of belief, and in the life of an African community there was a close relationship between the natural and the supernatural, the secular and the sacred."[1] By contrast, many of the elites of Europe and the Americas in the eighteenth century were adopting a scientific worldview that tended toward naturalism and a belief in an impersonal universe, but for Africans brought to the New World as slaves the heavenly world was not distant. Gods, spirits, ancestor spirits, and the like were part of everyday life and the welfare of the community depended on a close relationship with these supernatural elements. In other words, religion was central to the consciousness and worldview of the slaves. Moreover, the fundamental Africanness, or Africanity, continued in the New World to shape the religious experiences of slaves even as they converted to Christianity. As Raboteau has written, "Afro-American cults have modified traditions and added new ones. Yet, despite discontinuity and innovation, the fundamental religious perspectives of Africa have continued to orient the lives of the descendants of slaves in the New World."[2] Another scholar puts it this way, "The African/American was thus uniquely ready for the Great Awakenings. First, coming from a living mystery faith in Africa, he was prepared to participate in the Christian mystery. Second, because of his noncoherent world view he deeply yearned for new coherence and a new sense of unity and purpose."[3] What this scholar means by "noncoherent" worldview was the disconnect between desiring to be true to the African heritage of one's parents and grandparents while trying at the same time to fit into the world of white Europeans in the New World where the African heritage was threatened. It was difficult, if not impossible, to remain true to Africa and also be what in America was considered a "good slave."[4]

This discussion of worldview is difficult to document but interesting and plausible. We do not have many slave records testifying specifically to the psychic discontent of being caught between two worlds. What we have, however, is an abundance of evidence of the various ways that slaves behaved religiously. There is some indication that slaves believed that their gods did not come across the Atlantic to the New World. This belief caused a sense of loss that African Americans set out to remedy. They did so by constructing a new religious worldview and subculture based on both the common African heritage they shared and the common experience of slavery. This culture, in the words of one scholar, "was built upon the shared core of African understandings of man, spirit, and the world. Man's spirit was seen as dual. Spirit was viewed as pervasive and approachable, and the world as the present merging with the past. Man's soul was to join spirit after death."[5]

From the 1930s to the 1970s scholars debated whether or not North American slavery stripped slaves of their African identity. From the 1970s to the present, the view that a great deal of the African heritage has survived, religion especially, has prevailed. How much of African American religion is African and how much is revivalist Protestantism? However one balances these two influences, a consensus has emerged that both are present. Many scholars believe that the African influences, the experience of slavery during which African Americans converted to Christianity, and the revivalism of the First and Second Great Awakenings have combined to make African American religion something more than merely Protestantism among black people. Rather, African American religion is unique.[6]

The First Great Awakening and the Religion of the Slaves

From the mid-fifteenth century onward there are records of white slave traders using the conversion of African slaves as a justification for slavery. Expressing pity for Africans as well as guilt for the cruelty inherent in the slave trade, these accounts nevertheless say that all the pain and suffering will be worth it if the slaves become Christians. The following two quotes from a Portuguese chronicler illustrate how the pangs of guilt could be softened by the belief that slavery would result in conversion:

> But what heart could be so hard as not to be pierced with piteous feeling to see that company? For some kept their heads low and their faces bathed in tears, looking one upon another; others stood groaning very dolorously, looking up to the height of heaven . . . crying out loudly, as if asking help of the Father of Nature; others struck their faces with the palms of their hands, throwing themselves at full length upon the ground; others made their lamentation in the manner of a dirge, after the custom of their country. . . . But to increase

> their sufferings . . . those who had charge of the division of the cap-
> tives . . . began to separate one from another . . . to part fathers from
> sons, husbands from wives, brothers from brothers. No respect was
> shown either to friends or relations, but each fell where his lot took
> him.[7]

After recording such sadness, this same chronicler took solace in the
prospect of slave conversion, which was part of a general effort to make
slaves like whites:

> And so their lot was now quite the contrary of what it had been;
> since before they had lived in perdition of soul and body; of their
> souls, in that they were yet pagans, without the clearness and the
> light of the holy faith; and of their bodies, in that they lived like
> beasts, without any custom of reasonable beings—for they had no
> knowledge of bread or wine, and they were without covering of
> clothes, or the lodgement of houses; and worse than all, they had
> no understanding of good, but only knew how to lie in bestial
> sloth.[8]

Like almost all whites, this chronicler believed that in the long run
enslavement would be for the best, as Africans would acculturate and
become like Europeans.

Even though salvation was often used as a justification for slavery,
white churches in colonial North America were relatively indifferent to
slave conversion during the seventeenth and early eighteenth centuries,
and preachers often criticized this lack of concern. In 1682, one
preacher charged that as long as slaves worked hard and made a profit,
owners cared little for the state of their souls. In 1685, the publication
of a sermon with the title "Trade preferr'd before Religion and Christ
made to give place to Mammon" illustrated this concern.[9] The belief
that conversion might lead to freedom contributed to the reluctance to
evangelize slaves actively. The laws were somewhat vague on this point,
but many colonists believed that if their slaves were converted, English
law would require their emancipation. For this reason, some owners
denied missionaries access to their slaves. By 1706 this legal situation
was clarified and corrected in some of the colonies, with new laws that
stated clearly that conversion did not equal freedom.[10]

In addition to the fear of freedom, white prejudice also inhibited
efforts to convert Africans. Many masters believed their slaves were too

brutish to be saved. This belief was based largely on the language barrier and resulted in missionaries concentrating on slave children. Missionaries would bypass the adult slaves and teach the children English in hopes that this would prepare them for conversion. Some planters, however, went beyond the cultural and language differences and argued flatly that Africans were a different specie. This view was remarkably similar to the English view of Native Americans in the early colonial period. Again, ministers were the ones who protested this view, often reminding owners that Africans were human and therefore equal to whites in the sight of God. This plea for equality sometimes made matters worse, however, as many owners could not escape the logic that if Africans were equal to whites and eligible for conversion, then slavery itself could no longer be justified. These owners were correct. The belief in equality and the call for conversion were related, and even after legislation made it clear that conversion would not result in legal equality, many owners feared that preachers and missionaries would inadvertently plant ideas of equality in the minds of slaves. These owners feared that even if slaves were not freed legally, the spiritual claim to equal fellowship with whites would cause slaves to become "saucy." As if to confirm this view, there was a slave rebellion in 1729 that resulted when baptized slaves concluded that they should be freed.[11]

Responding to the fears of slave owners, some missionaries and preachers denied that conversion would arouse slaves and argued instead that it would actually make better slaves. The Anglican bishop of London wrote in 1727, "And so far is Christianity from discharging Men from the Duties of the Station and Condition in which it found them, that it lays them under stronger Obligations to perform those Duties with the greatest Diligence and Fidelity; not only from the Fear of Men, but from a Sense of Duty to God, and the Belief and Expectation of a future Account."[12] Some missionaries pointed directly to the profit motive, arguing that converted slaves would work harder and be more loyal, thus insuring greater productivity and more money for the owner. These missionaries and preachers drew a distinction between spiritual and physical freedom. Conversion resulted only in the spiritual freedom of slaves, they argued. In these instances, the Christian gospel became a means of slave control in much the same way that it was sometimes used by urban business owners for social control of their workers.

The preponderance of slaves in the South also served as an impediment to slave conversions. Before the Second Great Awakening, religion was weakest in the South. In Anglican areas such as Virginia, there were too few priests. In non-Anglican areas there were simply too few churches of any kind. One chronicler in 1701 reported that in South Carolina more than half of the colony's 7,000 white inhabitants had no access to religion. This report did not even consider Native Americans or slaves. In 1724 another observer reported that in North Carolina there was a real need for missionaries to the British, let alone the slaves and Native Americans. New England, by contrast, had a lot more churches and ministers but far fewer African slaves to convert. There, leading ministers such as John Eliot and Cotton Mather advocated missionary efforts to Christianize slaves.[13]

When all these conditions are taken into account, it is small wonder that there was little successful evangelization of slaves during the first century of slavery in the American colonies. This began to change during the First Great Awakening (1730–1750) as Baptists and Presbyterians (Methodists later) began to evangelize African Americans. Because these revivalist denominations believed that conversion could happen instantaneously as the first step in the Christian life, they were well suited to slave evangelism. By contrast, Anglicans struggled to evangelize illiterate slaves because they stressed learning the catechism of Christian doctrine as necessary to full conversion and baptism. In this case, literacy had to precede conversion. The task of evangelization proceeded very slowly because there simply were not enough teachers in most areas. As one scholar writes about the difference between Anglican and revivalist methods, "The Anglican usually taught the slaves the Ten Commandments, the Apostles' Creed and the Lord's Prayer; the revivalist preacher helped them to feel the weight of sin, to imagine the threats of Hell, and to accept Christ as their only Savior."[14] Revivalist preaching had an immediacy and simplicity that appealed to illiterate slaves who could barely understand English, let alone the Apostles' Creed. Moreover, as Baptists and Presbyterians began to preach revivals, Africans recognized several doctrines. God the creator, the divinity of Jesus, the Holy Spirit all made sense in light of the religious influences slaves had brought with them from Africa. They thought it unusual that there was only one Holy Spirit and only one human manifestation of divinity, but otherwise these ideas were similar to tribal beliefs. Moreover, the concepts of evil, punishment, and an afterlife were all familiar.

Religious worship, however, would have seemed very different. Slaves were accustomed to drumming and dancing, and one can be sure that white Presbyterians in the early eighteenth century did neither. In a culture with a strong Puritan influence, such activities were considered worldly and sinful. As Raboteau has written, "The differences between Protestant Christianity and African religious belief were, of course, much more numerous and much more important than the similarities, but there were enough similarities to make it possible for slaves to find some common ground between the beliefs of their ancestors and those of the white Christians."[15] The differences between white and black religious experience began to abate somewhat during the First Great Awakening as the Baptist revivals among whites began to include ecstatic religious experience. African Americans welcomed this. The intensity of religious emotion was new for whites, but not for slaves who had brought such experiences with them from Africa. They responded in significant numbers.[16]

In the "preliminary showers" of the First Great Awakening, as the early revivals were called, the great theologian Jonathan Edwards recorded, "There are several Negroes who, from what was seen in them and what is discernable in them since, appear to have been truly born again in the late remarkable season."[17] The most prolific of the First Great Awakening preachers, George Whitefield, also noted that as the revivals swept the colonies African Americans were converted in significant numbers, and revivalist Gilbert Tennent wrote approvingly of this phenomenon. One scholar has called the presence of African American slaves at the revivals of the First Great Awakening "one of the most important happenings for blacks in America."[18] The reverend Samuel Davies wrote of the importance of conversion, telling African Americans, "You will say perhaps 'other Negroes are baptized; and why not I?' But, consider some other negroes have been in great trouble about their souls; their hearts have been broken for sin; they have accepted Christ as their only Savior; and are Christians indeed; and when you are such, it will be time enough for you to be baptized."[19] Notice here the emphasis on conversion first and foremost. Neither Davies nor any other revivalist of the First Great Awakening disapproved of Christian instruction; all believed it was essential to the Christian life. But, it was secondary in both importance and in time, as conversion to Christ was preeminent, the first step in one's Christian walk. Such revivalism was quite the opposite of the Anglican way, and was one of the primary reasons that slave conversions only began in significant numbers with the coming of the revivals of the First Great Awakening.

While religious statistics in the eighteenth and nineteenth centuries are not always reliable, they do suggest patterns of growth. In other words, scholars often do not rely heavily on the accuracy of the actual numbers recorded in denominational record books, but they do pay attention to statistical increases or decreases. Some fragmentary statistics suggest significant growth in African American slave conversions during the years of the First Great Awakening and thereafter. Methodists in 1786 (the first year they distinguished black from white members) recorded 1,890 black members out of a total of 18,791 in the American colonies. By 1790, the figure was 11,682 and in 1797, 12,215. These figures represented almost one-fourth of the total Methodist membership in America. Baptist records are sparse, consisting largely of estimates. One estimate is that African Americans were one-fourth of total Baptist membership by 1793, which would have been about 18,000 or so. According to another study, the number increased from 18,000 in 1793 to about 40,000 by 1813.[20] For a variety of reasons having to do with the independent status of Baptist congregations and the ease with which Baptist preachers can be ordained, Baptist churches became the preferred denomination of African Americans and remain so to this day. Any local group of black baptized believers could form a Baptist congregation and ordain a minister. Moreover, the simplicity of Baptist preaching often appealed to illiterate slaves as did water baptism, which resembled some African religious rituals.

As a result of the conversion of African Americans during the First Great Awakening, white Protestants envisioned using freed slaves to evangelize Africa. This dream would be reenacted again in the nineteenth century. In 1773, Samuel Hopkins, one of the leading preachers of the late colonial era, first hit upon this idea. He persuaded the influential colonial politician Ezra Stiles to participate. They raised funds and picked two African Americans to head the effort. One was a slave, Bristol Yamma, who was from Hopkins' church in Rhode Island, and the other was a freedman, John Quamino. The two were sent off to the College of New Jersey, as Princeton was then called, for training under Presbyterian theologian John Witherspoon. The whole effort collapsed, however, when Quamino died and the Revolutionary War diverted the attention of the others.[21] The plan was a testament nevertheless to the First Great Awakening's vision of converting American slaves as well as Africans in Africa.

By the end of the First Great Awakening the old fear that conversion meant freedom for slaves had abated significantly. Slaves were slaves whether Christianized or not. It was also becoming clear that free African Americans were second-class citizens even if they were Christians. In 1785, African American preacher Henry Evans established a black Methodist church in Fayetteville, North Carolina, which began to thrive. Whites came to observe, were impressed, and began to join. As they did, they took control of the church, forcing the African Americans into a side shed. Evans himself concurred with this development and was seen by the whites as being "properly respectful." White Christians often exhibited this type of prejudice. They not only had trouble believing that African American Christians could run their own churches, but also feared such independence. On the other hand, black deference to white power, like that of Evans, was not uncommon. The more important story of African American religion, however, would be the development of the theme of liberation during the Second Great Awakening.

The Second Great Awakening and African American Religion

As important as the First Great Awakening was for normalizing the idea that slaves should be evangelized, most of the conversion of African Americans would take place during the Second Great Awakening. As this happened, white Christians once again feared that evangelization of slaves would lead to independence. The most significant aspect of the mass conversion of slaves during the Second Great Awakening was the way they combined African heritage, their common experience as slaves, and elements of biblical teaching to fashion a distinctly African American brand of Protestant Christianity.

One of the reasons for the appeal of the Second Great Awakening among slaves was that, by opposing slavery, the Baptists and Methodists, the most revivalistic denominations, had won the right to be heard. In the late-eighteenth century Baptist associations in Virginia, Kentucky, New York, Indiana, Illinois, and Ohio issued strong antislavery manifestoes. One of the leading Baptist activists of the time, John

Leland, was actually from Massachusetts but preached revivals and pastored churches in Virginia from 1777 to 1791. An advocate of religious liberty, he apparently influenced James Madison and Thomas Jefferson in 1785 when those two founding fathers wrote Virginia's bill establishing religious freedom. Ever the champion of conscience, Leland demanded that religious liberty be extended to slaves so they could travel to night revival meetings, and he linked slavery with religious persecution as twin examples of oppression.[22] In 1789, Leland introduced an antislavery resolution at the meeting of the Baptist General Committee of Virginia, the state association of Baptists. The resolution read, "Resolved that slavery is a violent deprivation of the rights of nature, and inconsistent with a republican government; and we, therefore, recommend it to our brethren, to make use of every legal measure to extirpate this horrid evil from the land and pray Almighty God that our honorable legislature may have it in their power to proclaim the great Jubilee consistent with the principles of good policy."[23] Just four years later Virginia Baptists backtracked on the strong 1789 statement and decided that slavery was a matter of conscience that should be left to individuals to decide—individual owners, that is. This retreat was but a prelude to the more thoroughgoing reversal that Baptists in the South would make on the issue of slavery.

Methodists prior to 1800 had also opposed slavery, requiring traveling preachers to emancipate their slaves and declaring that slavery was contrary to God's will. A conference in Baltimore in 1780 issued a statement that "[S]lavery is contrary to the laws of God, man, and nature—hurtful to society; contrary to the dictates of conscience and pure religion, and doing that which we would not others should do to us and ours."[24] Four years later, this declaration was stiffened to include threat of expulsion for any Methodist who failed to comply with the antislavery proclamation within 12 months. For Methodists at that time, it was a violation of church rule to buy or sell slaves except for the purpose of freeing them. As one slave recalled, "I had recently joined the Methodist Church, and from the sermon I heard, I felt that God had made all men free and equal, and that I ought not be a slave."[25] The attitude toward African Americans and slavery was quite different at the beginning of the Second Great Awakening than during the First. George Whitefield, Samuel Davies, and the other great preachers of the earlier revivals all advocated preaching to African Americans but were careful to say or do nothing that might disrupt the institution of slavery. On the eve of the Second Great Awakening, slaves were already joining the Baptists and Methodists in significant numbers, largely, it would seem, because these denominations preached equality and advocated freedom.[26]

Such egalitarianism was not to last, however, as Baptists and Methodists in the South backtracked, then reversed themselves on the issue of slavery. This change showed how denominations tend to accommodate themselves to the norms of culture as they become larger.[27] There has been a general trend in American religion that when groups move from sectarian status to become more mainstream, they soften their radicalism and take on the views of the majority. At the same time Baptists and Methodists were accommodating to the larger society, it became apparent that slavery was not going to go away. Baptists and Methodists, therefore, gave in and just learned to live in peace with an institution they had previously denounced as evil. Once again, as had happened in the late seventeenth and early eighteenth centuries, the idea developed that conversion would make African Americans better but not free. It was a short step from conversion making slaves better, to conversion making better slaves, at which point the message was as much for owners who wanted to control their slaves as for the slaves who wanted to be free.[28]

When the Second Great Awakening began at places like Gaspar River and Cane Ridge, Kentucky, in 1800 and 1801, the emotional expression of the camp meeting revivals eclipsed the experiences of the First Great Awakening, and African Americans embraced this development. As Raboteau has written, "The camp meeting proved to be a powerful instrument for accelerating the pace of slave conversions."[29] In addition to the emotional appeal were the mere demographics of the Second Great Awakening and the methods employed by the preachers involved. The Second Great Awakening revived religion in the South where most slaves lived. Planters became more religious themselves and became interested in promoting revival among their slaves for a variety of reasons, some altruistic and others more self-serving. The Awakening took place primarily among Baptists, Methodists, and Presbyterians. These denominations were well suited to carry the Christian gospel around the countryside because they were able to articulate its message in simple ways that the uneducated and illiterate could comprehend. The populist approach to religion appealed to slaves, just as it appealed to poor white farmers and urban workers. Revivals were egalitarian and individualistic, carrying the central message that all were equally sinners in need of salvation. Moreover, revival preachers had no qualms about preaching to mixed-race crowds. The desire to see all people converted drove them to ignore societal taboos as they stressed a non-Calvinist (Arminian) gospel.[30] The Arminian belief that all people have free will and the capacity to convert to Christ motivated preachers to take their message to the slaves.

The extent to which the Methodists, Baptists, and Presbyterians appealed to slaves is illustrated in a narrative by John Thompson, a slave from Maryland. He told how his Episcopalian mistress and her family would travel five miles to church and five miles back home every Sunday. Thompson and the other slaves understood almost nothing of the doctrine preached at the Episcopalian Church. "So we went to the Episcopal church," he remembered, "but always came home as we went, for the preaching was above our comprehension, so that we could understand but little that was said." Eventually, a Methodist preacher came within proximity of the plantation where Thompson lived, and "preached in a manner so plain that the way faring man, though a fool, could not err therein. This new doctrine produced great consternation among the slaveholders. It was something that they could not understand. It brought glad tidings to the poor bondman; it bound up the broken-hearted; it opened the prison doors to them that were bound, and let the captive go free."[31] Thompson told how the simple Methodist message spread from one plantation to another until it reached his own. Nearly every slave he knew was converted. Richard Allen, one of the founders of African American Methodism put it simply when accounting for Methodist successes among black people, "[T]he unlearned can understand. . . . The Methodists were the first people that brought glad tidings to the colored people . . . for all other denominations preached so high-flown that we were not able to comprehend their doctrine."[32]

Because Baptists and Methodists put less emphasis on education for clergy and instead stressed ability to communicate and enthusiasm for the gospel, they were open to black preachers who could learn the rudiments of the biblical story of Christ's death and resurrection as redemption for human sin. Beyond such basic knowledge, which could be gleaned from white revival preachers, the only test was whether a black preacher was effective in winning converts. The development of

African American preachers was crucial for the increase in conversion of slaves because they preferred black preachers to white. Leland told stories of slaves walking 20 miles one-way on Sunday to hear a black preacher. He stated flatly that slaves "put more confidence in their own color than they do in whites."[33] Likewise, the Presbyterian preacher Charles Colcock Jones, commenting on the success of Baptists in revival preaching among slaves, wrote, "In general the Negroes were followers of the Baptists in Virginia, and after a while, as they permitted many colored men to preach, the great majority of them went to hear preachers of their own color."[34] As early as the 1780s, a slave named Lewis preached to crowds as large as 400. In 1792, following the resignation of the preacher of the Portsmouth, Virginia Baptist Church, the congregation called a black preacher to be its pastor. People in the church liked him so much that they purchased his freedom and that of his whole family. The same year the Roanoke Baptist Association purchased a slave preacher and set him free, while another black preacher pastored a white congregation in Gloucester County.[35]

Several scholars have concurred that the appearance of black preachers was the most important turning point in the development of African American religion.[36] The importance of slave preachers was heightened as racist conditions persisted in the face of black conversions to Protestant Christianity. The era of egalitarian preaching on the part of Baptists and Methodists came to a close pretty quickly after 1800. While there continued to be many mixed-race congregations in the early nineteenth century, African Americans were required to sit in the back or in the balcony of the churches. This type of discrimination gave rise to one of the most important denominations in African American religion, the African Methodist Episcopal Church.

The African Methodist Episcopal Church did not begin its separate existence for ecclesiastical or theological reasons. Rather, it was the racist practices of the white Methodist Episcopal Church in Philadelphia and elsewhere that gave rise to the first separate African American denomination in American history. In 1792, at St. George's Methodist Episcopal Church in Philadelphia, black worshippers were asked to move to the balcony because they were seated in an area of the church that, unbeknownst to them, was for whites only, When they moved too slowly, some of the African Americans were literally pulled from their knees during prayer and forced out of their pews. Richard Allen and Absolom Jones promptly led the black Methodists out of the church. Allen was a former slave who had been licensed by the Methodists in New Jersey and Pennsylvania. He had already been active in forming prayer meetings and had even suggested prior to the incident at St. George's that African Americans have their own separate place of worship. "Our only design is to secure to ourselves our rights and privileges to regulate our affairs, temporal and spiritual, the same as if we were white people."[37] Allen and Jones secured temporary meeting places for the next several years before dedicating the St. Thomas African Episcopal Church, which was to be separate from the white-controlled Methodist denomination. Jones became the pastor after Allen declined. As Allen put it, he could never be anything other than a Methodist.[38] Allen then founded Bethel Methodist Church, which was a separate black congregation within the Methodist Episcopal Church. Allen's strategy was apparently to exert autonomy for African Americans within the white denomination. His approach worked only in part and only for a few decades. Eventually, because of continued interference from the white leaders of the denomination, Allen was forced to join with other African Americans in forming the African Methodist Episcopal (A.M.E.) denomination, which has been one of the most important black institutions in American history.

This desire of whites to control predominately black congregations was repeated in other areas of the country within the Methodist Episcopal Church and within various Baptist associations and congregations. In some Baptist churches African American membership exceeded white membership, but by the 1820s most black congregations were under white control. This shift can be illustrated by two regulations in the Virginia association of Baptist churches. In 1794, the association allowed African American congregations to send black representatives to associational meetings. In 1828, the rules were changed and African American congregations had to be represented by whites. As in the case of the Methodists, such prejudice led eventually to the founding of black Baptist associations and later, nationwide black Baptist denominations. By the second decade of the nineteenth century the pattern was pretty much set. Black preachers became exasperated with white harassment and so formed separate institutions in an effort to take control of their own religious affairs.[39]

As African Americans began to assert religious independence, white and black Protestants continued to evangelize slaves. Some scholars estimate that during the first two decades of the nineteenth century only a minority of slaves were touched by Christianity. The converted tended to be house slaves, urban slaves, and artisan slaves. The vast majority of slaves were rural plantation workers, and here the gospel message was yet to penetrate. Concern for rural slaves gave rise in the 1830s and 1840s to the plantation mission, which became a key institution in the further evangelization of slaves. Plantation mission societies were often adjuncts to Baptist associations and were very similar to a myriad of other reform voluntary organizations founded during the first third of the nineteenth century. Members gave lectures to planters, urging them to take responsibility for Bible teaching and worship among their slaves, held conferences to discuss methods of evangelization, issued committee reports, circulated pamphlets, and so on. While plantation missions were motivated primarily by concern for spreading the gospel among slaves, the message by this time had been made safe, as the denominations that formerly had opposed slavery had come to accept it. Pamphlets, for example, tried to show that while the Bible did not forbid slavery, it did require evangelization.[40] This attitude would be part of a reform theme that would pervade the South until the Civil War ended slavery altogether. Essentially, southern Baptist, Methodist, and Presbyterian preachers began to call for the reform of slavery, which included the effort to meet the religious needs of slaves as well as to treat them more humanely. Preachers defended slavery but also warned that if slavery were not made more humane and just, God's judgment would come upon the South. Many believed that is precisely what happened in the Civil War.[41]

Lurking in the background of the plantation missions and all other such efforts to evangelize slaves was the fear of abolition. This fear had the potential to seriously hamper efforts to take the gospel to slaves. The answer among those involved in plantation missions was that evangelization was the best answer to Christian abolitionists in the North who condemned slavery as unjust, partly because it kept slaves in sin. The logic was that if slavery facilitated conversion of African Americans, then the institution itself might be proved to be good. In 1829, C. C. Pinckney said it was important to improve the religious state of slaves as a way to gain the "advantage in argument over . . . Northern Brethren," while a county Baptist association report included this defense: "One of their [the North] repeated charges is, that we do not afford religious instruction to the Negroes; . . . To this it may briefly be replied, that they themselves have greatly retarded this work."[42] The implication of that last sentence was that northern abolitionists, by planting ideas of freedom in the heads of slaves, made it too dangerous to evangelize them. This was probably a reference to David Walker's famous 1829 *Appeal,* a strenuous attack on slavery that was believed to incite slaves to rebellion.

Plantation mission methods consisted of Sunday preaching to slaves "at their level of understanding," a lecture on doctrine during the week, and Sunday schools to train children. Mission literature encouraged masters to attend meetings with slaves in order to set a good example. Instruction had to be oral because several slave states had antiliteracy laws that made it a crime to teach slaves to read and write. Nevertheless, several catechisms were prepared to instruct slaves how to live the Christian life following their conversion. Plantation mission literature almost always contained a warning to the slaves themselves and to plantation missionaries that no large meetings were to take place without the express permission of the plantation owner or manager.[43]

Various associational minutes listed all sorts of reasons for supporting plantation missions, among these were a desire to reach the poor with the gospel, control slaves, defend slavery against abolitionists, and promote the dream of the ideal plantation. A motivation that can be teased out of the records of the slaveholders themselves was the deep misgivings that owners may have had about the injustice of slavery. As one scholar has written, "The conversion of his slave would . . . please a Christian slaveholder who was concerned with the state of their souls, and who might even have had some secret misgivings about owning them."[44] In 1859, the North Carolina *Christian Advocate* summed up the southern Christian view of slavery that helped plantation missions flourish: "Everybody who believes in religion at all, admits that it is the duty of Christians to give religious instruction to the slave population of the Southern States. To deny the safety and propriety of preaching the Gospel to the Negroes, is either to abandon Christianity, or to admit that slavery is condemned by it."[45]

As the revivals of the Second Great Awakening contributed to the growth of Christianity among African Americans, a distinctly black style of worship emerged, the integration of African heritage and culture with American Protestantism. Various observers of the early revivals of the Second Great Awakening noticed that African Americans were the most enthusiastic worshippers. One wrote, "By no class is a camp meeting hailed with more unmixed delight than by the poor slaves." Georgia evangelist Jesse Lee in 1807 recorded, "The first day of the meeting, we had a gentle and comfortable moving of the spirit of the Lord among us; and at night it was much more powerful than before, and the meeting was kept up all night without intermission. However, before day the white people retired and the meeting was continued by the black people." John Leland in 1790 wrote of his observations as to the style of worship among slaves, "[They] commonly are more noisy in time of preaching than the whites, and are more subject to bodily exercise, and if they meet with an encouragement in these things, they grow extravagant."[46]

The most common distinctly African American worship exercise was the ring shout. This was the practice of forming a circle, or ring, and singing, dancing, shouting, and stomping as participants either chanted or sang religious verse. In the early twentieth century, black sociologist W. E. B. Du Bois would group all black vocal expressions of worship into what he called "the Frenzy." Whether ring shout or frenzy, African American worship could be controversial, and not just among whites. African Methodist Episcopal bishop Daniel Payne opposed overt emotion, once attempting to stop a ring shout at a camp meeting. He recorded the event this way: "After the sermon they formed a ring, and with coats off, sung, clapped their hands and stamped their feet in a most ridiculous and heathenish way." When he tried to intervene to get the men to stop, one of them told just how important the ring shout was for the black revival experience. "[T]he spirit of God works upon people in different ways," this man told Payne. "At camp-meeting there must be a ring here, a ring there, a ring over yonder, or sinners will not get converted."[47] Richard Allen opposed the frenzy precisely because it was a holdover from African tribal religion. He rejected nearly all emotional expressions such as groaning, shouting, clapping, ring dancing, and the like.

Opinions such as those of Payne and Allen were in the minority, however, as African Americans almost universally took up the ecstatic religion of the Second Great Awakening and made it a staple of the black experience. Among whites, many Baptist preachers approved as well. Whites may or may not have viewed the African American religious ecstasy as an expression of African heritage, but those who supported the frenzy saw it as genuine religious experience, and that was enough. Scholars today believe that the frenzy, the ring shout, and other emotional expressions were both genuine religion and experiences in keeping with the slaves' African past. Raboteau has written, "The Protestant revivalist tradition, accepted by the slaves and their descendants in the United States, proved in this instance to be amenable to the influence of African styles of behavior. . . . While the North American slaves danced under the impulse of the Spirit of a 'new' God, they danced in ways their fathers in Africa would have recognized."[48]

Just as revivalism seemed to put the message of Christianity into the language of white commoners, so too it proved adaptable to African styles. As African culture merged with Protestant theology within the context of slavery, the central theme of African American religion emerged—liberation. This theme can be best illustrated by the stories of three religious visionaries who led slave revolts during the era of the Second Great Awakening.

"Three Generals in the Lord's Army"

During the period of the Second Great Awakening, there were three significant slave revolts that were inspired by religious visions of liberation and led by men who saw themselves in religious terms.[49] The first of these took place shortly after Toussaint L'Ouverture's successful slave revolt in Haiti in 1800, and was probably inspired by the Haiti rebellion.

Gabriel was a slave of Thomas Prosser. He was a student of the Bible and was especially drawn to Samson, the Old Testament figure who single-handedly killed a thousand Philistines. From his childhood forward, Gabriel believed that he was a black Samson called by God to liberate his people. He even wore his hair long, which had been a source of strength for the biblical Samson. Gabriel and his fellow conspirators formulated a plan whereby they would kill all whites they encountered, seize arms from a Richmond, Virginia, armory, then take money from the state treasury. These actions would send a signal to other slaves that an uprising was underway. The pressure of the revolt would then allow Gabriel to negotiate freedom for the slaves. If the plot failed, they would retreat to the mountains to carry on guerilla warfare for as long as it took to win their freedom.

Gabriel estimated that he had 10,000 followers, while others put the figure somewhere between 2,000 and 6,000. The governor of Mississippi believed that as many as 50,000 were ready to join in Gabriel's rebellion. However many slaves there were who had heard of the plan or who stood ready to jump into any rebellion that began, it is estimated that 1,000 slaves met on August 30, 1800, at night to begin the operation. A rainstorm interrupted the plans and the group dispersed. After this initial failure it became more and more difficult to communicate orders, and word began to leak out to authorities that there was a revolt afoot. Authorities began to round up suspects, and the plot was crushed. About 35 people were eventually executed, including Gabriel on October 7. While the revolt was clearly inspired by L'Ouverture's Haiti rebellion, and by the egalitarianism of Jeffersonian democracy, religious themes were clearly present as well. There were several other minor revolts or plans for them in the months and years to come. In these, biblical themes were often integrated with the African religious practice of Vodun, in which a medicine man would use various herbs that were believed to provide protection and knowledge of the future.

The second revolt with heavy religious overtones was that of Denmark Vesey, whom scholar Gayraud Wilmore calls a "Methodist Conspirator." Denmark Vesey purchased his freedom from Joseph Vesey the same year that Gabriel planned his revolt, 1800. Even while a slave, Vesey was an articulate, sophisticated, well-traveled man because his master had used him as a personal assistant. After gaining his freedom he moved to Charleston and worked for the next 20 years as a carpenter, reading everything he could and traveling to the Sea Islands off the coast as well as into the interior of South Carolina. In his travels he made extensive contacts with slaves. As an active Methodist layman he had conversations with other Methodists outside the South and had access to radical literature that came from the North and from the African colony of Sierra Leone, which was populated in part by freed American slaves. Vesey became fascinated with certain passages of scripture that he believed designated him for a special calling. The first was from Zechariah 14 that reads in part, "Behold, a day of Jehovah commeth, when thy spoil shall be divided in the midst of thee. For I will gather all nations against Jerusalem to battle; and the city shall be taken, and the houses rifled, and the women ravished."[50] The second was the story of Joshua fighting the battle of Jericho, where the

Israelites marched around the city, and God caused the walls to come tumbling down.

> So the people shouted, and the priests blew the trumpet: and it came to pass, when the people heard the sound of the trumpet, that the people shouted with a great shout, and the wall fell down flat, so that the people went up into the city, every man straight before him, and they took the city. And they utterly destroyed all that was in the city, both men and women, both young and old, and ox and sheep, and ass, with the edge of the sword.[51]

This use of divinely sanctioned violence resonated with Vesey.

In addition to these biblical stories Vesey was also inspired by Gabriel and L'Ouverture, and his movement had elements of African religion in the person of Gullah Jack. Gullah Jack was born in Africa and was a conjurer. He told people to eat nothing but parched corn and ground nuts on the day of the planned rebellion and to carry a crab claw in their pocket. This, he believed, would protect them from harm. Black Methodists in the African Methodist Episcopal denomination also aided Vesey's rebellion. After the A.M.E. Church split from the white Methodist denomination in 1816, white Methodists harassed black churches, sometimes attempting to take away their property and expel their preachers. It is likely that these actions played a part in furthering plans for revolt. Within the A.M.E. Church, the Methodist class meetings, as they were called, became the communications network for spreading information about the plan. A.M.E. pastor Morris Brown, who advised Vesey's group, was a protégé of Richard Allen and would later become a bishop. Some scholars believe that Allen himself knew and approved of Brown's support for Vesey's revolt.

The revolt was originally scheduled for June 16, 1822, by which time there were somewhere between 3,000 and 9,000 ready to take orders. One of Vesey's lieutenants had written to the president of Haiti informing him of the plan. The area of operation consisted of an 80-mile stretch around Charleston. Vesey instructed that all whites were to be killed except the few who were believed to be ready to join the revolt. Things began to come apart in late May when a house slave heard of the plan and informed his master. Arrests began on May 30, and one of the first two arrested confessed and gave names of the other conspirators. When the appointed day arrived, the militia surrounded Charleston, and the plan could not be put into effect. More arrests followed, including that of Vesey who was executed on July 2. Gullah Jack was arrested a few days later. In all, 131 were arrested, 37 executed, 43 transported out-of-state or banished from the United States, and 48 whipped and discharged. Rather than dampening the revolutionary spirit, however, Vesey's plan seemed once again to inspire other revolts and harden black sentiment in favor of ridding the nation of slavery, by violence if necessary.

It became apparent to the white powers that religion and rebellion seemed to go together in slave communities. For this reason, some states enacted laws strictly regulating religious activities. In 1800, South Carolina passed legislation forbidding slave church meetings from sunset to sunrise. At the request of the Charleston Baptist Associ-ation the law was relaxed three years later to allow meetings until 9 P.M. It was relaxed again in 1819 to allow slave meetings anytime there was at least one white present. All such laws were widely broken and some-times not even enforced. Typically, the level of enforcement was directly related to the perceived threat of rebellion.

The most famous slave rebellion in American history was led by Nat Turner. Turner, a Baptist preacher from Southampton, Virginia, seems to have found something in the Bible that whites had missed. "Nat Turner, . . . " Wilmore has written, "discovered that the God of the Bible demanded justice, and to know him and his Son Jesus Christ was to be set free from every power that dehumanizes and oppresses."[52] Turner was born the same year Vesey gained his freedom and Gabriel attempted to lead his revolt. A slave to Benjamin Turner, Nat was a pre-cocious child with the birthmarks of an African conjurer. These marks led his parents to believe that he had been chosen by God for a special work. Benjamin Turner was one of those slaveholders who followed the advice of the plantation missions organizations and promoted religion among his slaves. He saw to it that they received Bible instruction and ample opportunities for worship. Master Turner and others were amazed at young Nat's ability to absorb this religious training. He could read, write, and think proficiently. With encouragement from family, master, and friends, it is little wonder that Nat himself came to believe that God had called him to be a preacher and had set him apart for some special purpose.

While growing up, Turner was struck by the passage from the gospel of Luke 12:31, which reads in part, "I am come to send fire on the earth."[53] Turner began to read his own messianic calling in this and other verses, essentially believing that he, like Christ, was destined to save his people. He made a connection between Jesus and the Old Testament prophets, something white preachers rarely did. Whites tended to portray Jesus as the meek and mild lamb, led to slaughter for the sins of the world. By contrast, the Old Testament prophets called down judgment on the nation of Israel. Turner put these two images together; the savior of the world was also the prophet of justice.

On one occasion, long before he would lead a revolt, Turner ran away and survived by hiding in the woods for 30 days. He willingly returned to his plantation, saying God had instructed him to do so. This event has been subjected to various interpretations, but the most plausible seems to be that he believed he had acted precipitately and needed instead to wait on God for the right time to move against slavery. Luke 12 was again important at this juncture: "But and if that servant says in his heart, My lord delayeth his coming; and shall begin to beat the menservants and maidens, and to eat and drink, and to be drunken; the lord of that servant will come in a day when he looketh not for him, and at an hour when he is not aware. . . . And that servant who knew his lord's will, and prepared not himself, neither did according to his will, shall be beaten with many stripes."[54] Turner believed he needed to wait and prepare for the time of his calling.

Shortly after returning from his runaway, Turner had a vision of white and black spirits engaged in a great battle. In the midst of the vision he heard a voice saying, "Such is your luck, such you are called to see, and let it come rough or smooth, you must surely bear it."[55] This was his call. After 1825 the visions increased as he began to preach extensively across the countryside. One day he found blood on corn in a field, on another, hieroglyphics on leaves. Then, in 1828, he had another pivotal experience. Recalling it later, in his famous confession of 1831, he said, "[A]nd on the appearance of the sign I should arise and prepare myself, and slay my enemies with their own weapons. And immediately on the sign appearing in the heavens, the seal was removed from my lips, and I communicated the great work laid out for me to do, to four in whom I had the greatest confidence. It was intended by us to have begun the work of death on the 4th of July last."[56]

Turner waited for more than two years for the "sign" he had envisioned in 1828. In July 1831 he fell ill and was, therefore, unable to

meet the July 4 date with destiny. In August there was a strange atmo-
spheric haze in the sky over Virginia and North Carolina that became
known as the "Three Blue Days." This, he believed, was the sign for
which he had waited. On August 21, Turner met with his closest associates, all dedicated to winning their freedom by any means necessary.
They were convinced that this was the right time—God's time of
vengeance and justice. With an axe and hatchet they set out for the
home of John Travis, Turner's master, killing him, his wife, and five others. Collecting arms and more slaves, they continued over a 20-mile
swath of Southampton County. All told, 70 slaves joined in the rebellion, killing 57 whites. It was the bloodiest slave uprising in American
history. The plan was to take the county seat, procure more arms, and
widen the revolt. Alarmed whites gathered, along with the militia.
There were offers of support in suppressing the rebellion from as far
away as Philadelphia and New London, Connecticut. After experiencing brief success against the militia, Turner's men were dispersed and
were never able to regroup. Turner eluded authorities for more than six
weeks, hiding first in a cave, then in a hole he dug under a tree. On
October 30 he was apprehended at gunpoint. He was tried and con-
victed, then executed on November 11. During the 11 days between
arrest and hanging he made his famous confession to Thomas R. Gray,
the primary source of information about his rebellion. He died defiant,
showing no sign of sorrow and making no request for mercy. When
Gray asked him if he had been mistaken in his belief that God had
called him to lead the revolt, he replied, "Was not Christ crucified?"[57]

In all, 53 slaves were arrested and tried. Twenty-one were acquitted and 12 others taken out of the state. Twenty were hanged. Probably
a hundred more slaves died in fighting that continued before the movement was completely smashed. Turner's rebellion sent a wave of fear
across the slaveholding South, prompting the passage of laws in several
states against teaching slaves to read and write and against slaves
preaching the gospel. As Wilmore has written, "The southern whites
who observed the slave preachers at close range knew about the possible amalgam of African religion and radical Christianity. They sensed
the ability of those men and women to inspire revolt and threw up the
ramparts of repressive legislation and the lynch law against them."[58]

The slave revolts planned or carried out by these three figures
were all inspired by visions that were made possible in part by the

revivals. The impact of the revivals was unmistakable and enduring. African Americans were Christianized and there developed subsequently a distinctly African American religion that had liberation as its central theme. All slave revolts were crushed, but African American religion thrived in the context of freedom following the Civil War, providing black communities with the one institution they controlled. Little more than a century after the Second Great Awakening, African American churches would carry the theme of liberation to victory in the Civil Rights Movement of the 1960s with another black prophet. Martin Luther King, Jr., was a black Baptist preacher who would have been very much at home in the revivals of the Second Great Awakening.

Notes

1. Albert J. Raboteau, *Slave Religion: The "Invisible Institution" in the Antebellum South* (New York: Oxford University Press, 1978), 15.

2. Ibid., 42.

3. Mechal Sobel, *Trabelin' On: The Slave Journey to an Afro-Baptist Faith* (Westport, Conn.: Greenwood Press, 1979).

4. Ibid., 101.

5. Ibid., 224.

6. See, for example, Gayraud S. Wilmore, *Black Religion and Black Radicalism: An Interpretation of the Religious History of Afro-American People,* 2nd ed. (Maryknoll, N.Y.: Orbis Books, 1983).

7. Quoted in Raboteau, 96.

8. Quoted in ibid., 97.

9. Quoted in ibid., 98.

10. Ibid., 98–100.

11. Ibid., 100–102.

12. Quoted in ibid., 103.

13. Ibid., 104–5.

14. Ibid., 133.

15. Ibid., 127.

16. Sobel, 98.

17. Quoted in Raboteau, 128.

18. Sobel, 97.

19. Quoted in Raboteau, 130.

20. Ibid., 131.

21. Ibid., 109.

22. Nathan Hatch, *The Democratization of American Christianity* (New Haven, Conn.: Yale University Press, 1989), 103.

23. Quoted in Sobel, 86.

24. Quoted in Raboteau, 143.

25. Quoted in Hatch, 102.

26. Ibid., 103.

27. Sobel, 89; See also Christine Leigh Heyrman, *Southern Cross: The Beginnings of the Bible Belt* (New York: Knopf, 1997).

28. Raboteau, 145.

29. Ibid., 132.

30. Ibid.

31. Quoted in Hatch, 104.

32. Quoted in ibid., 104.

33. Quoted in ibid., 106.

34. Quoted in ibid., 106.

35. Raboteau, 133–34.

36. Ibid., 137.

37. Quoted in Hatch, 107.

38. C. Eric Lincoln and Lawrence H. Mamiya, *The Black Church in the African American Experience* (Durham, N.C.: Duke University Press, 1998), 50–51; see also Albert J. Raboteau, *A Fire in the Bones: Reflections on African-American Religious History* (Boston: Beacon Press, 1995), 79–102. Lincoln and Mamiya say the St. George's incident took place in 1787.

39. Hatch, 112; Raboteau, *Slave Religion,* 137; Lincoln and Mamiya, 20–46.

40. Raboteau, *Slave Religion,* 154–55.

41. Eugene D. Genovese, *A Consuming Fire: The Fall of the Confederacy in the Mind of the White Christian South* (Athens: University of Georgia Press, 1998).

42. Quoted in Raboteau, *Slave Religion,* 160.

43. Ibid., 161–62.

44. Quoted in ibid., 174.

45. Quoted in ibid., 175.

46. Quoted in ibid., 61.

47. Quoted in Sobel, 143.

48. Raboteau, *Slave Religion,* 72.

49. The three stories that follow come from Gayraud Wilmore's *Black Religion and Black Radicalism,* 53–73.

50. Quoted in ibid., 58.

51. Quoted in ibid., 58–59.

52. Ibid., 64.

53. Quoted in ibid., 65.

54. Quoted in ibid., 67.

55. Quoted in ibid., 67.

56. Quoted in ibid., 68.

57. Quoted in ibid., 71.

58. Ibid., 72.

CHAPTER 5

THE SECOND GREAT AWAKENING, TRANSCENDENTALISM, AND THE ANTISLAVERY IMPULSE

In addition to the conversion of African American slaves, one of the most significant outgrowths of the revivals of the Second Great Awakening was the heightened sense of social reform. Historian Gilbert Barnes, writing in the 1930s, was the first to make the connection between Charles Finney's revivals in the early 1830s and the upsurge in the antislavery movement. Since Barnes' work, the revivals have been connected to a whole array of reform impulses, including temperance, moral reform, missionary societies, women's rights, prison reform, and education.[1] Before the Second Great Awakening, during the colonial period, Americans appropriated the "city on a hill" mentality of the Puritans. In this vision, America was to be the place where godly communities would serve as a model of what a good society should be. The revolutionaries of 1776 in many ways operated within a somewhat secularized version of this vision. They believed that a great work, a millennial work, was dawning in America, and the Revolution was part of it. Those from the Old World of Europe were welcomed and encouraged to join the project that would start with republican government in America but would continue with all of western civilization being transformed. America was the vanguard of the millennium, and America's destiny was to lead the rest of western civilization in a millennial transformation.

During the Second Great Awakening, the vision of Americans narrowed. No longer was the nation merely the starting place for the transformation. Rather, America came to be seen as exceptional. In other words, America was different, and what was happening here was not going to happen in Europe or anywhere else unless Americans themselves transplanted the message of Christianity and the institutions of democracy. As historian William McLoughlin put it, "[America's] destiny was not Europe's or mankind's but their own. . . . God had created a unique people and elected them to establish these institutions throughout the world; they were to uplift inferior peoples who, lacking the innate capacity for republicanism, might at least be converted or adapted to it if they could learn to assimilate the ways of Christian America."[2] In other words, the revivals of the Second Great Awakening created in many Americans a sense that it was their God-ordained task to reform their own society and export that reform impulse to other lands.

Early in the Second Great Awakening, Baptist pastor Richard Furman of South Carolina contended that America was "originally designed as [an] asylum for religion and liberty." He said that the advantages of America should cause Americans to look forward to the day when the nation will be the "praise of the whole earth; and shall participate, largely, in the fulfillment of those sacred prophecies which have foretold the glory of Messiah's kingdom: when 'there shall be abundance of peace;' 'when God shall build the cities,' and 'cause them to be spread abroad;' 'when righteousness shall dwell in the fruitful field, and the wilderness shall rejoice and blossom as the rose.'"[3] In this view, God had prepared America for its role in world history, and the revivals were the main part of that preparation. Indeed, the revivals led some to believe that the millennium (Christ's thousand year reign on earth) was dawning and that it was their job to help usher in that era by reforming society. At times this reform effort was corporate—that is, people believed that the institutions of society must be remade. At other times, the revivals tended to bring about a more personal and individual approach where reformers believed that if individuals could be shown their social sins, they would stop sinning and society would automatically become better as a result. For example, as will be discussed later in this chapter, many abolitionists believed that if slaveholders could be convinced that slavery was a sin, they would voluntarily free their slaves and treat African Americans justly. One historian actually compares this quest for personal holiness and individual reform to Transcendentalism's individualism, putting the case this way: "The quest of personal holiness became in some ways a kind of plain man's transcendentalism, which geared ancient creeds to the drive shaft of social reform."[4]

This reform impulse was a product of the shift from Calvinism to Arminianism. The social outgrowth of the idea that anyone could choose to be saved was that men and women, once they were transformed, could change society merely by choosing to do so. They need not wait for God; they were called to put their faith in action in a voluntary way. This impulse gave rise to the age of voluntary societies that still exists to a large degree in America. Typically, from the Second Great Awakening to the present, when Americans see a social problem, their impulse is to band together in a voluntary reform society and fix it. It takes little imagination to see how if individuals can determine voluntarily whether or not their souls will be saved, they can surely decide to change society in accordance with the demands of justice. As McLoughlin writes, "It was from this assumption, pervasive in the nation after 1830, that perfectionism and millennial optimism grew to such importance."[5]

Even Christ's own act of sacrifice on the cross came to be seen as voluntary and therefore as a model for believers. In following Christ, revival converts were to sacrifice themselves for the conversion and betterment of others, either by becoming missionaries or evangelists or by joining voluntary societies.[6] This spirit was captured well in the wake of the Finney revivals of 1831 when the Brick Presbyterian Church of Rochester rewrote its covenant to read in part:

> We promise to renounce all the ways of sin, and to make it the business of our life to do good and promote the declarative glory of our heavenly Father. . . . We promise to make it the great business of our life to glorify God and build up the Redeemer's Kingdom in this fallen world, and constantly to endeavor to present our bodies a living sacrifice, holy and acceptable to Him.[7]

While there were several different issues in which this reform impulse manifested itself, none was more important than antislavery.

Theodore Weld and the Evangelical Antislavery Movement

The connection between the revivals of the Second Great Awakening and abolition was so strong that it would hardly be an overstatement to say that the revivals were responsible for antislavery becoming a radical national movement. This connection can be demonstrated in the lives of several individuals, most notably Theodore Dwight Weld.

Weld was born in Hampton, Connecticut, on November 23, 1803, the son of a Congregational minister. He and everyone around him assumed he would follow in his father's footsteps and become a preacher. He attended Andover Academy with that intention. Weld, who was a restless and active young boy, often roamed the hills and fields near Hampton and would usually run a mile uphill before retiring for the evening. He tackled his studies with the same energy, doing well as a student. While at Andover he developed eye problems that left him temporarily blind and required him to convalesce for a time. To help support himself after his preparatory studies, Weld became a traveling lecturer and salesman for a program of mnemonics, the art of memorization. But the most important part of Weld's endeavor as a mnemonics salesman was that he became accustomed to lecturing to substantial groups of people. This experience would serve him well in his career as one of the chief spokespersons for antislavery.[8]

In 1824, Weld's family moved west to upstate New York in what has been called the "burned-over" district, the place where revival fires would sweep back and forth across the region and from which so many reform and religious movements would spring. The family move also placed Weld in the burgeoning Erie Canal region, where Finney's revivals would soon flourish. Weld spent much of his time in Utica at Hamilton College where he lived with a friend. The college permitted him to attend classes for free without actually being enrolled. As revivals began to sweep the area, Weld heard that Finney was a ranting maniac, and he believed these reports. Nevertheless, in the spring of 1826, his aunt Sophia was able to persuade him to attend one of Finney's meetings. Sophia slyly maneuvered Weld into the middle of a pew where he would be unlikely to bolt if Finney's preaching made him uncomfortable.

For his part, Finney had also heard that Hamilton College students looked up to Weld as a leader, and, as was often Finney's style, he decided to direct his preaching at Weld. While staring directly at him, Finney said, "One Sinner destroyeth much good." Then he followed with, "And yes! You'll go to college and use all your influence against the Lord's work." As Weld later put it, "He just held me up on his toasting-fork before that audience." Weld squirmed in his seat and made a move to leave, but Sophia whispered, "You'll break my heart if you go."[9]

The next day when Weld encountered Finney at a local store, he verbally assaulted the evangelist in an attempt to get back at him. Finney calmly replied, "Mr. Weld, are you the son of a minister of Christ, and is this the way for you to behave?"[10] Embarrassed, Weld fled the scene. Later, he went to find Finney to apologize and ended up on his knees sobbing, then spent that evening at Sophia's house once again in a rage against Finney. After a sleepless night coming to grips with his behavior, he attended Finney's meeting the next evening and stood to confess his sins and be converted. He immediately joined the Finney crusade and spent the next year promoting revivals and defending Finney against the very attacks he had once believed. In conjunction with his revival work, Weld became active in the temperance movement. For most of the next five years Weld was one of the most active and effective temperance lecturers in western New York. He was also involved in the manual labor movement at Oneida Academy. Reformers believed that manual labor was a character-building endeavor and so set up academies where young boys could be educated while they worked to support themselves.

Weld's conversion to the antislavery cause came in the early 1830s partly in conjunction with a near-death experience. In February 1832 he was traveling in a stagecoach attempting to ford the Alum River near Columbus, Ohio. The stage overturned, and Weld was trampled by the horses then swept downstream in the frigid water. He eventually washed up on the river shore and was rescued from overexposure by some locals. While Finney interpreted this as an attack by Satan, Weld's mother and other family members took it as a sign that God had spared him for a special work. Weld was already thinking about slavery, as were all reformers. The most significant reform effort dealing with slavery before the early 1830s was colonization. Colonizationists opposed slavery but believed that African Americans would never live successfully in white America. The solution to slavery, therefore, was to free the slaves and send them back to Africa. The American Colonization Society had been founded in 1817 and was supported by many influential people in the North and the South. The lasting result of colonization was the formation of the African colony of Liberia.

Weld favored the colonization movement in the 1820s. By 1831, however, he had moved from colonization to abolition and was in contact with William Lloyd Garrison. Through his newspaper the *Liberator,* Garrison had become the voice of immediate emancipation, the most radical stance on abolition. Immediatists such as Garrison believed that slaves should be freed immediately. Essentially, by the 1830s there were colonizationists, gradual abolitionists who believed that slaves should be freed some day and that slaveholders should be compensated, and immediate abolitionists who sided with Garrison and his *Liberator.*

Garrison's immediatist abolition was closely related to the Second Great Awakening's revivals. As one scholar has put the case, "The movement for 'immediate abolition' began as a direct extension of evangelical Christianity."[11] Garrison's creed articulated in the *Liberator* was just what revivalism taught, "the conviction that sin was conscious, active disobedience to God."[12] Garrison wrote like an evangelist preached, "I take for granted that slavery is a crime—a damning crime: therefore my efforts shall be directed to the exposure of those who practice it."[13] Immediatists promoted their doctrine just as revivalists preached conversion, believing that once convinced of the evils of slavery, slaveholders would voluntarily emancipate their slaves. Garrison and others could brook no complicity with slavery, no gradualism. They denounced the British plan to compensate owners and the apprenticeship program of British abolitionist William Wilberforce to prepare slaves for freedom. Gradual abolition would have been like preaching that men and women should gradually stop sinning.

Weld, like most evangelical abolitionists who were products of revivals, became an immediatist. He wrote to Garrison in 1833:

> From what I infer that the Society is based upon the great bottom law of human right, that nothing but crime can forfeit liberty. That no condition of birth, no shade of color, no mere misfortune of circumstances, can annul that birth-right charter which God has bequeated [sic] to every being upon whom he has stamped his own image, by making him a free moral agent, and that he who robs his fellow man of this tramples upon right, subverts justice, outrages

humanity, unsettles the foundations of human safety, and sacrilegiously assumes the prerogative of God.[14]

Here Weld was joining the egalitarian principles of the revival, the work ethic of the manual labor movement he had been part of at Oneida Academy, and the Declaration of Independence. Weld truly believed that just as individuals like himself could be persuaded to convert, so slaveholders could be persuaded to emancipate their slaves. This was the special call for which God had spared him in the river accident.

The groundwork for Weld's conversion to abolition had probably been laid in part by his boyhood experiences: his mother telling him the Bible story of Hagar the slave, one of his family's friends owning a slave whom Weld knew personally, his friendship with a black classmate in school, something that was a social taboo at the time, and seeing slavery firsthand while traveling as a lecturer for mnemonics. His conversion was made simpler, though not necessarily easy, by several other considerations. Because he already believed in social equality among whites, he only needed to apply this principle to African Americans as well, and because he was of secure Puritan stock, he did not fear losing his own station to freed slaves who might take the jobs of laborers. Moreover, he had no wife or daughter who might be subjected to retribution should freed slaves decide to get back at whites for years of injustice. This latter fear was compounded for many whites by the belief that freed black males would prey sexually on white women. Rather than these fears, so prevalent among even northern whites, Weld, in pure revivalist fashion, feared God's retribution against America if something were not done about the sin of slavery. Perhaps most important was the revival mentality that put all human beings on the same level before God. All were sinners in need of salvation. All needed freedom from spiritual bondage, and slaves needed freedom from physical bondage as well.

Weld's agony over slavery took place in the wake of Nat Turner's rebellion of 1831 and freed slave David Walker's famous *Appeal* of 1829, which was one of the most radical antislavery tracts ever written. Weld was not alone in his pilgrimage. Many of his acquaintances were moving from supporting colonization to abolition at the same time, including James G. Birney, a slaveholder from Alabama who would eventually run for president on the Liberty Party ticket, and the Tappan brothers, two wealthy New York businessmen whom Weld had befriended at Oneida Academy. Weld also knew Charles Stuart who had recently joined the abolitionist crusade and was touring Great Britain, lecturing, in the early 1830s. By the time Weld wrote to Garrison in 1833, he was thoroughly convinced that abolition was the only just approach to slavery and that he was called to dedicate himself to immediate emancipation.

Weld became one of the most visible and highly regarded antislavery lecturers in part because of his activities at Lane Seminary in Cincinnati, Ohio. The seminary was involved in the manual labor movement, and in his work with the Manual Labor Institute Weld had been instrumental in convincing Lyman Beecher to move from his church in Boston to Lane to become president in 1832. In 1834, Weld and other abolitionist students planned a series of debates on slavery that took place in February over the course of 18 days, every other night for about two-and-a-half hours. One scholar has called these "a protracted meeting," which was what Finney's extended revival meetings were called, and, indeed, the slavery debates functioned like a revival.[15] Many of the students converted to the antislavery cause, and with Weld's leadership they formed an antislavery society dedicated to immediate emancipation. The group's constitution called for, "Immediate emancipation of the whole colored race, within the United States . . . and the elevation of [blacks] to an intellectual, moral, and political equality with the whites." The African American slave was considered "a moral agent, the keeper of his own happiness, the executive of his own powers, the accountable arbiter of his own choice."[16] The constitution went on to argue that slavery violated these truths and subjected the nation to the judgment of God. However, the Lane Anti-Slavery Society rejected either rebellion or political action as the means to emancipation. Rather, the goal was to persuade slaveholders to free their slaves. Following emancipation, blacks were to be protected by law equally with whites and employed as free laborers. These were essentially the same principles put forth by Garrison and his followers at the beginning of the immediatist movement in 1831. Believing that words alone were not enough, the Lane rebels, as they were soon to be called, set up a school for the freed African Americans of Cincinnati. As Weld wrote to Lewis Tappan, "We believe that faith without works is dead. We have formed a large and efficient organization for elevating the colored people in Cincinnati—have established a Lyceum among them, and lecture three or four evenings a week, on grammar, geography, arithmetic, natural philosophy, etc."[17]

It was quite enough that Weld and the others had come out in favor of immediate abolition in a city directly across the Ohio river from slaveholding Kentucky, but when they began to actually work side-by-side with African Americans, attempt to educate them, and then even bring them onto the Lane campus, fierce opposition erupted. The Lane abolitionists also stayed in the homes of blacks and on one occasion escorted a black female to the seminary and then back to the black section of town. Cincinnati newspapers editorialized against these and other activities and other journals followed, accusing the students of being rebellious against teachers, parents, and public opinion. An 1834 anonymous tract coined the term Weldites for the Lane abolitionists and suggested that the following definition be included in *Buck's Theological Dictionary*, a standard reference work at the time: "This is the name of a most deluded sect, the leader of which was a fanatic by name Theodore D. Weld, who under the show of great discernment, unequalled powers of mind, and more than apostolic self-denial, was at heart, a most proud, arrogant, self-conceited, disorganizing man."[18]

President Beecher, while opposed to slavery, believed the students were going too fast. He visited antislavery leader and Lane benefactor Lewis Tappan in New York, telling him that if a more moderate approach were adopted, thousands more would join the movement. Tappan was unimpressed by this line of argument and retorted, "If you, doctor, were a thorough antislavery man, how easy it would be for you and Mr. Weld to go on harmoniously."[19] But, the Weldites and President Beecher did not go on harmoniously. When trustees passed what the students believed were unreasonable restrictions on political activities on campus, the students promptly withdrew from Lane, gutting the institution.

The unwillingness to compromise has been attributed to the students' belief that antislavery was part of God's work that would help usher in Christ's millennial reign on earth. No matter how badly things might be at any given moment, Weld and the others believed that God's will would ultimately triumph. For this reason, they saw no need to alter their course in the face of stiff opposition; God was on their side.[20] On the other hand, the unwillingness of the Lane trustees, Cincinnati newspapers, and others to tolerate the students should be understood in the context of the time. Walker's *Appeal* had called for violence against slavery, Turner's rebellion had actually carried out such violence, and there was always lurking in the background of Jacksonian democracy the fear of social disorder. The authorities wanted the students to go slower and to respect established institutions. President Beecher greatly respected the students, but he knew that race mixing was too controversial. He urged the students to teach in black schools but not to stay in the homes of African Americans or walk the streets in mixed company, but Weld and the others could not accept any distinction based on color. As he responded to Beecher, "[A]ny reference to color, in social intercourse, [is] an odious and sinful prejudice."[21]

Most of the Lane rebels set up a school of their own briefly then went to Oberlin, Ohio, where a new school dedicated to abolition and racial equality was instituted with Finney as the head of the theological department. But Weld did not go to Oberlin. Instead, he became a full-time antislavery lecturer and for the next year and eight months traveled extensively through Ohio and Pennsylvania. Part of his work was with the Presbyterian General Assembly. By his count there were in 1834 only two commissioners in the denomination who were antislavery. After two weeks of his persuasion during the Assembly meeting of June 1835, there were 48. Much as Finney and other revivalists won converts to Christ, Weld won Christians to the abolition movement in a sort of second conversion. Weld even described his work much as Finney and other revivalists described theirs. He told how often when he spoke the first reaction of the congregation was opposition, followed by "anxious inquiry," a term synonymous with Finney's "anxious bench." Weld believed that when people's consciences had been pricked, they would become uncomfortable and rise up in opposition. He called such opposition the work of the devil. As he wrote to Birney, "The Devil will not give up his hold without a death struggle."[22] Like the revivalists, however, Weld believed that if he could preach long enough and hard enough, he could effectively wear down resistance and reach the souls of his listeners. Their consciences would see and feel the truth, and they would convert to the antislavery cause. As Weld once wrote, "If it is not FELT in the very tissues of the spirit, all the reasoning in the world is a feather thrown against the wind."[23] Weld's biographer has argued that the colonization movement asked people to contribute time and money to solve an unfortunate problem elsewhere; abolition asked them to confront the sin of slavery as their own and to experience a change of heart.[24]

A change of heart, however, did not always take place. At times Weld faced fierce opposition, and on one occasion in the western New York town of Troy anti-abolitionists actually forced him to cancel speaking engagements. This experience seemed to shatter his confidence that the millennium would start in the West and that antislavery would be its beginning. Following this defeat, Weld experienced the worst fate that can befall a public speaker; he lost his voice. From November 15 to December 2, 1836, Weld attended a large Anti-Slavery Society meeting in New York. As usual, he engaged in intense lecturing, and by the time the meeting was over he could scarcely speak above a whisper. With the Troy lecture cancellations still weighing heavily on his mind and heart, and now with this new setback, Weld retired from slavery oratory, renounced the West, and moved to New Jersey. He would continue to agitate against slavery, largely through writing, but his days as the backwoods orator were for the most part over. With more time on his hands, he would marry Angelina Grimke, have children, farm, and get involved in personal improvement schemes such as Grahamism and Phrenology. Grahamism was named for Sylvester Graham who advocated a healthy diet as the key to well-being. Today's Graham Crackers are the continuing legacy of this movement. Phrenology was the study of lumps on one's head, basically the idea that a trained phrenologist could give guidance by feeling these lumps, a kind of pseudo-scientific form of fortune-telling. More importantly, Weld wrote *The Bible Against Slavery* in 1837, which was intended to combat the southern idea that the Bible condoned the institution. Weld argued that Hebrew slavery in the Old Testament and southern slavery in the United States were two very different things. Hebrew slaves were treated like human beings, African Americans like property. Most abolitionists hailed the book, but one critic pointed out that even if Hebrew slavery were real slavery, this did not mean that God approved of it or that if he did, he necessarily approved of southern slavery.

Weld's most significant contribution to abolition after he retired from oratory was *American Slavery As It Is: Testimony of a Thousand Witnesses*. Beginning in 1838, he, his wife Angelina, and her sister Sarah began scouring southern newspapers, clipping out evidence of the brutality of slavery. In addition, they sent out letters to those who had lived in the South or were still living there, recruiting testimonials. This marked a change in Weld's strategy. Before, he had emphasized freedom first, then the horrors of slavery. In *American Slavery As It Is* he turned the priority around. The book sold over 100,000 copies the first year and continued to sell many more thereafter.

In the early 1840s, Weld began to lose faith in reform. In conjunction with travels to Washington, D.C., for a reform meeting, he observed the nation lurching toward conflict over slavery. By this time he had two sons, and Angelina would soon give birth to the couple's daughter. Turning more and more inward and becoming less and less optimistic about the prospects for abolishing slavery, he began to emphasize personal holiness and individual religion. The Weld family virtually stopped going to church as they devoted themselves increasingly to home religion. This was an emphasis on a different revival theme, personal holiness. Before, Weld had believed that as individuals were revived they could construct new church and educational institutions to replace ones that were either corrupt or moribund. Now he saw these institutions as standing between the individual and God. Instead of being reformed, such institutions needed to be ignored for the sake of individual purity.

In February 1844, Weld wrote what has been considered his valedictory on reform entitled "Truth's Hindrances." In this essay, he concluded that truth had no place in American public life. "Dare thou for the truth's sake withdraw from thy sect and abjure opinions which thou hast zealously propagated . . . ? Disavow measures, modes of action and systems of policy with which thou hast long been publicly identified." Weld's views here became like the Transcendentalist Emerson's in his work "New England Reformers." There, Emerson pointed to the limitations of public-reform efforts and called people to instead seek "the man within man." Weld's final farewell to reform came a few months later when Lewis Tappan wrote to encourage Weld to stay in the movement. Weld answered, "God does not call me to such a position."[25]

The Tappan Brothers and Antislavery

While Weld was one of the most visible abolitionist figures, two of the most important but less visible supporters were Arthur and Lewis

Tappan. The Tappan brothers, as they were often called in revivalist and reform circles, believed that the wealthy should be primarily responsible for funding reforms in education, public health, religion, and so forth.[26] The Tappans' mother, Sarah, had grown up in Northampton, Massachusetts, where the First Great Awakening preacher Jonathan Edwards had pastored until 1744. She was converted in a revival in 1769. Arthur was born in 1786 and Lewis in 1788, and there were three other Tappan boys in the family. Despite their orthodox mother's best efforts, Lewis converted to Unitarianism under the preaching of William Ellery Channing, who significantly influenced several of the Transcendentalists. In the 1820s, some of Lewis Tappan's business associates began to sponsor revival meetings for their workers, and Tappan attended. He was impressed with the commitment and zeal that the evangelicals had for foreign missions and domestic revivals, and he noticed that Unitarians did little in these areas. He called on Lyman Beecher for a consultation to discuss theology, especially the nature of God, which was the main issue between orthodox evangelicals and Unitarians, the latter denying the trinity.

All this was happening in the period when Tappan's financial situation was deteriorating. He had gotten into manufacturing just as the recession of 1826 hit, and he was deeply in debt. He visited his brother Arthur in New York, whose silk import business was thriving. Arthur spoke of his concern for Lewis's unorthodox Unitarianism. Lewis returned to Boston and sometime later went to his home library to write a letter to his father. There, he fell on his knees and converted. He would write about this experience, "I felt a constraining influence to address God in three persons, and then to pray to Jesus. I was unwilling to rise until the scales had fallen from my eyes, but I did." He then wrote his letter to his father, saying, "I shall therefore withdraw my self from the influence of a denomination with which I have cordially and for a long period acted, and shall put myself under the influences of the orthodox denomination."[27] While Lewis Tappan's conversion had not taken place at a revival meeting, revival influence was clearly part of the process that led to his experience. He would later write a pamphlet outlining his reasons for converting. In addition to unorthodoxy on the issue of the trinity, he also argued that the Unitarians were not fervent and active enough in their faith and, therefore, had little social benefit. Shortly after his conversion he would move to New York to join

Arthur's business, and the two would become major financial backers of revivals and evangelical social reform causes.

Arthur was already a fervent evangelical supporter of revivals and a Christian philanthropist of the first rank. In the 1820s he had given $5,000 to the American Bible Society and $4,000 to the American Sunday School Union, contingent on its raising $100,000 from other sources. He had given another $5,000 to the American Tract Society, which he had helped to found in 1825. The organization printed and distributed thousands of tracts explaining how a person could be converted to Christianity. Over the course of several years he paid the tuition of over one hundred college students, most of them at Yale University, and most preparing for the ministry. One admirer wrote of Arthur, "Our great benevolent system owes its expansion and power . . . to his influence. His example inspired the merchants of New York . . . , leading them to give hundreds and thousands where before they gave tens or fifteens."[28] Most of the institutions Arthur helped to found still exist. The benefactions listed above were merely the start of a life of Christian philanthropy for Arthur, and these were before he ever became involved in abolition. The story of how the Tappan brothers became abolitionists brings Weld and Garrison back into the picture.

Weld met Lewis Tappan when the latter brought his two sons to the Oneida Academy while Weld was there in the early 1830s. Lewis was so impressed that he placed his sons under Weld's spiritual tutelage. The sons were converted to revivalist Christianity, while the father was converted to abolition, largely by Weld. Before 1833, Lewis had been only a nominal abolitionist, largely because he spent most of his time promoting revivals. By the early thirties Arthur was already a moderate antislavery advocate and had even started an antislavery newspaper called the *Emancipator,* which was much more moderate than Garrison's *Liberator.*

In 1830, Garrison was imprisoned briefly in Baltimore for libel. He accused a shipmaster of piracy for transporting slaves to the deep South and said that the man was destined for the "lowest depths of perdition" for his sin. When released from jail, Garrison traveled to New York to visit the Tappans. This visit was the beginning of the transformation of the Tappans from moderate to fervent abolitionists. It was also a transforming moment for the entire abolitionist movement. As Lewis's biographer writes, "Garrison's trip from the Baltimore jail cell to Arthur

Tappan's store thus signaled more than a new beginning for the young reformer. It represented the end of one era in antislavery history and the opening of another."[29] The first era had been the moderate antislavery effort that had included colonization and other schemes such as gradual emancipation with compensation for slaveholders. Before Garrison, the American Colonization Society was the only national organization addressing the issue of slavery. The Society provided a brief union of evangelical abolitionists and those who favored colonization and other gradualist schemes. This form of moderate or gradualist antislavery is usually called "liberal antislavery" because it was supported by Enlightenment liberals such as Thomas Jefferson and other founding fathers, most of whom were dead by the 1830s. Liberal antislavery had advocates in the North and the South. The new era, marked by Garrison's teaming with the Tappans, would be a wholly northern phenomenon. By the mid-1830s it was difficult if not impossible to preach abolition in the South or to even find a copy of Garrison's *Liberator* below the Mason-Dixon line.

When the Tappans met Garrison they were already associated with Finney, having helped lure the great preacher to New York by financing the renovation of the Chatham Street Chapel, then the construction of the Broadway Tabernacle. From March to December 1833, as Finney preached at Chatham Street Chapel, some in the congregation gave increasing attention to slavery. Finney himself would write in his memoirs, "When I first went to New York I had made up my mind on the subject of the slavery question, and was exceedingly anxious to arouse public attention to the subject."[30] While pastoring at Chatham Street Finney refused to serve communion to slaveholders. Still, amalgamation repulsed him, and he required blacks to sit in a special section of the chapel. He told the Tappans that he did not think "that it always is a wicked prejudice" when a person had "a constitutional taste against associating with black people."[31] Later, after Finney went to Oberlin College, he ceased being prejudiced and supported the integration of African Americans into the college.[32]

In October, antislavery supporters met at Chatham Street, hurriedly formed the New York Antislavery Society, elected Arthur president, then disbanded just before an anti-abolition mob entered the church to attack them. Less than two months later, on December 4, delegates met in Philadelphia to form the American Anti-Slavery Society.

Garrison was the key figure, Lewis represented the Tappans, and Arthur was again elected president. The following year would see Weld agitating at Lane Seminary. These events would make the evangelical antislavery nexus complete with the Tappans, Garrison, Finney, Weld, and many others of like mind.

The degree to which this was radical activity can be seen in the sometimes-violent response to abolition. In the summer of 1834, just after Weld and his fellow Lane Rebels had encountered resistance in Cincinnati, there was a wave of violence in New York. Lewis Tappan's home was destroyed, as was the Quaker meeting hall next door. Quakers had been the first American denomination to take a stand against slavery back in the late eighteenth century. Arthur Tappan's business was threatened, as was Finney's Chatham Street Chapel. Newspapers tended to side with the rioters, and the police did little until the mobs turned against the more wealthy and socially established individuals in the antislavery movement. Then, the police cracked down, and the newspapers called for law and order. The violence gave the Tappans and others opportunity to reiterate that their cause was just and moderate; that violence and disorder were the domain of the pro-slavery and anti-black elements.[33]

The Tappans, Weld, Finney, and most others in the evangelical antislavery movement would join forces in 1840 to support the Liberty Party, with James G. Birney as their presidential candidate. While the party was unsuccessful politically, it succeeded in keeping the issue before the American people, as did the Free Soil Party of 1848. In the 1850s, antislavery would be one of the primary planks of the newly formed Republican Party. Republican candidate Abraham Lincoln won the presidency in 1860, but by that time a political solution to the slavery question was impossible, and the Civil War ensued.

Transcendentalists and Abolition

While the central and most forceful influences in the abolition movement came out of revivalist Protestantism, Transcendentalists also opposed slavery. Like everything else they did, much of the antislavery work of Transcendentalists was individualistic. They were much more reluctant to join voluntary associations than were evangelical reformers. Still, Transcendentalists often spoke out forcefully against slavery and lent their support to the abolition cause in whatever ways they could without compromising their beliefs.

As with most Transcendentalist enterprises, Emerson took the lead in antislavery. In 1837, in response to the murder of Elijah Lovejoy, he began to speak out. Lovejoy was a Presbyterian minister who ran an abolitionist press in Illinois, which anti-abolitionist forces targeted repeatedly. They destroyed three printing presses in an attempt to intimidate Lovejoy, but to no avail as he continued to order new machinery and print antislavery literature. When his fourth press arrived, a riot began and Lovejoy was killed as he attempted to protect the warehouse where the press was stored. Abolitionists across the nation were outraged, and in Concord, Emerson was asked to address a gathering. While the text of the address has not survived, much of what Emerson said has been reconstructed from his notes. "The professed aim of the abolitionists," was for him, "to awaken the conscience of the Northern states in hope thereby to awaken the conscience of the Southern States: a hope just and sublime."[34] At the same time, he showed his reluctance to join movements by distancing himself from the abolitionists' calls to action, instead emphasizing his commitment to free speech for those on all sides of the issue. At this point his commitment to abolition consisted of moral suasion only. As he put it, "When we have settled the right and wrong of the question, I think we have done all we can. A man can only extend his active attention to a certain finite amount of claims."[35]

By 1844, Emerson had become more willing to endorse abolitionist social action, as he showed in an address to the Women's Anti-Slavery Association of Concord. We are not sure why he moved to this more activist point of view, but it may be that he had been reading abolitionist literature such as Thomas Clarkson's *History of the Abolition of the African Slave Trade* and James Thome and J.H. Kimball's *Emancipation in the British West Indies*. Emerson's principal biographer believes that these books may have jarred Emerson out of his complacency but speculates that it is even more likely that Emerson's wife Lidian was a major influence in radicalizing him. She was a more committed abolitionist than Emerson, having met with the abolitionist Grimke sisters in September 1837 when they spent a week in Concord. Their visit left her determined "not to turn away my attention from the abolition cause till I have found whether there is not something for me personally to do and bear to forward it."[36]

Emerson's 1844 speech has been called his "emancipation address," and was given on the tenth anniversary of the emancipation of slaves in the British West Indies. Abolition was so divisive by that time that churches in Concord would not host the event. Instead, it was held in the courthouse. Henry David Thoreau went door to door urging Concordians to attend. When the sexton of the First Parish Church of Concord refused to ring the bell calling people to come, Thoreau did it himself. Lidian was also instrumental in encouraging her husband to speak. She was an active member of the Women's Anti-Slavery Association.

Emerson's emancipation address was a chronological narrative of the horrors of slavery. The narrative culminated with reference to the British Parliament's act to abolish slavery in the West Indies and contrasted it with the U.S. Congress's refusal to take action. Emerson rejected compromise and "political juggling" and called on Congress to outlaw slavery. He refuted the notion that African Americans were inferior to whites and said that pro-slavery sentiment could no longer be overlooked. Referring to his own moderate past he said, "[T]here have been moments, I said, when men might be forgiven who doubted. Those moments are past."[37]

Northern abolitionists were delighted by Emerson's speech. Thoreau arranged to have it published, and John Greenleaf Whittier, the Quaker poet and abolitionist, asked Emerson to be part of an upcoming antislavery convention. A few years later, Garrison wrote to Emerson, "You are not afraid publicly and pointedly to testify against the enslavement of three million of our countrymen."[38] Still, even with this sort of encouragement and applause, Emerson was never quite comfortable with his role as a public activist. He spoke out because he believed he had to.

In 1851, Emerson made another significant and nationally recognized speech, this time calling for civil disobedience against the Fugitive Slave Act. The occasion was the return and public whipping in Savannah, Georgia, of a slave named Thomas Sims who had stowed away on a ship to Boston. Emerson aimed his speech at neither Congress nor the South, but instead called on northern states to stop enforcing the law. "[M]ake this law inoperative," he implored. "It must be abridged and wiped out of the statute books. . . . If our resistance to this law is not right, there is no right."[39] Emerson would repeat this call to civil disobedience repeatedly over the next few years. He would also campaign actively for John G. Palfrey, a congressional candidate from the Free Soil Party, and began to help with the Underground Railroad, an effort to help slaves escape bondage and flee the South. His biographer has called Emerson's emotional speeches on slavery a practical validation of his lifelong affirmation of freedom of the will. As Emerson wrote, "America is the idea of emancipation."[40]

As Emerson's experience shows, the question was not so much what Transcendentalists did for the abolitionist movement, but what the abolitionist movement did for Transcendentalists. The vexing nature of the slavery question presented an insoluble challenge to the notion that individual freedom was sufficient to create a good society. Abolition drew Transcendentalists out of their extreme individualism by convincing some of them that more was needed. This is why Emerson began in the 1830s by merely condemning slavery, then moved by the 1850s to active participation in the Underground Railroad. Thoreau's development over time was very similar to Emerson's, but as was usually the case, Thoreau was more radical. In the 1830s, Nathaniel Rogers edited the antislavery newspaper *Herald of Freedom* in which he endorsed the individualistic approach to the slavery question. Rogers went so far as to call for the dissolution of all antislavery societies because they impeded the exercise of freedom on the part of individual abolitionists. Garrison rebuked Rogers, but Thoreau defended him, saying that Rogers was applying the principles of Transcendentalism.[41]

By the 1840s, although still quite individualistic, Thoreau was becoming more radical on slavery. In 1842, he invited activist Wendell Phillips to speak to the Lyceum meeting in Concord. Phillips's statements on slavery rankled the conservative members. Thoreau invited him back again the next year, and Phillips debated the conservative members, thoroughly refuting their arguments. When a motion arose in 1845 to invite Phillips for the third time, the conservative members of the Lyceum resigned and were replaced by Thoreau, Emerson, and Samuel Barrett. Thoreau viewed this replacement as a victory for free speech and wrote a letter to Garrison about the episode, which Garrison promptly printed in the *Liberator*.[42]

In the mid-forties, Thoreau was involved in the event for which he is perhaps most famous. The nation was preparing for war with Mexico, a war that abolitionists were convinced was to appease the South and open up new territory for the expansion of slavery. To protest the war, Thoreau refused to pay his poll tax. The local constable in Concord, who cared little for most Transcendentalists, especially Emerson, nevertheless respected Thoreau and did not arrest him until 1846. After a brief stay in jail, Thoreau's aunt paid his tax, and he was released. His aunt's actions angered Thoreau because he had hoped to stay in jail and call more attention to the abolitionists' cause. This event gave rise to the famous exchange between Emerson and Thoreau. Emerson visited his friend in jail and asked, "[W]hy did you go to jail?" Thoreau responded, "Why did you not?"[43] As Thoreau would say concerning civil disobedience:

> A minority is powerless while it conforms to the majority. . . . If the alternative is to keep all just men in prison, or give up war and slavery, the State will not hesitate which to choose. If a thousand men were not to pay their tax-bill this year, that would not be a violent bloody measure, as it would be to pay them, and enable the State to commit violence and shed innocent blood. This is, in fact, the definition of a peaceable revolution, if any such is possible."[44]

While Thoreau was still reluctant to join movements, he was here calling on individuals to act in concert with one another to oppose war and slavery. By the 1850s he taught that the state was subject to a higher law than its own and that through civil disobedience the individual avoided complicity with the state's evil actions. Moreover, the nonviolent radicalism of Transcendentalists like Thoreau was a recognition that reform could no longer be merely personal or even communal, but had to become political as well.[45]

Thoreau, like Emerson, also became involved with the Underground Railroad, although contrary to legend his cabin at Walden Pond was rarely used. Instead, he helped smuggle runaway slaves to his mother's house in Concord and then helped them move under cover of darkness toward Canada, often giving them money. In the 1850s, Thoreau became even more radical. When runaway Anthony Burns was arrested in Boston and the authorities were intent on shipping him back to slavery, Thoreau spoke at a rally organized by Garrison. Moving beyond passive resistance, he here sided with the abolitionists. When Garrison publicly burned a copy of the U.S. Constitution, Thoreau heartily approved.[46]

Thoreau's most controversial antislavery act was his support of John Brown. While nonviolent himself, Thoreau defended Brown's raid on Harper's Ferry, which was intended to incite a violent revolt against southern slavery. Condemned as a deluded vigilante by most, Brown was executed for his crimes. Nevertheless, Thoreau extolled Brown's idealism and courage, writing in his essay, "The Last Days of John Brown," "The North, I mean the living North, was suddenly all transcendental. It went behind the human law, it went behind the apparent failure, and recognized eternal justice and glory."[47] Thoreau also wrote "A Plea for Captain John Brown," in which he praised Brown's courage and denounced those who spoke timidly against slavery and were afraid to defend Brown. The highest praise he gave Brown was in calling him a Transcendentalist for his willingness to listen to the voice within even when it led him to oppose the state.[48] Needless to say, in his own time and since, Thoreau has been criticized for his support of Brown's actions.

A third Transcendentalist antislavery advocate was Theodore Parker. Although not one of the original Transcendentalists, Parker was perhaps the most important theologian the movement produced. Parker took practical action against slavery by writing to politicians, making his home a station on the Underground Railroad, and becoming an executive member of the Boston Vigilance Committee, which led resistance to returning runaway slaves. Many young people turned to Parker for antislavery leadership.[49] In the late 1830s and early 1840s, abolitionists celebrated Parker's denunciations of slavery, which were without the qualifications that Emerson and others were using at the time. While publishing articles in abolitionist journals, he was still hesitant to publicly identify fully with abolitionism because of the radicalism and strident tone of the movement. He praised and defended the work of associations but still emphasized that the best way to combat evil and apply religion to life was individual, not political. His most recent biographer describes Parker's reluctance to fully join the abolition crusade this way: "Perhaps Parker's principal reason for staying out of the antislavery movement was that, like Channing and Emerson, he preferred working independently for reform rather than in concert with others."[50]

The most outspoken antislavery Transcendentalists denounced slavery just as strongly as did evangelical abolitionists. They also eventually advocated that large numbers of people should resist the state's attempts to maintain or extend slavery. Thoreau even engaged in radical nonviolent civil disobedience and praised an individual who engaged in violent resistance. Where Transcendentalists and evangelical-revivalist abolitionists differed was in their approach to organizations and politics. The evangelicals believed in founding voluntary societies to engage in corporate action, while Transcendentalists were mostly individualistic. Even Transcendentalist calls for corporate action were usually made individually with little or no organizational support. While Emerson called on states to stop enforcing the Fugitive Slave Law, and Thoreau urged people not to pay their poll tax, neither founded nor joined an organization that would widen their calls or offer mutual support. Moreover, while Emerson eventually supported a candidate from the Free Soil Party, he and the other Transcendentalists rarely engaged in political action themselves. This was largely the province of the evangelicals.

The difference here was largely theological. Evangelicals believed in individual salvation, but they also believed that this experience instantly ushered one into the corporate body of believers, the church. The goal of the church was to usher in the kingdom of God by transforming individuals through revivalist conversions and society through reform. Transcendentalists believed that while all shared in the world spirit, each individual should listen to the voice within and stand alone in the truth as he or she understood it. The Transcendentalist goal was that individuals be free. Evangelicals also believed that God intended for individuals to be free, but they possessed as well the vision of a just society built on the principles of the kingdom of God. For them, the sin of slavery was not just that it denied African Americans their freedom, but also that it violated the biblical norms of a just society. They believed that God would judge America for this national sin.

Notes

1. Paul Johnson, *A Shopkeeper's Millennium: Society and Revivals in Rochester, New York, 1815–1837* (New York: Hill and Wang, 1978), 5.

2. William G. McLoughlin, *Revivals, Awakenings, and Reform: An Essay on Religion and Social Change in America, 1606–1977* (Chicago: University of Chicago Press, 1978), 105–6.

3. Quoted in John Boles, *The Great Revival: Beginnings of the Bible Belt* (Lexington: University Press of Kentucky, 1972), 106–7.

4. Timothy Smith, *Revivalism and Social Reform: American Protestantism on the Eve of the Civil War* (Baltimore: Johns Hopkins Press, 1980), 8.

5. McLoughlin, 114.

6. Ibid., 120.

7. Quoted in Johnson, 110–11.

8. Unless otherwise noted, the material in this chapter on Weld comes from his principal biography: Robert H. Abzug, *Passionate Liberator: Theodore Dwight Weld and the Dilemma of Reform* (New York: Oxford University Press, 1980).

9. Quoted in ibid., 48.

10. Quoted in ibid., 48.

11. Bertram Wyatt-Brown, *Lewis Tappan and the Evangelical War Against Slavery* (Cleveland, Ohio: The Press of Case Western Reserve University, 1969), 81.

12. Ibid., 81.

13. Quoted in ibid., 81.

14. Quoted in Abzug, 88.

15. Wyatt-Brown, 126.

16. Quoted in Abzug, 92.

17. Quoted in ibid., 94.

18. Quoted in ibid., 98.

19. Quoted in Wyatt-Brown, 128.

20. Abzug, 108.

21. Quoted in ibid., 111.

22. Quoted in ibid., 126.

23. Quoted in ibid., 129.

24. Ibid., 129.

25. Quoted in ibid., 241 and 243.

26. Unless otherwise noted, the information on the Tappans in this section is from Wyatt-Brown, *Lewis Tappan and the Evangelical War Against Slavery.*

27. Ibid., 33–34.

28. Quoted in ibid., 51.

29. Ibid., 81.

30. Quoted in Charles E. Hambrick-Stowe, *Charles G. Finney and the Spirit of American Evangelicalism* (Grand Rapids, Mich.: Eerdmans, 1996), 141.

31. Quoted in ibid., 142.

32. Quoted in ibid., 200.

33. Wyatt-Brown, 111–20.

34. Quoted in Robert D. Richardson, *Emerson: The Mind on Fire* (Berkeley: University of California Press, 1995), 269–70.

35. Quoted in ibid., 269–70.

36. Quoted in ibid., 270; see also 395–96.

37. Quoted in ibid., 399.

38. Quoted in ibid., 399.

39. Quoted in ibid., 496–99.

40. Quoted in ibid., 499.

41. Walter Harding, *The Days of Henry David Thoreau: A Biography* (New York: Dover Publications, 1962), 119–20.

42. Ibid., 175–76.

43. Quoted in ibid., 206.

44. Quoted in Anne C. Rose, *Transcendentalism as a Social Movement, 1830–1850* (New Haven, Conn.: Yale University Press, 1981), 222.

45. Ibid., 222–23.

46. Harding, 317–19.

47. Quoted in Donald N. Koster, *Transcendentalism in America* (Boston: Twayne Publishers, 1975), 55.

48. Harding, 418.

49. Rose, 218–22.

50. Dean Grodzins, *American Heretic: Theodore Parker and Transcendentalism* (Chapel Hill: University of North Carolina Press, 2002), 340.

A JOURNAL OF CIVILIZATION

ol. XI.—No. 563.]   NEW YORK, SATURDAY, OCTOBER 12, 1867.   [SINGLE COPIES TEN CE [$4.00 PER YEAR IN ADVA

Entered according to Act of Congress, in the Year 1867, by Harper & Brothers, in the Clerk's Office of the District Court for the Southern District of New York.

THE CIRCUIT PREACHER.—Drawn by A. R. Waud.—[See Next Page.]

"The Circuit Preacher." (Courtesy of the Billy Graham Center Museum, Wheaton, IL.)

"Camp Meeting." Attributed to Alexander Rider, ca. 1820. (Courtesy of the Billy Graham Center Museum, Wheaton, IL.)

Portrait of Charles Grandison Finney, 1834. (Courtesy of the Allen
Memorial Art Museum, Oberlin College, Ohio. Gift of Lewis Tappan to
Oberlin College, 1858.)

Angelina Grimke. (Library of Congress)

Sarah Grimke. (Library of Congress)

Ralph Waldo Emerson. (Library of Congress)

Henry David Thoreau. (Library of Congress)

CHAPTER 6

REVIVALISM AND FEMINISM

The woman's rights movement of the nineteenth century was closely associated with the abolition movement and both were influenced by the evangelical revivals of the Second Great Awakening. As feminist scholar Nancy Hardesty has written, "[T]he nineteenth-century American woman's rights movement was deeply rooted in evangelical revivalism. Its theology and practice motivated and equipped women and men to adopt a feminist ideology, to reject stereotyped sex roles, and to work for positive changes in marriage, church, society, and politics."[1] This influence sometimes went unacknowledged even though some women activists were heavily influenced by their evangelical upbringing even after having left the orthodox Christian faith. In the twentieth century, liberal religion was generally associated with civil rights for African Americans and equal rights for women. During the 1960s, it was more often liberal Protestants and Jews who worked with African Americans for civil rights, while evangelicals tended to be socially conservative. In the area of women's rights, the same was true. Liberal Protestants and some liberal Catholics supported equal rights for women, while many evangelical denominations issued statements emphasizing the duty of women to submit to their husbands and the belief that women should not be ordained preachers. During the era of the Second Great Awakening, however, very nearly the reverse was true. Liberal religion, such as Unitarianism and Transcendentalism, often sentimentalized and trivialized women's contributions and sought to confine women to domestic roles.[2] There were exceptions such as the Transcendentalist Margaret Fuller who wrote *Woman in the Nineteenth Century*. For the most part, however, leaders of the woman's rights movement before the Civil War tended to be products of the evangelical revivals.

There are many variations of feminism, but a reasonable definition for the purposes of the nineteenth century would stress the "basic equality of men and women, a commitment to woman's and man's freedom to choose their own destinies apart from gender-determined roles, social rules, or any of the social relationships in which they participate."[3] Evangelical feminists emphasized this basic equality in areas such as the right to control their own finances, sue for divorce and child custody, practice birth control, become educated, seek employment, and vote.[4]

The woman's rights movement was part of the Benevolence Empire in American history that is often dated from 1797 when Isabella Graham, a Presbyterian widow, founded the Society for the Relief of Poor Widows with Small Children. The Benevolence Empire was simply a period of widespread reform lasting until roughly the Civil War, resulting in the development of many benevolence organizations. The general spirit of reform and some of the organizations continue even today. Women were central to the Benevolence Empire. By the late 1820s, there existed a reform network consisting of the American Sunday School Union (1824), which was founded by Joanna and Divy Bethune, the American Board of Commissioners for Foreign Missions (1810), the American Bible Society (1816), the American Colonization Society (1817), the American Tract Society (1825), the American Education Society (1826), the American Home Mission Society (1826), the American Temperance Society (1826), the American Peace Society (1828), and the American Anti-Slavery Society (1833). These organizations ran largely on money raised by women, and many smaller reform organizations were actually led by women; they included agencies that sought to aid the handicapped, help the mentally ill, provide relief for the poor, and reform prisons. As women became involved in these reform efforts, speaking out in behalf of others, they learned to speak out on their own issues and to see themselves as agents of change in the area of equality for women. They used a variety of methods, including moral suasion, conversion, party politics, petitioning, and job training.[5]

One of the primary reasons that woman's rights became important in the first half of the nineteenth century was that industrialization was changing the way people's public lives were organized. During the colonial period of American history (1607–1787), social life, including labor and work life, revolved around the family. Parents and children worked at home on the family farm. Children were treated like miniature adults in that they were given responsibilities for some aspect of the farm work at a very early age. As urban industry began, the first businesses tended to be family-oriented, and the colonial pattern continued briefly in the early nineteenth century. In these businesses the workers and the owners tended to live in close proximity to one another or even in the same dwelling. The work patterns and living conditions tended to blur the distinction between owners and employees, and families of the ownership and working classes tended to work as units. Around 1825, these work arrangements began to change. Owners moved away from the working-class areas of the cities to "the big house" where they lived with their wives and children, heightening a sense of class difference between owners and workers. Also important was the effect these changes had on families. Increasingly, for the middle and upper classes, the business world came to be a public province of the man. It was considered a rough and dangerous place, often corrosive to the morality of those involved. As men entered the public sphere, middle-class wives stayed home to train the children to be moral, upright citizens. The woman's role was to nurture the children, while the man provided the family's economic well-being. As women took charge of domestic life, they came to be thought of as more moral than men, but oddly this strength was used as an excuse for tightly regulating women's lives. In other words, as the argument went, because women were strong morally, they must be confined to the home to nurture the children. If allowed into the public workplace, they might be corrupted, and if this happened society would be imperiled. The result of all this was that "mother was in charge but without real authority."[6]

At the same time these changes were taking place, the revivals of the Second Great Awakening began to exert a leveling, democratic influence on American life. Revivalists believed that all people—men, women, black, white, rich, and poor—were created equal, and all were sinners in need of salvation. Just as African American slaves often seized on this sense of equality, so too did women. As woman's rights activist Sarah Grimke wrote in the first of her *Letters on the Equality of the Sexes and the Condition of Women,* "God created us equal;—he created us free agents;—he is our Lawgiver, our King and our Judge, and to him alone is woman bound to be in subjection, and to him alone is she accountable for the use of those talents with which her Heavenly Father has entrusted her."[7] Sarah's younger sister, Angelina, in her *Letters to*

Catherine Beecher, wrote, "Human beings have rights, because they are moral beings; . . . the mere circumstance of sex does not give to man higher rights and responsibilities, than to woman. . . . Whatever it is morally right for man to do, it is morally right for woman to do."[8] Many other feminists couched their arguments in religious terms, saying similar things.

Reinterpreting Scripture

For feminists, as for abolitionists, the Bible was very important, and both types of reformers had to reinterpret scripture in order to make their claims. As revivalists engaged in antislavery, they read the slavery passages of the Bible differently than did southern slaveholders and their preachers. Feminists would follow this pattern in reinterpreting verses of scripture that address gender issues. Rather than freezing the ancient status quo in place for all time, abolitionists and feminists saw scripture as undermining that status quo. Just as preachers of the Second Great Awakening emphasized verses of scripture that seemed to stress free will and instantaneous conversion, moving away from Calvinist concepts of original sin and predestination, so, too, did women interpreters shift the emphasis to freedom and equality. Where the story of Adam and Eve in the Garden of Eden was often used to show that Eve sinned first, then Adam, women of the Second Great Awakening emphasized that Adam and Eve both sinned. Women activists then proceeded to highlight the role of women in the Old Testament and how God had often called them to be prophets. As feminist preacher Antoinette Brown said at the 1853 Woman's Rights Convention, "If we believe the bible to endorse the institutions of patriarchal times, must we therefore suppose those institutions to be obligatory, or even right, for the present age? Not if we believe Christ, for he told us that things such as polygamy, were permitted on account of the hardness of their hearts. . . . God's will comes to us progressively, and light increases as we are ready to receive it."[9]

While many feminists reinterpreted the Bible as a result of their experiences in the abolition movement, Lucy Stone started to question patriarchal readings as a little girl. She read the King James Version of Genesis 3:16 that says a woman's desire will be for her husband and that he will rule over her. Stone recalled later that while she knew that male-dominated societal structures were opposed to women, this was the first time she had contemplated the horror that God might be against her as well. She went to her mother and asked if there was anything she could take that would make her die. When her mother asked why she wanted to die, Stone told her what she had read. Her mother read other passages of scripture to her and explained that a woman was supposed to submit to her husband. Stone wrote later, "My mother always tried to submit. I never could."[10] Stone would not submit, but neither would she abandon the Bible. Her hunch was that scripture did not err but that male interpretations and translations did. She went to college, learned Greek and Hebrew, read the biblical texts in their original languages, and concluded that translation and interpretation were indeed the culprits. Stone was once sitting next to a minister on a riverboat who accused her of holding unorthodox interpretations. As Stone related the story years later, when this preacher began to lose the argument he told her she should study scripture more diligently, especially the passages on women. To this she replied, "I have read them in Greek and can translate them for you."[11] She then began to quote passages to him and explain what the various Greek words meant. Knowing nothing of the Greek language, he was humiliated.

Likewise, Phoebe Palmer, the most important woman Bible teacher of the nineteenth century, had a high view of the authority of scripture. She wrote, "My highest and all-consuming desire was to be a Bible Christian." Her most famous passage, which appears in almost every work that she wrote or that others wrote about her, was: "The BIBLE, THE BLESSED BIBLE, IS THE TEXT BOOK. Not Wesley, not Fletcher, not Finney, not Mahan, not Upham, not Mrs. Phoebe Palmer, but the Bible—the holy Bible, is the first and last, and in the midst always. The BIBLE is the standard, the groundwork, the platform, the creed."[12] In the first of her *Letters on the Equality of the Sexes,* Sarah Grimke said she depended "solely on the bible to designate the sphere of woman, because I believe almost everything that has been written on the subject, has been the result of a misconception of the simple truths revealed in the Scriptures, in consequence of the false translation of many passages of Holy Writ."[13] In response to a *Pastoral Letter* issued by the Congregational clergy of Massachusetts in 1837, Grimke wrote, "The New Testament has been referred to, and I am willing to abide by its decision, but must enter my protest against the false translation of

some passages by the MEN who did that work, and against the perverted interpretation by the MEN who understood to write commen-
taries thereon."[14]

Generally, these biblical feminists of the nineteenth century
showed that God had selected women of the Old and New Testaments
for important work: Deborah, Miriam, Huldah, Jael, Anna, Priscilla,
and Phoebe. They pointed to the inclusive and accepting attitude Jesus
had toward women, and they stressed that the Apostle Paul had referred
to Phoebe in the book of Romans as a "deacon," a word that male translators had rendered as "servant." Paul had also called other women "co-
workers in the gospel": Euodia and Syntyche in Philippians 4:2, and
Tryphena and Tryphosa in Romans 16:12. Among the most useful passage for patriarchs was 1 Corinthians 14:34, which told women to keep
silent in the church. The female Bible expositors argued that hardly
anyone took the passages literally, and pointed out that most churches
allowed women to sing hymns and speak in certain settings. Antoinette
Brown argued that the passage referred to women "chattering" in public
meetings and that this could not have been a blanket prohibition
because the author, Paul, in 1 Corinthians 11:5, speaks of women praying and prophesying. Another seemingly patriarchal passage was 1 Timothy 2:11–12, which says, "Let the woman learn in silence with all
subjection. But I suffer not a woman to teach, nor to usurp authority
over the man, but to be in silence." Brown argued that the key word was
usurp, which means to take authority one does not have. A woman like
herself, who was ordained and licensed to preach, was not usurping.
On the Genesis passage that had troubled the young Lucy Stone, Brown
and other woman interpreters said that the reference to the husband's
rule over the wife was descriptive of what would happen as a result of
sin, not prescriptive of what should happen as a result of God's created
order.[15] Thought of this way, when things were put back the way God
intended them before the fall into sin, there would be equality between
men and women.

Women also applied the Golden Rule to their situation in much
the same way they did to slavery. Angelina Grimke once asked a
Charleston, South Carolina, slaveholder if she would like to be a slave.
When the woman said no, Grimke quoted the Golden Rule, "Do unto
others as you would have them do unto you." Brown did the same thing
rhetorically with men, asking them if they would like to be ruled over

by women. "I claim that this movement is preeminently a great Christian movement," Brown wrote. "It is founded in the Christian doctrine, 'Thou shalt love the Lord thy God supremely, and thy neighbor as thyself'; and the Golden Rule of the new gospel."[16]

Perhaps the favorite biblical text of feminists was Galatians 3:28, "There is neither Jew nor Greek, there is neither bond nor free, there is neither male nor female; for ye are all one in Christ Jesus." This passage brought the abolition and woman's rights movements together because the apostle Paul referred to both race and gender. Woman's rights activists argued that when one is brought into the kingdom of Christ, all distinctions between people disappear. All are brothers and sisters in Christ; all are equal.

The millennial idea that the kingdom of God was imminent motivated many of the reforms of the nineteenth century, and this idea was used explicitly in the woman's rights movement. Phoebe Palmer, for example, often referred to the day of Pentecost recorded in Acts where the apostle Peter quoted from Joel 2:28–32, "And it shall come to pass in the last days, saith God, I will pour out of my Spirit upon all flesh; and your sons and your daughters shall prophesy, and your young men shall see visions, and your old men shall dream dreams: And on my servants and on my handmaidens I will pour out in those days of my Spirit; and they shall prophesy."[17] Palmer remarked sarcastically that when the tongues of fire fell on the women, the apostles did not think to call a vestry meeting to decide whether or not women should be allowed to speak. She and other feminists also frequently quoted Acts 2:4, "They were *all* filled with the Holy Ghost, and began to speak."[18] They emphasized that all received the spirit and all spoke. Palmer believed that the woman's rights movement was a signal that the last days were near and that Christ's millennial kingdom was about to dawn. She wrote in her diary, "The dispensation of the Spirit is now entered upon,—the last dispensation previous to the last glorious appearing of our Lord and Savior Jesus Christ. . . . Male and Female are now one in Christ Jesus. The Spirit now descended alike on all. And they were all filled with the Holy Ghost, and began to speak as the Spirit gave utterance."[19]

Charles Finney was criticized for allowing women to pray at his meetings. He defended the practice in his *Lectures on Revivals,* arguing that there should be enough prayer meetings for all who are moved by the spirit to pray in public, including women. In 1845, he wrote in response to a woman's questions about public praying, "[S]ome have supposed that the Scriptures plainly prohibit the speaking or praying of women in promiscuous assemblies. I do not so understand the teachings of the Bible."[20]

In the 1850s, some of the leaders of the woman's rights movement began to abandon the Bible in favor of legal and natural rights arguments. At the Woman's Rights Convention of 1852 in Syracuse and again the next year in Cleveland, Antoinette Brown submitted a resolution recognizing that the Bible favored woman's rights. Ernestine Rose, another feminist present, spoke against the resolution, arguing that rather than the Bible, the movement should base its plea on natural rights as did the leaders of the American Revolution. The president of the organization, Lucretia Mott, also spoke against Brown's resolution, saying that abolitionists had learned the futility of trying to match Bible verse-for-verse with slaveholders. Southern slaveholders used the Bible to defend slavery, while northern abolitionists used it to denounce the institution, leading to a biblical stalemate. When Brown put her resolution before the 1853 meeting, Rose rebuked her even more strongly than the year before, saying, "There is a time and a season for everything, and this is no time to discuss the Bible. I appeal to the universal experience of men, to sustain me, in asking whether theological quibbles, has not been a firebrand wherever they have been thrown? We have a political question under discussion; let us take that question and argue it with reference to right and wrong."[21]

Hardesty believes that the move away from the Bible weakened the woman's rights movement of the nineteenth century. In her view, woman's rights advocates would have done better to keep preaching that the denial of equality for women was morally sinful. The nineteenth century was still an era where the vast majority of Americans believed in sin and could be moved by a message that named particular practices as sinful. Abolitionists, Hardesty believes, tended to keep their focus on the sin of slavery whereas women, to the detriment of their movement, shifted from biblical language to an emphasis on individual rights. Hardesty writes rhetorically, "One wonders what might have happened if the feminists had instead followed the example of the abolitionists, who built their movement on the conviction that slaveholding was not only a violation of a person's political rights but morally sinful."[22]

Another equally plausible explanation for the sputtering of the first woman's rights movement after the Civil War is that it was tied too closely to abolition. At the 27th anniversary of the American Anti-Slavery Society in 1860, Elizabeth Cady Stanton contended that "this is the only organization on God's footstool where the humanity of woman is recognized, and these are the only men who have ever echoed back her cries for justice and equality. . . . [T]he mission of this Radical Anti-Slavery Movement is not to the African slave alone, but to the slaves of custom, creed and sex, as well, and most faithfully has it done its work."[23] When the slaves were freed, many men who had supported both abolition and woman's rights simply lost interest in the latter. Women would have to forge ahead without the support of male abolitionists. It would be two generations before this second, post-Civil War phase of woman's rights would culminate in passage of the Nineteenth Amendment to the Constitution (1920) granting women the right to vote.

Leading Woman's Rights Activists

Having analyzed the ways nineteenth-century feminists reinterpreted scripture, it is important to see how they were prepared for this task by earlier life experiences, especially the influence of revivalist religion. Most of the women discussed below who were at the forefront of feminism before 1850 were products of either evangelical Protestantism or Quakerism. Religion had greatly influenced their lives.

Although not born until near the end of the Second Great Awakening, Frances Willard was very much touched by revivalist influences. In Hardesty's view, Willard was the "woman of the century."[24] She was born in the burned-over district of western New York, where revival fires swept back and forth across the region. "Heir to the revivalist legacy of broad-based, gospel-rooted reform," Hardesty writes, "she sought to do everything within her power to empower and uplift women."[25] Willard was born in 1839 in the appropriately named town of Churchville, New York, which had experienced a revival in 1829. Willard attributed that revival to her father's efforts, but Churchville was only 14 miles from Rochester, where Finney's revivals occurred in 1830. It might be more accurate to say that the Churchville revival was part of the Finneyite movement that began to influence the region in

1827 and into the early 1830s. Willard's family moved to Oberlin in 1841 so that her father, Josiah, could attend Oberlin College to study for the ministry. Although he had been active in lay ministry for many years, he had never been ordained. The family also favored Oberlin because of the school's abolitionist stance. In 1844, when Josiah experienced lung problems, the family moved to Wisconsin. Typically, in the nineteenth century, people with health problems believed that the open spaces and clear air of the western frontier would help cure them. Frances grew up in Wisconsin where the family became Methodist. In 1857, the family moved again, this time to Evanston, Illinois, outside Chicago, where Frances would attend Northwestern Female College.

Willard was converted during the winter of 1859–1860, then, as a result of the influence of Bible teacher Phoebe Palmer, had what Methodists called "the second blessing." The second blessing, also known as holiness or perfection, was a form of spiritual sanctification whereby the believer reached a new level of spirituality. One reached this state by figuratively laying oneself on the altar as a sacrifice to God. To the degree one was able to present oneself as a spiritual sacrifice, God would accept the sacrifice, and the person would become perfect at least as far as the will was concerned. In other words, while a person might not ever live perfectly, he or she could will perfectly. After teaching for a time, Willard became president of Evanston College for Ladies, which merged with Northwestern University after the Chicago fire destroyed the property and wealth of many of the College for Ladies benefactors. She became dean of the Women's College of Northwestern University as well as professor but resigned in 1874 because of difficulties working with the university president, to whom she had been briefly engaged some years before. Willard joined the temperance movement in 1873 and would become president of the Women's Christian Temperance Union in 1879. She would serve in this post effectively for many years as one of the most significant reformers of her era. She was also involved in revivals again in the 1870s when she worked with Dwight L. Moody, the most important revivalist preacher of the late nineteenth century. Moody was nearly as significant for late-century revivalism as Finney had been during the Second Great Awakening.[26]

While Willard and most of the other significant woman activists made significant contributions to reform, Phoebe Palmer was first and foremost a spiritual leader and Bible teacher. Palmer was born Phoebe

Worrall in 1807 and grew up in New York the daughter of a doctor who practiced homeopathic medicine. Her sister Sarah was also a significant spiritual leader but not as famous as Phoebe. They converted at a young age and joined the Methodist Episcopal Church. In 1835, Sarah received the second blessing and soon thereafter started the Tuesday Meeting for the Promotion of Holiness, which would continue for the next 60 years.

Phoebe received the second blessing on July 26, 1837, and would become famous, traveling about with her doctor husband, preaching and teaching. She was perhaps the nineteenth century's most significant promoter of holiness. Phoebe helped shape the concept of holiness in her books *The Way of Holiness* (1843), *Faith and Its Effects* (1849), and *Present to My Christian Friend on Entire Devotion to God* (1853). She even influenced Finney. He received the second blessing in 1843 and began thereafter to teach it himself.[27]

Although not a Bible teacher in the same way that Palmer was, activist Elizabeth Cady Stanton was no less a student of scripture in her early years. Born in 1815, she was converted at a young age at a Finney revival in Troy, New York. When her brother died, her father said to her, "Oh my daughter, I wish you were a boy."[28] Rather than deflate her, the remark inspired Stanton to do all the things that boys were allowed to do. She convinced her Presbyterian pastor to teach her Greek with the boys, and she became such a proficient student that when he died he willed to her his Greek New Testament, Greek grammar, and lexicon. Stanton was involved in many reforms and after the Civil War became one of the leaders who kept the woman's rights movement going after male abolitionists lost interest. In 1895 she published *The Woman's Bible*, a two-volume commentary on various passages of scripture having to do with gender.

The abolition movement welcomed many women into the world of reform, and two of the earliest were from Great Britain. Frances Wright, born in 1775 in Scotland, visited the United States in the 1820s and published her impressions (*Views of Society and Manners in America*) making her a kind of female Alexis de Tocqueville. In her book she called slavery evil and argued that woman's education was neglected. Returning to America in 1824, she wrote *A PLAN For the Gradual Abolition of Slavery in the United States, without danger or loss to the Citizens of the South.* She then founded a model community in Nashoba, Tennessee, but it did not last. Wright was significant because she was one of the first women in America to speak publicly on slavery.

A second British woman was the Quaker Elizabeth Heyrick. Born in 1769, she was one of the earliest immediatists. Her book *Immediate, not Gradual Emancipation* was printed in Philadelphia in 1824. In it she not only called gradual emancipation "the very master-piece of satanic policy," but also called for the boycott of products produced with slave labor.[29]

Like Heyrick, Elizabeth Chandler was also a Quaker. Born in 1807, she grew up in Philadelphia. In the 1820s she began writing essays for a journal called *The Genius of Universal Emancipation*. In 1829 she became editor of the "Ladies Repository" section of the journal and in that capacity wrote many poems on slavery. Like all early abolitionist women, she was criticized for speaking publicly. In response she tied the woman's rights movement together with antislavery, especially as it related to slave women. She wrote, "[S]hould we not, every woman of us, north and south, east and west, rise up with one accord, and demand for our miserable sisters a restitution of the rights and privileges of her sex?"[30] Chandler also wrote a series of letters, entitled collectively *To the Ladies of Baltimore*, exhorting women to take up the mantle of antislavery.

Some women abolitionists, however, were apologetic about violating gender taboos. Lydia Maria Child was one of these more conservative activists, and, significantly, was not a product of revivalism. A Unitarian born in 1802, Child published a work entitled, *An Appeal in Favor of that Class of Americans Called Africans* (1833) that refuted gradualist colonization in favor of immediate emancipation. Like many men in the antislavery movement, Child appears to have feared that too much attention to woman's rights might imperil abolition. In her preface she wrote deferentially, almost apologetically, "Read [this book], from sheer curiosity to see what a woman (who had much better tend to her household concerns) will say upon such a subject."[31] Near the end of the book she timidly called on women to sign petitions to Congress to end slavery in Washington, D.C. She knew that abolition was radical enough; women abolitionists were doubly so. Two years after her book appeared, and after the number of subscribers to her children's magazine had plummeted, she wrote, *Brief History of the Condition of Women, in Various Ages and Nations*. Still somewhat apologetic, she explained in the preface, "This volume is not an essay upon woman's rights, or a philosophical investigation of what is or ought to be the relation of the sexes. . . . I have simply endeavored to give an accurate history of the condition of women, in language sufficiently concise for popular use."[32] Child's case shows one of the ironies of nineteenth-century reform, at least an irony from the perspective of the twenty-first century. She, the theologically liberal Unitarian, was more conservative on reform issues than the theological conservatives who were products of revivals and based their arguments on scripture. This relationship between conservative religion and progressive politics was not unusual in the nineteenth century for women or men.

Like Child, many abolitionist men were ambivalent about woman's rights, at least in the early 1830s. While generally welcoming women, men feared that attention and energy spent on woman's rights might divert efforts away from abolition. In 1832 Garrison's *Liberator* started a "Ladies Department" that reprinted Chandler's essay "Our Own Sex." Six months later the first female society in New England was formed in Providence, Rhode Island. The Boston Female Anti-Slavery Society was formed shortly thereafter, first as a fundraising unit for the New England Anti-Slavery Society, then as an independent organization. Maria Weston Chapman and her three sisters were most influential in the Boston Female Anti-Slavery Society.[33] Still, there were no women invited to Philadelphia for the founding of the American Anti-Slavery Society in 1833. On the second day of the meeting, Lucretia Mott and three others joined as spectators. When the organization wrote its "Declaration of Sentiments and Purposes" the women were not invited to sign. As one woman recalled, "It was not thought of in season."[34] This is precisely what many male abolitionists believed, even those men who supported woman's rights. Abolition had to come first, only then could the woman's rights issue be taken up. Many women disagreed, most notably the Grimke sisters.

The Grimke Sisters

While women such as Elizabeth Cady Stanton, Frances Willard, and a few others would become more famous later and have longer careers in woman's rights, during the era of the Second Great Awakening the most influential women were the Grimke sisters from Charleston,

South Carolina. Sarah and Angelina were the daughters of John F. Grimke and Mary Smith Grimke, slaveholding southern aristocrats. Sarah was born in 1792, the family's sixth child and second daughter. Angelina was born in 1805, the fourteenth and youngest child. John was a legislator and judge whose favorite subject was moral philosophy. He believed strongly in an individual's right to think for oneself and instilled this in his children. He was also an author who wrote three volumes on law. While John did not provide extensive formal education for his daughters, he did give them access to his library and allowed Sarah to participate in the debates he held to prepare his sons for law school. Mary was an understanding, compassionate, and affectionate mother to Sarah, Angelina, and the other 12 children she bore, and she was well-read in theology.[35]

Thirteen years older than Angelina, Sarah essentially raised her younger sister. This was not unusual in the era when families were large and children were treated as miniature adults. Often the older children were given responsibility to watch over and care for the younger ones. In the case of the Grimke sisters, there developed an unusual bond that would last for the rest of their lives. As a child Angelina called her older sister "mother," and the two lived together during their adult lives, even after Angelina married. They read the same books, had the same friends, read each other's writings, and mutually supported one another.[36]

Sarah's encounter with a Presbyterian revivalist Henry Kollock when she was a teenager proved critical. After a week spent in private conversation with him, Sarah experienced an evangelical conversion, although by her own reckoning she backslid into sin several times thereafter. In 1818 she accompanied her father to the North when he sought medical treatment. The two stayed for a time with a Quaker doctor in Philadelphia, then went to the New Jersey shore, hoping John would recuperate. He worsened, however, and died there. After Sarah returned alone to Charleston, she began to worship at the meeting-house of the Quakers, a simple and humble sect of Christians who had radical views on woman's rights and slavery. Because southern aristocrats did not regard Quakers highly, Sarah was ridiculed by friends and family members. Sarah persisted, however, and in 1821, after having a mystical experience, accompanied by her widowed sister Anna Frost, she returned to the Quaker community in Philadelphia. There she fell in love with Israel Morris, a Quaker widower she had met while returning to Charleston after her trip with her father. Although he proposed in 1826 and again in 1830, Sarah declined, perhaps because she was preparing for the Quaker ministry and may have thought it impossible to combine marriage with ministry.[37]

Like most women activists of her era, Sarah was drawn into the abolitionist movement. Raised in southern comfort, even as a child she was horrified at the treatment of African Americans. She attempted to counter the injustice by befriending her family's slaves and even attempting to teach her personal servant to read, a violation of South Carolina law.[38] Her first encounter with abolitionism came when she traveled with her ailing father to Philadelphia. The Quakers she met gave her a copy of the *Journal* of John Woolman, an eighteenth-century Quaker who was one of the first vocal opponents of slavery. He traveled in the South and was sometimes harassed and beaten for his views. He refused to wear or use items made from slave labor. Sarah read the *Journal* with great interest and after arriving home concluded she could no longer reside in Charleston or anywhere in the South. This resolution ultimately convinced her to move to Philadelphia. Once there she was disturbed by the inability or unwillingness of some Quakers to practice what they preached, especially with regard to African Americans.[39] Eventually, she and Angelina would become fully engaged members of the abolitionist movement as the most visible women opposing slavery.

Sarah's antislavery activism would lead eventually into woman's rights. Her principal biographer, Gerda Lerner, believes that Sarah was more the feminist than Angelina, while Angelina was more the abolitionist. This was merely a matter of balance, however, because both sisters believed in woman's rights and antislavery and saw the two movements as interconnected. As Angelina worked diligently for abolition she often found herself having to fight for the right of women to speak in public. Obviously, the right to speak against slavery in public implied the right of women to speak in public on other issues as well. The woman's rights and abolition movements could scarcely be separated at that point.

In the words of Lerner, "Sarah's argument for the emancipation of women was almost entirely theological; her language was biblical; her images were derived from Christian iconography."[40] Lerner sees Sarah as a major feminist thinker and the first woman in America to write a coherent feminist argument. Like many other women covered in this chapter, Sarah believed that biblical arguments for the subordination of women were faulty either in interpretation, translation, or both. Men and women, she insisted, were created equal. Adam and Eve had both sinned. "They both fell from innocence, and consequently from happiness, but not from equality," Sarah believed. As for the curse on Eve she wrote, "[T]he curse . . . is simple prophecy. The Hebrew, like our French language, uses the same word to express shall and will. Our translators having been accustomed to exercise lordship over their wives, and seeing only through the medium of perverted judgment . . . translated it shall instead of will, and thus converted prediction to Eve into a command to Adam."[41] In words that her sister Angelina and others would echo, Sarah wrote, "WHATSOEVER IT IS MORALLY RIGHT FOR A MAN TO DO IT IS MORALLY RIGHT FOR A WOMAN TO DO . . . she is clothed by her Maker with the same rights, and . . . the same duties."[42]

Sarah's most important work was her *Of Letters on the Equality of the Sexes*. It was perhaps the most influential book in the nineteenth-century woman's rights movement. Lucy Stone called it "first rate," and Elizabeth Cady Stanton acknowledged its influence on her own work. Lucretia Mott called it the most important book since Mary Wollstonecraft's *Rights of Women*.[43] The book was a compilation of letters that Grimke had written to a number of women dealing with a variety of gender issues and answering questions that had been posed to her by other woman's rights activists. She appeared as the reigning authority on woman's rights.

Angelina's pilgrimage in the faith and in reform was greatly influenced by Sarah's example. Angelina refused confirmation in the Episcopal Church when she was 13, then converted to Presbyterianism at the age of 20. While she was young she taught Bible studies and held prayer meetings for her family's slaves, and urged members of her Presbyterian church to speak out against slavery. In 1828, she began to record her frustrations with southern society in her diary, then left for Philadelphia to join Sarah the next year. Generally, Angelina was more confident in her own judgments and more willing to act on her instincts than was Sarah. She would become the more visible of the sisters. She was also more critical of the Quakers for not living up to their antislavery heritage, and she began to read abolitionist literature outside the Quaker community. By 1834 she was urging one of her brothers to leave the colonization movement and become an abolitionist. Both sisters joined the Free Produce movement, which boycotted products made with slave labor, and Angelina joined the Philadelphia Female Anti-Slavery Society in 1835. That year she wrote a letter to William Lloyd Garrison that he published in the *Liberator.* Her Philadelphia Quaker community, fearing reprisal for being associated with abolition, pressured Angelina to renounce the letter. She refused. The next year both sisters defied the Quakers, moved to New York, and became the first female agents for the American Anti-Slavery Society. At the "parlour meetings" of the society they began to speak to mixed audiences.[44]

This speaking to "promiscuous" audiences, as mixed audiences were then called, caused a significant controversy among abolitionists. Leading abolitionist Theodore Dwight Weld supported the right of women abolitionists to speak publicly, arguing "it was downright slave-holding to shut them out. . . . Why! Folks talk about women's preaching as tho' it was next to highway robbery—eyes astare and mouth agape. Pity women were not born with a split stick on their tongues!"[45] Weld even suggested at one point that a woman had as much right to ask a man to marry her as the other way around. While we do not need to doubt Weld's sincerity, it is worth noting that he and Angelina were corresponding with each other on both public issues such as abolition and woman's rights and personal issues. In short, they were falling in love and would eventually marry.

Still, while advocating equality for women, Weld initially believed that antislavery was of primary importance. He, therefore, wanted women to be cautious about allowing woman's rights, "lesser work" as he called it, to obscure what he thought was the more important issue. He wrote to Sarah and Angelina, "Let us all first wake up the nation to lift millions of slaves of both sexes from the dust, and turn them into MEN and then when we all have our hand in, it will be an easy matter to take millions of females from their knees and set them on their feet, or in other words transform them from babies into women."[46] Angelina was stung by Weld's position and did not hesitate to rebuke him. Reminding him of how abolitionists were once told to go slow, she wrote, "Now my dear brothers this invasion of our rights was just such an attack upon us, as that made upon Abolitionists generally when they were told a few years ago that they had no right to discuss the subject of Slavery. Did you take no notice of this assertion? Why no! [W]ith one heart and one voice you said, We will settle this right before we go one step further. The time to assert a right is the time when that right is denied."[47] Alluding to their budding romance, she also said that while she agreed with Weld that women should be allowed to propose marriage, she was too proud ever to do that, perhaps implying that she was ready for him to ask.

The two debated back and forth on the relative importance and immediacy of abolition and woman's rights. At one point Weld suggested that when the Grimke sisters met resistance for speaking publicly, they should use their Quakerism as an excuse, essentially arguing that because Quakers taught woman's rights, they should be exempted from the general societal taboo against women speaking to mixed audiences. Angelina replied, "Now we want thee to sustain us on the high ground of MORAL RIGHT, not Quaker peculiarity." She continued, "We do not stand on Quaker ground, but on the Bible ground and moral right. What we claim for ourselves, we claim for every woman whom God has called and qualified with gifts and graces."[48]

Following their intense debate over antislavery and woman's rights, Weld finally admitted that he was in love with Angelina. She confessed that she had felt the same way for some time but had been unwilling to break society's taboo against the woman saying it first.[49] The two were married in 1838, moved to a farm in New Jersey in the early 1840s, raised a family, and continued to work for woman's rights, antislavery, education, and other reforms until Angelina's death in 1879. Sarah lived and worked with Angelina and Theodore, often serving as nanny for the children. Together, the three reformers lived in the belief that all people, regardless of race or gender, were equal in God's sight and should be so treated by law and society. Moreover, they believed they should labor to bring righteousness to the earth in order to prepare the way for God's millennial kingdom. Like the nation itself, they were shaped by the revivals of the Second Great Awakening.

Notes

1. Nancy A. Hardesty, *Women Called to Witness: Evangelical Feminism in the Nineteenth Century* (Knoxville: University of Tennessee Press, 1999), x.

2. See, for example, Ann Douglas, *The Feminization of American Culture* (New York: Anchor Press/Doubleday, 1988); and Nancy F. Cott, *The Bonds of Womanhood: 'Woman's Sphere' in New England, 1780–1835* (New Haven, Conn.: Yale University Press, 1977).

3. Hardesty, x–xi.

4. Ibid.

5. Ibid., 21.

6. Ibid., 23.

7. Larry Ceplair, ed., *The Public Years of Sarah and Angelina Grimke: Selected Writings, 1835–1839* (New York: Columbia University Press, 1989), 207.

8. Ibid., 194–95.

9. Quoted in Hardesty, 58–59.

10. Quoted in ibid., 54.

11. Quoted in ibid., 63.

12. Quoted in ibid., 56.

13. Quoted in Ceplair, 204–5.

14. Quoted in ibid., 213.

15. Hardesty, 63.

16. Quoted in ibid., 64.

17. Quoted in ibid., 64.

18. Quoted in ibid., 65.

19. Quoted in ibid., 65.

20. Quoted in ibid., 72–73.

21. Quoted in ibid., 66–67.

22. Ibid., 67.

23. Quoted in Ceplair, 2.

24. Hardesty, 1.

25. Ibid., 12.

26. Ibid., 1–12.

27. Ibid., 38–42.

28. Quoted in ibid., 53.

29. Quoted in Ceplair, 7.

30. Quoted in ibid., 8.

31. Quoted in ibid., 9.

32. Quoted in ibid., 9.

33. Ibid., 8.

34. Quoted in ibid., 9.

35. Ibid., 12–13.

36. Gerda Lerner, *The Feminist Thought of Sarah Grimke* (New York: Oxford University Press, 1998), 7–11.

37. Ibid., 11.

38. Ibid., 6.

39. Ceplair, 13–14.

40. Lerner, 4.

41. Quoted in ibid., 23.

42. Quoted in ibid., 26.

43. Ibid., 26–27.

44. Ibid., 12–13.

45. Quoted in Robert H. Abzug, *Passionate Liberator: Theodore Dwight Weld and the Dilemma of Reform* (New York: Oxford University Press, 1980), 176.

46. Quoted in ibid., 178.

47. Quoted in ibid., 179.

48. Quoted in Hardesty, 59–60.

49. Quoted in Abzug, 188.

BIOGRAPHIES

Amos Bronson Alcott (1799–1888)

A close friend of Ralph Waldo Emerson, Alcott was one of the inner circle of Transcendentalist founders. Growing up in Connecticut, he taught himself to read. He left home at the age of 17 and went door-to-door as a salesman in the South, returning home after five years to become a teacher and to marry Abigail May in 1830. One of his daughters, Louisa May, became a famous writer, while another became an artist.

As an educational reformer in the 1830s, Alcott applied Transcendentalist principles to teaching. Essentially, he believed that children were born with an innate sense of right and wrong and that they could be best taught through dialogue and example instead of lecture and memorization of facts. His two-volume *Conversations with Children on the Gospels* appeared in 1836 and 1837. Alcott's educational ideas were controversial and sometimes misunderstood. The Temple School he founded in the late 1830s was short-lived in part because his educational methods and approaches to moral development were unorthodox for that time.

In the 1840s, Alcott joined forces with Charles Lane in an ill-fated attempt to form a commune called Fruitlands. Believing that all creatures were related, Fruitlands did not allow the butchery of animals or even the use of animal products for food or clothing. Intended to be an ideal agricultural community that would shun the negative side effects of capitalist business enterprise, the community did not survive the winter because of the lack of food and adequate warm clothing.

After recovering from the despondency that followed the Fruitlands' failure, Alcott traveled successfully throughout the Midwest as a lecturer. During the Civil War he served as the superintendent of schools for Concord and in 1879 established his Concord School of Philosophy, which was a summer institute for adults. For nearly a decade people from across the United States flocked to Concord to attend the institutes.

Richard Allen (1760–1831)

Allen was the founder of the first African American Protestant denomination. Raised as a slave in the Philadelphia area, he was converted in 1777 and began Methodist lay preaching shortly thereafter. He subsequently converted his owner who then allowed him to purchase his freedom. Because of his success as a circuit-riding preacher, prominent Methodist leaders, including Francis Asbury, began to mentor him. In 1786, Allen began to assist in the ministry of St. George's Methodist Episcopal Church in Philadelphia. As a result of his efforts, many African Americans joined the church. Allen and his associate Absalom Jones, also a former slave, formed the Free African Society in 1787, which was a benevolence and mutual aid society for African American Methodists.

In either 1787 or 1792 (scholars disagree as to which date is correct), Allen and Jones led an exodus of black worshippers from St. George's after whites established segregated seating. Jones started a new congregation aligned with the Episcopal Church, but Allen formed Bethel Church, which remained Methodist. He worked for two more decades to maintain a black identity within Methodism and was ordained as a deacon by Francis Asbury in the Methodist Episcopal Church in 1799. White Methodists often resisted black autonomy, however, and in 1816, following a battle with St. George's officials who sought to bring Bethel back under their jurisdiction, Allen left the Methodist Episcopal Church and formed the African Methodist Episcopal (A.M.E.) Church.

Allen disapproved of the excessive emotionalism of the Second Great Awakening among African Americans. Still, his work within Methodism took place within the context of the revivals that helped convert blacks to Christianity. While desiring a calmer approach to religion than the frontier camp meetings, he nevertheless dedicated himself to the conversion of both blacks and whites and worked diligently to carve out a Christian identity that African Americans could claim as their own.

Susan B. Anthony (1820–1906)

Along with Elizabeth Cady Stanton, Anthony was one of the leading woman's rights reformers of the nineteenth century. Born in South Adams, Massachusetts, into a Quaker family, by the 1840s she had become a schoolteacher and reformer. She was active in the abolition temperance movements. The centerpiece of her reform efforts, however, was always equality for women.

She teamed with Stanton to lead the fight for woman's suffrage. Together they published a weekly periodical called *The Revolution,* and in 1869 organized the National Woman Suffrage Association, which would later become the National American Woman Suffrage Association after it merged with a rival organization. Anthony served as its president from 1892–1900. From 1881–1902 she published her own account of the movement in her four-volume *The History of Woman Suffrage.*

Although not a convert of the revivals of the Second Great Awakening, Anthony was nevertheless a product of the reform emphasis of her Quaker upbringing. As far as anyone can tell, she was never romantically involved and remained single throughout her life. Just as Catholic nuns are symbolically married to the work of Christ, Anthony was singularly committed to woman's rights.

Lyman Beecher (1775–1863)

Beecher was one of New England's and America's most influential clergymen in the nineteenth century. He was also the patriarch of a very influential family. His daughter, Harriet Beecher Stowe, wrote the classic *Uncle Tom's Cabin,* which inspired many in the North to take action against slavery, and his son, Henry Ward Beecher, was one of the great preachers and religious statesmen of the later nineteenth century and one of America's first influential liberal Protestant preachers.

Beecher grew up in Connecticut, entering Yale in 1793 when the college was under the presidency of Timothy Dwight. Beecher came under Dwight's evangelical, revivalistic influence and was converted in 1796. The two subsequently became friends. Beecher was licensed as a Congregational minister, but his first significant pastorate was at the East Hampton Presbyterian Church where he began work in 1799. He preached revivalistic Protestantism there until 1810 when he moved to the Congregational Church in Litchfield, Connecticut.

Connecticut was one of the last two states to have an established (i.e., tax-supported) church. When the state legislature considered disestablishment in 1817, Beecher was at first opposed, believing that the church needed the state's support to thrive. In the months following disestablishment, however, Beecher changed his mind and concluded that churches actually flourished best when they were free and had to support themselves without state aid.

Beecher moved from Litchfield to Boston in 1826, where he became the pastor of the Hanover Street (Congregational) Church. In Boston the most controversial religious issue prior to the development of Transcendentalism was the influence of Unitarianism, which denied the divinity of Christ, the Trinity, and other orthodox Protestant doctrines. Beecher became a vigorous defender of orthodox, evangelical Protestantism in the face of the Unitarian challenge, but he was alarmed at what appeared to be the unbridled revivalism of fellow evangelical Charles Finney. His concern led in 1827 to a historic meeting in New Lebanon, New York, between Beecher's supporters and Finney's group. Prepared to fight Finney and resist his entrance into New England, Beecher was instead persuaded that Finney's revivalism was genuine and orthodox. While never as extemporaneous or populist as Finney, Beecher became more revivalistic than he had been. In addition to revivals, Beecher was equally supportive of social reform. His first published sermon that caught the attention of a wide public audience was entitled "Remedy for Dueling," which he published in 1806 after Aaron Burr shot and killed Alexander Hamilton in a duel. He also supported the temperance movement, moderate antislavery, and a host of other voluntary social movements.

Like many other Protestants, Beecher was convinced that religion was the greatest need on America's western frontier and believed that New England religion in its moderately revivalistic form was the only hope for civilizing the West. Largely for this reason, he became president of Lane Seminary in Cincinnati, Ohio, in 1832 and also simultaneously pastor of Cincinnati's Second Presbyterian Church. There, he continued to preach and promote reform while leading the seminary, even surviving a heresy trial after being accused of departing from the Calvinist Westminster Confession of Faith. During his presidency, a group of radical abolitionist students led by Theodore Dwight Weld left the school and went to Oberlin College. While against slavery, Beecher was moderate and opposed the students' call for immediate abolition.

Beecher retired from the pastorate of Second Presbyterian in 1843 and from the seminary presidency in 1850. He continued to write and speak until his death in 1863.

Alexander Campbell (1788–1866)

Campbell was the key leader in the Restoration movement. His father, Thomas, who visited America in 1807, decided to stay and brought Alexander and the rest of the family to join him in 1809. In Ireland, the Campbells had been evangelical Presbyterians who dissented from the national church. After coming to America, Thomas helped form the Christian Association of Washington County Pennsylvania, which was intended to promote unity across denominational lines. Like the Presbyterian revivalist Barton Stone and some others, he was beginning to view denominational divisions as unbiblical and counterproductive to the gospel. Attempts to unify denominations were often controversial, and by the time Alexander arrived in America the Campbell name was suspect among Presbyterians. The Campbells tried being Baptist but eventually became independent of all denominations in their attempt to restore the unified Christian church of the New Testament. By 1830, those in Alexander's movement were often called Campbellites, but they preferred to be called merely Christians or Disciples because those are New Testament terms. In 1832, the Disciples joined together with Stone's "Christians" to form one of America's truly indigenous denominations. Ironically, their efforts to end denominationalism led to the formation of yet another denomination.

In addition to his efforts to restore a unified New Testament Christianity, Campbell also promoted Christian education and journalism. He had studied in Scotland where he spent nearly a year after being shipwrecked enroute to America. At the University of Glasgow he was influenced significantly by the Scottish Common Sense School of Enlightenment philosophy as well as by the great English thinker John Locke. Common Sense philosophy taught that the real world can be known directly, as opposed to our knowing only ideas we form about the material world. Against skeptics such as David Hume, the Common Sense approach posits that certain knowledge such as the existence of the external world and our own existence can be taken for granted without having to be proven. Common Sense philosophy, as well as other moderate Enlightenment thought, contributed to Campbell's becoming more a debater than revivalist. Some of his debates were published and circulated widely. He was more rational in his approach to Christianity than was the norm for revivalist Protestantism during the Second Great Awakening, believing that people could be convinced of the truths of Christianity through well-articulated arguments instead of emotional appeals. Unlike many products of the Enlightenment, however, he remained orthodox and biblical in his emphases, arguing vigorously for the traditional truths of scripture. His frontier biblical rationalism manifested itself in the periodicals he founded, the first in 1823 called *The Christian Baptist,* then after 1830, *The Millennial Harbinger,* which he edited until his death in 1866. He also published several books and pamphlets and in 1840 established Bethany College in present-day West Virginia.

When Campbell died, an estimated 200,000 people belonged to the Disciples of Christ movement, and it was one of the fastest growing denominations of the nineteenth century. The Disciples eventually divided into the Disciples, the Churches of Christ, and the Independent Christian Churches and today have roughly five million members collectively worldwide. The Restoration movement was a product of the Second Great Awakening's emphasis on reestablishing the Christian faith in its pure New Testament form.

Peter Cartwright (1785–1872)

Cartwright was one of the leading Methodist revivalists of the nineteenth century. Born in Virginia, as a boy he moved with his family to Kentucky where he was converted in 1801 at a camp meeting that occurred in the aftermath of the Cane Ridge revival, the largest revival of the Second Great Awakening. He subsequently joined the Methodist denomination and was ordained as a circuit-riding preacher. By 1812, he was a presiding elder, overseeing Methodist churches in Kentucky, then transferred to Illinois in 1824 and served as a presiding elder and preacher until his death.

In Illinois, Cartwright got involved in politics, winning a seat in the Illinois legislature in 1828. In his re-election bid in 1832, he defeated Abraham Lincoln. Lincoln avenged his loss 14 years later when he beat Cartwright for a seat in the U.S. House of Representatives. Allegedly, during that election campaign, Lincoln attended one of Cartwright's revivals. When the preacher asked everyone to stand who wanted to go to heaven, all stood except for Lincoln. Cartwright then asked Lincoln where he intended to go, and Lincoln responded, "I intend to go to Congress."

Politics aside, Cartwright was most influential as a preacher, and this was where he focused most of his time and energy. He delivered an estimated 15,000 sermons and baptized an estimated 12,000 individuals in his Illinois years alone. He was a vigorous promoter of evangelical, revivalist Methodism and, like Presbyterian and later independent revivalist Barton Stone, described and defended the emotional "exercises" of the frontier camp meetings. He was populist and democratic, opposing pew rentals in churches, and generally defending common people. His church in Pleasant Plains, Illinois, remains to this day an active Methodist parish and historical landmark of the Methodist denomination.

Timothy Dwight (1752–1817)

Timothy Dwight, the grandson of America's greatest theologian Jonathan Edwards, was president of Yale College from 1795 until his death in 1817. During this time of Enlightenment, rationalist influences became significant in many American colleges, challenging the traditional beliefs of Protestantism. Dwight fought to keep Yale in the orthodox, evangelical Protestant fold. While not himself a revivalist of the Second Great Awakening, he was an ordained Congregational minister who influenced many of the preachers who would promote revivalism, perhaps most significantly, Lyman Beecher who was converted by Dwight in 1796.

As college president, Dwight taught the capstone course to all Yale students in their senior year and preached to the student body every Sunday. He initiated campus debates in which he vigorously and successfully defended orthodoxy against rationalistic ideas emanating from French Enlightenment thinkers such as Voltaire and Condorcet and their American counterparts, Thomas Jefferson and Thomas Paine. Dwight vigorously defended the divinity of Christ, his bodily resurrection, the Trinity, and miracles, all of which were attacked by Enlightenment intellectuals. During the first year of his presidency he initiated campus debates on the question of whether the Old and New Testaments were uniquely the word of God. He also preached a four-year series of sermons explaining and defending the essentials of the Christian faith. The sermons were later published and used regularly as a theological textbook for nearly half a century. Under his preaching and lecturing, a campus revival began in 1802 in which many students who had developed an attachment to rationalism converted to orthodox Protestantism. The Yale revivals took place just a year after "The Great

Revival" at Cane Ridge, Kentucky, which marked the beginning of the Second Great Awakening.

Ralph Waldo Emerson (1803–1882)

While never intending to found a movement, Emerson was the leader of Transcendentalism. Born into an influential family, with a Unitarian minister as his father, Emerson initially followed New England social conventions. He was educated at Harvard College and Divinity School and became a Unitarian minister. In the 1830s, however, he rejected Unitarian theology, just as Unitarians had earlier rejected Calvinism, and resigned his pastorate at Second Church in Boston.

Emerson's 1836 book, *Nature*, the most important treatise of the Transcendentalist movement, both rejected orthodox Christianity's view of creation as being other than God, and critiqued the Enlightenment view that human reason and the natural world were separate from one another. Where orthodox Christianity taught that individuals were sinful and in need of a transcendent God to save them, Emerson believed that human beings possessed a spirit that was itself capable of divinity. Where science taught that through the application of the mind nature could be understood, described, and quantified, Emerson believed that nature should be experienced so that one's conscious existence became one with all that was, which was none other than the divine. For Emerson, nature, God, and humanity were all part of an "over soul," world spirit, or divine mind. The way to truth was neither through understanding God's revelation nor through scientific mastery of data but through experiencing, intuiting, and feeling the oneness of all things. In his 1838 Harvard Divinity School address, he told students to reject the literal teachings of the Bible and to instead read scripture as merely a myth that was intended to foster in individuals an intuition or feeling of God and nature. For Emerson, Jesus was a model of how to live, but neither Jesus nor scripture were ultimately authoritative, as evangelical Protestantism taught.

In an era dominated theologically by revivalist Protestantism and intellectually by the Enlightenment, Emerson helped create an American tradition of Transcendentalism that was the counterpart to European romanticism. The romantic idea that truth could be intuited and experienced directly from nature, as opposed to revealed by God or discovered by science, became an important inspiration for poets and novelists throughout American history.

Charles Finney (1792–1875)

Finney was the leading preacher of the Second Great Awakening and one of the greatest revivalists in American history. He has been called "the Father of modern revivalism."

Born in Warren, Connecticut, Finney and his family moved west into New York state in 1794. He returned to Connecticut in 1812 to attend Warren Academy for preparatory education. The natural route would have been to continue at Yale College, but Finney never attended college, instead continuing his education through his own study with the help of tutors. He was a schoolteacher briefly, then studied law and practiced as an attorney from roughly 1818 until his conversion in 1821. Following his conversion he allegedly told a client, "I have a retainer from the Lord Jesus Christ to plead his cause, and I cannot plead yours." After theological training with a preacher/tutor, he was licensed to preach as a Presbyterian minister.

Finney began to preach in western New York, and held revivals regularly in several small towns and in the mid-sized industrial cities of Utica and Rochester. By the mid-1820s he was quickly becoming the most famous preacher in the region and would begin to hold revivals in major cities such as Philadelphia, New York, Boston, and even Great Britain. His most intense period of revivalism came in the five-year period from 1827 to 1832. After 1832, he curtailed his travels somewhat and served in settled pastorates in New York City at the Chatham Street Chapel and then Broadway Tabernacle. In 1835, he moved to Oberlin, Ohio, as a professor at the newly founded Oberlin College and pastor of the town's First Congregational Church. He would serve as president of Oberlin College from 1851 to 1866. Even as a settled pastor and professor, he continued to preach revival campaigns on many occasions.

Beginning early in his career as a revivalist, Finney developed what came to be called the "new measures," which were methods geared toward generating conversions at revival meetings. Among these were the protracted meeting, which was simply a series of revival meetings at one location over a several-week period, and the anxious bench, which was a special section of the meeting hall, usually near the front, where potential converts who were anxious about the state of their souls could sit during the services. Finney believed that while God brought revivals, there were specific things that human beings could do that would make revivals likely to occur. In other words, whereas Calvinist theology taught that revivals were purely the work of God; Finney believed that the effort of human beings could help to generate revivals. This idea meshed with his view of salvation. Calvinists believed God chose who would be converted, while Finney urged all his listeners to drop their excuses and decide for themselves to accept salvation. In 1835, he published *Lectures on Revivals of Religion* in which he outlined the methods he believed would generate revivals. He would write several other books during his career as well. In addition to his new measures, Finney also became famous for promoting women's participation in revival services, even allowing them to pray in public.

Finney's brand of revivalism was bound together with voluntary notions of social reform. Leaders in temperance, abolition, woman's rights, education, prison reform, and other movements were often converts from Finney revivals. He believed that once converted, Christians should work diligently in voluntary associations to reform society and help inaugurate the kingdom of God on earth.

Margaret Fuller (1810–1850)

Fuller was one of the central figures of Transcendentalism and was a very significant voice for women during the early years of the nineteenth-century woman's rights movement. Because her Unitarian parents thought she was precocious, they paid close attention to her education. In addition to instruction from her father and other tutors, Fuller attended a grammar school, the Boston Lyceum, and the Young Ladies' Seminary in Groton, Massachusetts. She then continued her studies on her own and mastered European literary figures such as Goethe, translating some of his works into English.

In 1836, Fuller met Emerson just as he was completing his book *Nature,* the manifesto of Transcendentalism. Through Emerson she became friends with many of the central figures of the Transcendentalist movement and by 1838 had been invited to join the Transcendentalist Club. In 1839, she became editor of the Transcendentalist journal the *Dial,* where she would serve for three years not only editing the works of the most prominent Transcendentalists but also writing many articles. One of her most significant essays, "The Great Lawsuit: Man vs. Men and Woman vs. Women," appeared in the *Dial* after Emerson took over as editor. In 1845 an enlarged version was published as a groundbreaking book *Woman in the Nineteenth Century,* which was important for the advancement of the woman's movement. By that time Fuller was writing for Horace Greeley's New York *Tribune.* Several of her essays and reviews from the *Tribune* were published collectively in 1846 as *Papers on Literature and Art.*

Like most Transcendentalists, Fuller rejected the Unitarianism of her upbringing in favor of the romantic philosophy of Transcendentalism. She claimed that she believed in Christ because she could do without him but that she chose not to do so. She may have meant that she retained the model of Jesus' life as worthy of emulation but that she did not believe he was uniquely the Son of God. Others could be messiahs as well as Christ. While retaining a certain sense of the value of churches, worship for Fuller was a natural phenomenon experienced best in solitary contemplation of the great outdoors.

Fuller traveled to Europe on the eve of the 1848 Revolutions. In Italy she met Giovanni Angelo Ossoli, a handsome 26-year-old nobleman, more than a decade her junior. The two fell in love and had a son together. Ossoli fought in the republican revolution while Fuller worked in a hospital. A brief republic was declared, but it did not last, and Fuller and Ossoli fled Italy. In May 1850, they were shipwrecked off the coast of Long Island; their bodies and property were never recovered.

Sarah (1792–1873) and Angelina (1805–1879) Grimke

The Grimke sisters were prominent abolitionists and woman's rights activists. They were born into a wealthy slaveholding family in South Carolina. More than 12 years younger than Sarah, Angelina was put in her older sister's charge and while growing up even called Sarah "mother." Originally Episcopalians, they moved to Philadelphia in the 1820s and became Quakers, partly because of that denomination's reputation for opposing slavery and supporting equal rights for women. In 1836, Angelina published *An Appeal to the Christian Women of the South,* which was a strenuous antislavery tract. Popular in abolitionist quarters in the North, it was publicly burned in South Carolina. When Massachusetts ministers criticized the Grimkes for speaking publicly against slavery, Sarah authored a biblical defense of the right of women to speak in public entitled *Letters on the Equality of the Sexes, and the Condition of Women* (1838). Because the tract enhanced their reputations as feminists, soon they were nearly as well known for woman's rights as for abolition. The sisters believed that abolition and woman's rights could not be separated; both were issues of equality.

In 1838, Angelina married Theodore Dwight Weld, one of the leading abolitionists in America. Sarah, who remained single throughout her life, moved in with the Weld couple, and all three continued their antislavery efforts. Both Grimke sisters assisted in the research that produced Weld's monumental *Slavery As It Is*, which appeared in 1839. They cut back their public appearances as their time was taken up with domestic life when Angelina began having children.

James McGready (c. 1758–1817)

James McGready was instrumental in organizing and promoting the early frontier revivals of the Second Great Awakening. After his family moved to western North Carolina, McGready returned to Pennsylvania in his late teens to study theology with Princeton graduate John McMillan. He experienced an evangelical conversion shortly thereafter and was licensed to preach by Presbyterians when he was about 30.

He returned to western North Carolina as a controversial revival preacher, often emphasizing God's wrath toward sinners. While some converted, including Barton Stone, who would become one of the leading revival preachers of the era, McGready also encountered such strong opposition among some resisters that he had to flee the area in 1796. He headed for the frontier of southwestern Kentucky where he resumed his preaching. In Kentucky he served three small river communities—Red River, Gasper River, and Muddy River—all in Logan County. The rough and often irreligious frontiersmen responded enthusiastically to McGready's preaching and many converted.

In the summer of 1800, McGready actively promoted a meeting at Gasper River that became one of the first significant events of the Second Great Awakening. The protracted revival was probably the first camp meeting in American history, and as such set the stage for what would become a staple in American religion for more than a century. At camp meetings people traveled to a common rural place, camped for several days, and listened to preachers throughout the day and into the night. Hundreds and eventually thousands of frontier folk were converted at these meetings. People came from as far away as one hundred miles to the Gasper River meeting, and when news of the revivals spread, camp meetings were planned for many other areas of rural America. The following year the largest (estimated at 10,000 to 25,000) of the early meetings took place at Cane Ridge.

Following the "Great Revival," as Cane Ridge was called, McGready moved to northern Kentucky and spent his final years ministering there.

Lucretia Coffin Mott (1793–1880)

While neither a product nor promoter of revivals or Transcendentalism, Lucretia Mott was an important reformer during the period of the Second Great Awakening and beyond. Born in Nantucket Island, Massachusetts, Lucretia Coffin was raised as a Quaker and educated in a Quaker boarding school. In 1811, she married James Mott, a teacher at the school she had attended. The couple raised six children while running cotton and woolen businesses. In the 1820s, Lucretia became increasingly active in Quaker life, even serving as the equivalent of a Quaker minister (Quakers did not have formal ordination). She also became active as a reformer.

Mott was most significant as a voice for abolition of slavery and woman's rights. She and her husband helped to found the American Anti-slavery Society in 1833, and Lucretia helped to establish the Philadelphia Female Anti-Slavery Society the same year. She was part of a delegation to the World Anti-Slavery Convention in London in 1840, but the male delegates refused to seat her because she was a woman. In 1848, along with Elizabeth Cady Stanton, she helped organize the famous Seneca Falls, New York, Woman's Rights Convention, which issued the *Declaration of Sentiments,* a manifesto for the woman's rights movement. In 1870 she became president of the Pennsylvania Peace Society.

Mott, Stanton, and Susan B. Anthony are memorialized in a sculpture at the United States Capitol.

Phoebe Worrall Palmer (1807–1874)

Phoebe Palmer was one of the leading figures of the Second Great Awakening. As a Methodist Bible teacher and author she promoted the doctrine of holiness, also known as perfectionism. She participated in more than 300 camp meetings and urban revivals in the United States, Canada, and the British Isles.

Palmer was born Phoebe Worrall and took her last name from her physician husband Walter C. Palmer, whom she married at the age of 19. In 1835, she began to attend Tuesday meetings held in her sister's home. Soon she was leading the study of scripture and discussions of the Wesleyan doctrine of holiness or perfection, which taught that subsequent to conversion one should experience a second blessing of God's grace that would lead to sanctification, a higher and purer form of the Christian life. While a person would never become sinless in actions, perfectionism taught that one's will could become pure. In other words, one would never intend to sin. Phoebe helped shape the concept of holiness in her books *The Way of Holiness* (1843), *Faith and Its Effects* (1849), and *Present to My Christian Friend on Entire Devotion to God* (1853). Charles Finney received the holiness second blessing in 1843. The theology that Palmer helped to develop in her writings and teachings was later adopted by holiness denominations such as the Nazarenes, the Free Methodists, the Wesleyans, and the Keswick Movement in England.

As a Bible teacher, Palmer often encountered resistance from those who opposed women in the ministry. In response she strenuously defended the right of women to pray and teach in public. She once wrote that when the Holy Spirit fell at the day of Pentecost in New Testament times, the apostles did not form a committee to decide whether women should be allowed to talk. She believed God worked through men and women equally and viewed the increase in the number of women Bible teachers as a sign that God's kingdom was near.

Like most spiritual leaders of the Second Great Awakening, Palmer was also a vigorous promoter of social reform. In 1850, she established a mission in the Five Points region of New York City that provided schoolrooms, baths, rent-free apartments, and other programs for poor families. She also worked to develop rescue agencies for the poor and homes for the deaf. She believed that compassion for the poor was a moral issue. On slavery, however, she was neutral, believing that this was a political question.

Theodore Parker (1810–1860)

Parker was one of the leading preachers of the mid-nineteenth century. Nearly forgotten for decades, a recent biography attempts to restore his reputation as one of the leading Transcendentalists and liberal preachers in America.

Born in Lexington, Massachusetts, Parker was educated privately mostly through his own study. He passed examinations at Harvard in 1831, then entered the Divinity School and graduated in 1836. In his 1841 sermon *A Discourse on the Permanent and Transient in Christianity* he laid out his belief that the creeds and scriptures of historic Christianity are imperfect reflections of the truth. He did not believe that Christianity had to be grounded in revelation or even in the deity of Christ. In Transcendentalist fashion he urged people to experience God intuitively and center their religious authority in such experience. The Transcendentalist emphasis on experience would become a central feature of liberal Protestantism, of which Parker was an early exponent. Unlike Ralph Waldo Emerson, Parker never left the ministry and saw Transcendentalism as deeply religious, not as a retreat from religion as it has sometimes been portrayed. Parker was also a dedicated reformer, supporting abolition and most other progressive reforms of his day.

Elizabeth Palmer Peabody (1804–1894)

Elizabeth Peabody was a friend to virtually every significant Transcendentalist and was something of a mentor for Margaret Fuller. Peabody was primarily interested in the education of children, using the Transcendental concept of intuition in her approach. For her, education was less a matter of transmitting knowledge to children than in evoking from them their own inner sense of morality and aesthetics. Education should be geared toward the development of the whole person, she believed, with the spiritual and intellectual considered part of the whole, not separate entities. Her educational ideas helped lead to the founding of the first kindergarten in America in 1859.

In the 1830s, Peabody was a partner with Bronson Alcott in his short-lived educational experiment known as the Temple School. His two-volume *Conversations with Children on the Gospels* (published in 1836 and 1837) developed from his editing of notes Peabody had taken while observing Alcott with the students. In the 1840s, she managed a circulating library and bookstore in Boston that served as a meeting place for Transcendentalists. Fuller's famous "conversations" took place there as did the planning sessions for the Brook Farm community. Peabody also became a significant publisher of periodicals such as the *Dial* and *Aesthetic Papers* and of books by William Ellery Channing and Nathaniel Hawthorne.

Elizabeth Cady Stanton (1815–1902)

Stanton was one of the leading woman's rights leaders of the nineteenth century. She was converted as a young girl at a Charles Finney revival in Troy, New York. Her father clearly preferred his sons and once told Elizabeth that he wished she were a boy. This slight seemed to inspire her to achieve beyond what was expected or allowed of women in the nineteenth century. She convinced her pastor to teach her Greek so she could become proficient in biblical studies, which would serve her well when she published her *Woman's Bible* in 1895. She also studied in Emma Willard's Female Seminary in Troy, New York, graduating in 1832.

As an organizer and activist Elizabeth Cady was at the center of the antislavery movement as a result of her marriage to abolitionist Henry Stanton. She became convinced that antislavery and woman's rights should not be separated and was often highly critical of male reformers who supported abolition and voting rights for African American males without supporting woman's suffrage as well. In the 1840s, Stanton helped to organize the first major woman's rights convention, which took place at Seneca Falls, New York, in 1848, and she drafted the convention's *Declaration of Sentiments.* She continued to organize a number of other conventions, to lecture throughout the East and Midwest, and to work for a variety of reforms such as suffrage, changes in divorce laws, and property rights for women. Stanton and Susan B. Anthony worked together closely on many woman's rights projects. Together they edited a periodical called *The Revolution,* and in 1869 started the National Woman Suffrage Association, which would later become the National American Woman Suffrage Association.

Religiously, having been converted in the Second Great Awakening, Stanton moved from evangelical Protestantism to Unitarianism, then to skepticism. Unlike the evangelical feminists, she eventually concluded that there was very little in the Bible that could be used to support equality for women.

Barton Stone (1772–1844)

Stone was a significant figure in the early revivals of the Second Great Awakening, especially the "Great Revival" at Cane Ridge, Kentucky, in 1801. Born near Port Tabacco, Maryland, Stone was converted in his late teens by the preaching of James McGready and others. In the 1790s, he applied for and received a license to preach in the Presbyterian denomination. After preaching briefly in North Carolina, Virginia, and Tennessee, he moved west to Kentucky and became pastor of churches at Cane Ridge and Concord.

Stone attended McGready's Logan County revivals and observed what he believed were genuine manifestations of the spirit of God. He later categorized these as "religious exercises"—the falling exercise, jerking exercise, dancing exercise, running exercise, laughing exercise, singing exercise, and even barking exercise. These behaviors during frontier revivals were viewed as excessive by more conservative Protestants, but Stone and other revival promoters believed otherwise.

Following McGready's revivals at Gaspar River, Stone actively promoted a camp meeting at Cane Ridge, which became the largest of the early frontier revivals with an estimated 10,000 to 25,000 people in attendance. The revivals crossed denominational lines as Baptists, Methodists, Presbyterians, and others attended. As a result of the mixing of these denominations and of his interpretation of the Bible, Stone believed that people from various denominations could be united merely as Christians. Moreover, they believed that much of what denominations taught was not in accordance with the Bible. Stone and some others, therefore, left the Presbyterian Church and began a movement that came to be known simply as the Christian Church. Attempting to be biblical Christians without denominational labels, they nevertheless became very much like a new denomination. In 1832, Stone's Christian Church merged with that of Alexander Campbell, who had become the leader of a very similar movement. This Stone-Campbell merger produced the Disciples of Christ that later divided into the Churches of Christ, the Independent Christian Churches, and the Disciples.

The broader effort to transcend denominations and be merely "Christian" in the first century, New Testament fashion became known as the Restoration movement in American religious history because of the attempt to restore a unified New Testament Christianity without denominational differences. The Restoration movement was part of the Second Great Awakening and to a large extent a direct product of the early revivals of the period.

Arthur (1786–1865) and Lewis (1788–1873) Tappan

The Tappan brothers were wealthy backers of revivals and social reform, especially abolition. They also served in leadership positions in a variety of voluntary agencies promoting distribution of Bibles, development of Sunday Schools, education, temperance, and mental health. They helped to build the Broadway Tabernacle in New York City and were instrumental in bringing Charles Finney there as first pastor. They also supported Lane Seminary and Oberlin College. Fervent evangelical Christians, they believed that reform was the logical outgrowth of the Christian life simply because injustice and immorality were inconsistent with God's will.

Lewis was a more public figure than Arthur and gained renown as a lecturer as well as philanthropist. Having originally been a Unitarian under the influence of the famous minister William Ellery Channing, he converted to evangelical/revivalist Protestantism in the 1820s, partly under the influence of Lyman Beecher. Lewis worked with others to gain freedom for the slaves aboard the famous ship *Amistad,* a story that became the subject of a film in the 1990s. Arthur seems never to have strayed from the orthodox, Calvinist upbringing the Tappans received from their mother. He usually worked behind the scenes, giving money and serving in executive positions of reform organizations. In addition to Arthur's influence and benefactions to several voluntary associations in the 1820s, the Tappans were influential in the formation of the American Anti-Slavery Society in 1833, with Arthur serving as first president, and the American and Foreign Anti-Slavery Society in 1840.

Henry David Thoreau (1817–1862)

If Ralph Waldo Emerson was the leading thinker of the Transcendentalist movement, Thoreau was its leading practitioner. Even though Thoreau was 14 years younger than Emerson, the two became friends in 1837 just after Thoreau's graduation from Harvard. Thoreau's most famous book is *Walden.* In 1845, he moved into a small hut that he had built near Walden Pond on Emerson's property and lived there alone for a little more than two years. His immediate goal was to write what would become another book, an account of an 1839 trip down the Merrimac River taken with his brother, but he set that project aside temporarily to write of life at Walden Pond. The Walden experience facilitated the Transcendentalist goal of communing with nature. Thoreau spent his days observing and experiencing the natural world around him and learning to enjoy solitary individualism. He believed that peace, happiness, and right living required self-reliance and that the only way to achieve self-reliance was through simplifying one's life. One had to forsake worldly possessions and live as simply and naturally as possible.

Thoreau's independent pursuit of truth also showed itself in his resistance to injustice, particularly during the 1840s when the United States went to war with Mexico. Convinced that this action was part of a plan to extend slavery in the territories that would be annexed from Mexico, Thoreau refused to pay his poll tax and was eventually jailed briefly. His plan was to draw attention to injustice and to inspire others to refuse participation with evil. He subsequently wrote an essay, known today usually as "On Civil Disobedience," that influenced Martin Luther King, Jr., Mahatma Gandhi, and others who engage in nonviolent protest.

In addition to his books, Thoreau wrote many essays that have influenced and shaped American literature, helping to create an American romantic tradition that thrives even today.

Nat Turner (1800–1831)

Turner was a Baptist slave preacher from Southampton, Virginia, who led the most famous slave rebellion in American history. A slave of Benjamin Turner, Nat was an obviously gifted child who had birthmarks resembling those of an African conjurer. These marks led his parents to believe that he was chosen by God for a special work, a belief that Nat came to embrace as well. His master was a pious Christian who saw to it that his slaves received biblical instruction, something in which Nat excelled.

In the 1820s, Turner had visions and experienced other supernatural phenomena that convinced him he was called to liberate his people. He adopted a messianic view of himself, believing that just as Christ was a liberator, so, too, was he. One of his favorite verses of scripture while growing up was Luke 12:31, "I am come to send a fire on the earth." After 1825 Turner's visions seemed to increase in intensity and frequency as he preached across the Virginia countryside. In 1828, he had a pivotal vision that convinced him that he was to slay his enemies with their own weapons in an effort to end slavery. In August 1831, Turner and 70 others revolted, killing whites across a 20-mile swath of territory. They hoped to enlist many more slaves, take the county seat, procure more arms, and widen the rebellion, but they were dispersed, then rounded up, arrested, and tried. Turner himself eluded the white militia until October 30, but was finally apprehended and executed on November 11 after giving his famous "Confession," from which we get most of our information about him.

While highly controversial, Turner exhibited one of the central themes of African American religion—liberation. He learned that theme in the context of the Second Great Awakening's emphasis on the Bible.

Theodore Dwight Weld (1803–1895)

Weld was one of the most important and influential antislavery reformers of the nineteenth century. The son of a Congregational minister, he was converted by Charles Finney in 1825 and for two years worked with Finney promoting revivals. In 1827 he devoted himself full-time to temperance and antislavery reform and was instrumental in convincing the wealthy Tappan brothers to join these movements.

Weld studied theology at Lane Seminary in Cincinnati from 1832 to 1834. In 1834, he organized a campus debate on slavery and won the majority of the student body to the antislavery cause. In addition to opposing slavery, the students started education services in the African American section of the city and even brought black young people onto the Lane campus. The school's trustees complained of such radicalism and convinced the president, Lyman Beecher, that it had to stop. Refusing to follow new regulations curtailing their activities, over 50 students left Lane. Most went to Oberlin College, but Weld did not. Instead, he returned to full-time abolitionism and entered his most intense period of antislavery lecturing.

Stricken with voice problems in 1836, Weld began to work primarily as an organizer and author. In 1837, he published *The Bible Against Slavery,* and in 1839, with the help of his wife Angelina Grimke and her sister Sarah, he published *Slavery As It Is,* an exposé of the injustices of slavery that consisted mostly of newspaper clippings and testimonials from slaves, ex-slaves, and slave owners. In the 1840s, Weld moved even further from the center of abolitionist reform, in large part retiring to a farm in New Jersey where he and Angelina raised their family. He taught school and continued to write and occasionally speak against slavery. He was reluctant to engage in political activity, however, and eventually concluded that such was not his call in life. After the

Civil War ended the slavery question in America, Weld moved to Hyde Park, Massachusetts, where he lived out the final 28 years of his life.

Weld was both a product of and participant in the Second Great Awakening. After his conversion, he utilized revivalist techniques to spread the gospel of antislavery and win converts to the abolitionist cause.

PRIMARY DOCUMENTS

Document 1
Richard Allen, Excerpt from Autobiography re: the founding of the African Church

Richard Allen (1760–1831) was the founder of the first African American denomination, the African Methodist Episcopal (A.M.E.) Church. While the A.M.E. Church was not founded until 1816, below is Allen's telling of a historic event at St. George's Methodist Episcopal Church in 1792 (some say 1787). After having helped build up St. George's, the African Americans were relegated to segregated balcony seating. Instead of complying, they left the church and started what Allen cites as the first African American congregation in history, separate from the Methodists. Allen refused to become pastor of a church that was not Methodist. Instead, his friend Absalom Jones led that congregation into the Episcopal Church. Allen became pastor of a separate black congregation within the Methodist Episcopal Church until 1816 when he helped form the A.M.E.

A number of us usually attended St. George's Church on Fourth street; and when the coloured people began to get numerous in attending the church, they moved us from the seats we usually sat on, and placed us around the wall, and on Sabbath morning we went to church and the sexton stood at the door, and told us to go in the gallery. He told us to go, and we would see where to sit. We expected to take the seats over the ones we formerly occupied below, not knowing any better. We took those seats. Meeting had begun, and they were nearly done singing, and just as we got to the seats, the elder said, "let us pray." We had not been long upon our knees before I heard considerable scuffling and low talking. I raised my head up and saw one of the trustees, H—M—, having hold of the Rev. Absalom Jones, pulling him up off of his knees, and saying, "You must get up—you must not kneel here." Mr. Jones replied, "wait until prayer is over." Mr. H—M—said "no, you must get up now, or I will call for aid and force you away." Mr. Jones said, "wait until prayer is over, and I will get up and trouble you no more." With that he beckoned to one of the other trustees, Mr. L—S—to come to his assistance. He came, and went to William White to pull him up. By this time prayer was over, and we all went out of the church in a body, and they were no more plagued with us in the church. This raised a great excitement and inquiry among the citizens, in so much that I believe they were ashamed of their conduct. But my dear Lord was with us, and we were filled with fresh vigour to get a house erected to worship God in. Seeing our forlorn and distressed situation, many of the hearts of our citizens were moved to urge us forward; notwithstanding we had subscribed largely towards finishing St. George's Church, in building the gallery and laying new floors, and just as the house was made comfortable, we were turned out from enjoying the comforts of worshiping therein. We then hired a store room, and held worship by ourselves. Here we were pursued with threats of being disowned, and read publicly out of the meeting if we did continue to worship in the place we had hired; but we believed the Lord would be our friend. We got subscription papers out to raise money to build the house of the Lord. By this time we had waited on Dr. Rush and Mr. Robert Ralston, and told them of our distressing situation. We considered it a blessing that the Lord had put it into our hearts to wait upon those gentlemen. They pitied our situation, and subscribed largely towards the church, and were very friendly towards us, and advised us how to go on. We appointed Mr. Ralston our treasurer. Dr. Rush did much for us in public by his influence. I hope the name of Dr. Benjamin Rush and Mr. Robert Ralston will never be forgotten among us. They were the two first gentlemen who espoused the cause of the oppressed, and aided us in building the house of the Lord for the poor Africans to worship in. Here was the beginning and rise of the first African church in America. . . .

In 1793 a committee was appointed from the African Church to solicit me to be their minister, for there was no colored preacher in Philadelphia but myself. I told them I could not accept of their offer, as I was a Methodist. I was indebted to the Methodists, under God, for what little religion I had; being convinced that they were the people of God, I informed them that I could not be any thing else but a Methodist, as I was born and awakened under them, and I could go no further with them, for I was a Methodist, and would leave you in peace and love. I would do nothing to retard them in building a church as it was an extensive building, neither would I go out with a subscription paper until they were done going out with their subscription. I bought an old frame that had been formerly occupied as a blacksmith shop from Mr. Sims, and hauled it on the lot in Sixth near Lobard street, that had formerly been taken for the church of England. I employed carpenters to repair the old frame, and fit it for a place of worship. In July, 1794, Bishop [Francis] Asbury being in town I solicited him to open the church for us which he accepted.

Source: Richard Allen, *The Life, Experience, and Gospel Labours of the Rt. Rev. Richard Allen. To Which is Annexed the Rise and Progress of the African Methodist Episcopal Church in the United States of America. Containing a Narrative of the Yellow Fever in the Year of Our Lord 1793: With an Address to the People of Colour in the United States* (Philadelphia: Martin & Boden, 1833).

Document 2
Peter Cartwright on Cane Ridge and the New Lights

Peter Cartwright (1785–1872) was first converted in a camp meeting that took place in the aftermath of the great Cane Ridge Revival of 1801. He became a Methodist circuit-riding preacher then a presiding elder in the denomination. In Illinois, where the denomination sent him to serve from 1824 until his retirement, he became involved in politics, once defeating Abraham Lincoln for a seat in the state legislature, then losing to Lincoln in a race for the U.S. House of Representatives.

Notice below that while Cartwright supports camp meeting revivals, he opposes those like Barton Stone who left the settled Presbyterian or Methodist denominations in an attempt to be merely Christians without denominational affiliation. Cartwright was an ardent believer in the Methodist Church and opposed those who tried to work independently of well established Protestant denominations.

Somewhere between 1800 and 1801, in the upper part of Kentucky, at a memorable place called "Cane Ridge," there was appointed a sacramental meeting by some of the Presbyterian ministers, at which meeting, seemingly unexpected by ministers or people, the mighty power of God was displayed in a very extraordinary manner; many were moved to tears, and bitter and loud crying for mercy. The meeting was protracted for weeks. Ministers of almost all denominations flocked in from far and near. The meeting was kept up by night and day. Thousands heard of the mighty work, and came on foot, on horseback, in carriages and wagons. It was supposed that there were in attendance at times during the meeting from twelve to twenty-five thousand people. Hundreds fell prostrate under the mighty power of God, as men slain in battle. Stands were erected in the woods from which preachers of different Churches proclaimed repentance toward God and faith in our Lord Jesus Christ, and it was supposed, by eye and ear witnesses, that between one and two thousand souls were happily and powerfully converted to God during the meeting. It was not unusual for one, two, three, and four to seven preachers to be addressing the listening thousands at the same time from the different stands erected for the purpose. The heavenly fire spread in almost every direction. It was said, by truthful witnesses, that at times more than one thousand persons broke into loud shouting all at once, and that the shouts could be heard for miles around.

From this camp-meeting, for so it ought to be called, the news spread through all the Churches, and through all the land, and it excited great wonder and surprise; but it kindled a religious flame that spread all over Kentucky and through many other states. And I may here be permitted to say, that this was the first camp-meeting ever held in the United States, and here our camp-meetings took their rise.

As Presbyterian, Methodist, and Baptist ministers all united in the blessed work at this meeting, when they returned home to their different congregations, and carried the news of this mighty work, the revival spread rapidly throughout the land; but many of the ministers and members of the synod of Kentucky thought it all disorder, and tried to stop the work. They called their preachers who were engaged in the revival to account, and censured and silenced them. These ministers then rose up and unitedly renounced the jurisdiction of the Presbyterian Church, organized a Church of their own, and dubbed it with the name of Christian. Here was the origin of what was called the New Lights. They renounced the Westminster Confession of Faith, and all Church discipline, and professed to take the New Testament for their Church discipline. They established no standard of doctrine; every one was to take the New Testament, read it, and abide his own construction of it. Marshall, M'Namar, Dunlevy, Stone, Huston, and others, were the chief leaders in this trash trap. Soon a diversity of opinion sprang up, and they got into a Babel of confusion. Some preached Arian, some Socinian, and some Universalist doctrines; so that in a few years you could not tell what was harped or what was danced. They adopted the mode of immersion, the water-god of all exclusive errorists; and directly there was a mighty controversy about the way to heaven, whether it was by water or by dry land.

In the meantime a remnant of preachers that broke off from the Methodist Episcopal Church in 1792, headed by James O'Kelly, who had formed a party because he could not be a bishop in said Church, which party he called the Republican Methodist Church, came out to Kentucky and formed a union with these New Lights. Then the Methodist Episcopal Church had war, and rumors of war, almost on every side. The dreadful diversity of opinion among these New Lights, their want of any standard of doctrines, or regular Church discipline, made them an easy prey to prowling wolves of any description.

Soon the Shaker priests came along, and off went M'Namar, Dunlevy, and Huston, into that foolish error. Marshall and others retraced their steps. B. W. Stone stuck to his New Lightism, and fought many bloodless battles, till he grew old and feeble, and the mighty Alexander Campbell, the great, arose and poured such floods of regenerating water about the old man's cranium, that he formed a union with this giant errorist, and finally died, not much lamented out of the circle of a few friends. And this is the way with all the New Lights, in the government, morals, and discipline of the Church.

This Christian, or New Light Church, is a feeble and scattered people, though there are some good Christians among them. I suppose since the day of Pentecost, there was hardly ever a greater revival of religion than at Cane Ridge; and if there had been steady, Christian ministers, settled in Gospel doctrine and Church discipline, thousands might have been saved to the Church that wandered off in the mazes of vain, speculative divinity, and finally made shipwreck of the faith, fell back, turned infidel, and lost their religion and their souls forever. But evidently a new impetus was given to the work of God, and many, very many, will have cause to bless God forever for this revival of religion throughout the length and breadth of our Zion.

Source: Autobiography of Peter Cartwright, The Backwoods Preacher, edited by W. P. Strickland (New York: Carlton & Porter, 1856), 30–33.

Document 3
Lyman Beecher—The Government of God Desirable

Beecher (1775–1863) was one of the leading preachers in America during the Second Great Awakening. He was a pastor in Boston before becoming president of Lane Theological Seminary in Cincinnati, Ohio. Although more a theological statesman than revivalist itinerant, he nevertheless supported revivals and believed they should lead to social reform. While pastoring in Boston he championed Calvinist orthodoxy against the challenges of Unitarianism, but later he modified his Calvinism, moving toward Arminian revivalist theology that taught all were eligible for salvation. Eventually, he was tried by the Presbyterian Church for departing from the Calvinist Westminster Confession of Faith. He was acquitted of the charges.

In the sermon below one can see how Beecher retained the Calvinist emphasis on God's sovereignty while still believing that human beings had free will and were responsible for living the way God instructed in the Bible. This modified form of Calvinism was a product of the Second Great Awakening, but it was also the beginning of the end of Calvinism's dominance in American Protestant theology. From the Second Great Awakening on, Calvinism waned. Compare Beecher's reliance on God's will with Charles Finney's belief that human beings were largely responsible for making their own decisions about salvation and even for bringing about revivals by utilizing the right methods.

Thy will be done in earth as it is in heaven. Matthew vi., 10. . . .

I shall, therefore, suggest several considerations, to confirm this most obvious truth, that it is desirable that God should govern the world entirely according to His own good pleasure.

1. It is desirable that God should govern the world, and dispose of all events, according to His pleasure, because He knows perfectly in what manner it is best that the world should be governed.

The best way of disposing of men and their concerns is that which will effectually illustrate the glory of God. The glory of God is His benevolence, and His natural attributes for the manifestation of it, and sun of the moral universe, the light and life of His kingdom. All the blessedness of the intelligent creation arises, and ever will arise, from the manifestation and apprehension of the glory of God. It was to manifest this glory that the worlds were created. It was that there might be creatures to behold and enjoy God, that His dominions were peopled with intelligent beings. And it is that His holy subjects may see and enjoy Him, that He upholds and governs the universe. The entire importance of our world, therefore, and of men and their concerns, is relative, and is great or small only as we are made to illustrate the glory of God. How this important end shall be most effectually accomplished none but Himself is able to determine. He, only, knows how so to order things as that the existence of every being, and every event, shall answer the purpose of its creation, and from the rolling of a world to the fall of a sparrow shall conspire to increase the exhibitions of the divine character, and expand the joy of the holy universe. . . .

2. It is desirable that God should govern the world according to His own pleasure, because He is entirely able to execute His purposes.

A wise politician perceives, often, both the end and the means; and is still unable to bring to pass his counsels, because the means, though wise, are beyond his control. But God is as able to execute as He is to plan. Having chosen the end, and selected the means, his counsels stand. He is the Lord God omnipotent. The whole universe is a store-house of means; and when He speaks every intelligence and every atom flies to execute His pleasure. The omnipotence of God, in giving efficacy to His government, inspires and perpetuates the ecstasy of heaven. "And a voice came out from the throne, saying, Praise our God. And I heard as it were the voice of a great multitude, and as the voice of many waters, and as the voice of many thunderings, saying Alleluia, the Lord God omnipotent reigneth." What will that man do in heaven, who is afraid and reluctant to commit to God the government of the earth? And what will become of those who, unable to frustrate His counsels, murmur and rebel against His providence?

3. It is desirable that God should govern the world according to His pleasure, because the pleasure of God is always good. . . .

The sole object of the government of God, from beginning to end, is, to express His benevolence. His eternal decrees, of which so many are afraid, are nothing but the plan which God has devised to express His benevolence, and to make His kingdom as vast and as blest as His own infinite goodness desires. . . .

4. It is greatly to be desired that God should govern the world according to His pleasure, because it is His pleasure to rule as a moral governor.

A moral government is a government exercised over free agents, accountable beings; a government of laws, administered by motives. . . .

Has Omnipotence formed minds, which, the moment they are made, escape from His hands, and defy the control of their Maker? Has the Almighty erected a moral kingdom which He cannot govern without destroying its moral nature? Can He only watch, and mend, and rectify, the lawless wanderings of mind? Has He filled the earth with untamed and untamable spirits, whose wickedness and rebellion He can merely mitigate, but cannot control? . . . We may safely pray, then, "Thy will be done in earth as it is in heaven," without fearing at all the loss of moral agency; for all the glory of God, in His Law and Gospel, and all the eternal manifestations of glory to principalities and powers and heavenly places, depend wholly upon the fact, that men, though living under the government of God, and controlled according to His pleasure, are still entirely free, and accountable for all the deeds done in the body. There could be no justice in punishment and no condescension, no wisdom, no mercy, in the glorious gospel, did not the government of God, though administered according to His pleasure, include and insure the accountable agency of man. . . .

5. It is greatly to be desired that God should rule in the earth according to His pleasure, because it is His pleasure to govern the world in mercy, by Jesus Christ. . . .

Our only hope of heaven arises from being entirely in the hands of God. Our destruction could not be made more certain than it would be were we to be given up to our own disposal, or to the disposal of any being but God. Would sinful mortals change their own hearts? Could the combined universe, without God, change the depraved affections of men? Surely, then, we have cause for unceasing joy, that we are in the hands of God; seeing He is a God of mercy, and has decreed to rule in mercy, and actually is administering the government of the world in mercy, by Jesus Christ. . . .

6. It is greatly to be desired that God should dispose of mankind according to His pleasure, because, if He does so, it is certain that there will be no injustice done to anyone.

He will do no injustice to His holy kingdom by any whom He saves. He will bring none to heaven who are not holy, and prepared for heaven. He will bring none there in any way not consistent with His perfections, and the best good of His kingdom; none in any way but that prescribed in the gospel, the way of faith in Jesus Christ, of repentance for sin, and of good works as the constituted fruit and evidence of faith.

Earthly monarchs have their favorites, whom, if guilty of a violation of the laws, they will often interpose to save, although the welfare of the kingdom requires their punishment. But God has no such favorites—He is no respecter of persons: He spared not the angels: and upon the earth distinctions of intellect, or wealth, or honor, will have no effect; he only that believeth shall be saved. The great and the learned shall not be obtruded upon heaven without holiness because they are great or learned; and the humble and contrite shall not be excluded because they are poor, or ignorant, or obscure. God has provided a way for all men to return to Him. He has opened the door of their prison, and set open before them a door of admission into the kingdom of His dear Son; and commanded and entreated them to abandon their dreary abode, and come into the glorious liberty of the sons of God. . . .

7. It is greatly to be desired that God should govern the world according to His pleasure, because His own infinite blessedness, as well as the happiness of His kingdom, depends upon His working all things according to the counsel of His own will.

Could the Almighty be prevented from expressing the benevolence of His nature, according to His purposes, His present boundless blessedness would become the pain of ungratified desire. God is love, and His happiness consists in the exercise and expression of it, according to His own eternal purpose, which He purposed in Christ Jesus before the world began. It is therefore declared, "The Lord hath made all things for himself;" that is, to express and gratify His infinite benevolence. The moral excellence of God does not consist in quiescent love, but in love active, bursting forth, and abounding. Nor does the divine happiness arise from the contemplation of idle perfections, but from perfections which comprehend boundless capacity, and activity in doing good. . . .

From the character of God, and the nature of His government, as explained in this discourse, may be inferred, the nature and necessity of unconditional submission to God. Unconditional submission is an entire surrender of the soul to God, to be disposed of according to His pleasure,—occasioned by confidence in His character as God. . . .

The change produced, then, is the effect of benevolence, raising the affections of the soul from the world, and resting them upon God. Holiness is now most ardently loved. This is seen to dwell in God and His kingdom, and to be upheld and perfected by His moral government.

It is the treasure of the soul, and all the attributes of God stand pledged to protect it. The solicitude, therefore, is not merely, What will become of me? but, What, O Lord, will become of Thy glory, and the glory of Thy kingdom? And in the character of God, these inquiries are satisfactorily answered. If God be glorified, and His kingdom upheld and made happy, the soul is satisfied. There is nothing else to be anxious about; for individual happiness is included in the general good, as the drop is included in the ocean.

Source: The World's Great Sermons (Volume IV), comp. by Grenville Kleiser (New York: Funk and Wagnalls Company, 1909), 1–25.

Document 4
Charles G. Finney, "How to Promote a Revival"

Charles Finney (1792–1875) was the leading preacher of the Second Great Awakening and has been called the "father of modern revivalism," largely because of the techniques he advocated to promote revivals. In opposition to Calvinism, which had been the dominant theology in America until the Second Great Awakening, Finney believed that human beings could prepare their hearts for God's salvation then decide for themselves whether or not to be converted. Moreover, he believed that there were certain methods that would make revivals likely to take place. The Calvinist position was that only God could choose who was to be saved and that revivals took place only when God decided they should happen. Compare the text below with the modified version of Calvinism in the document by Lyman Beecher.

Biblical text—Break up your fallow ground; for it is time to seek the Lord, till he come and rain righteousness upon you.—HOSEA 10:12. . . . My design in this lecture is to show HOW A REVIVAL IS TO BE PROMOTED.

A revival consists of two parts; as it respects the church, and as it respects the ungodly. I shall speak to-night of a revival in the church. Fallow ground is ground which has once been tilled, but which now lies waste, and needs to be broken up and mellowed, before it is suited to receive grain. I shall show, as it respects a revival in the church,

    1. What it is to break up the fallow ground, in the sense of the text.
    2. How it is to be performed.

I. WHAT IS IT TO BREAK UP THE FALLOW GROUND?

To break up the fallow ground, is to break up your hearts—to prepare your minds to bring forth fruit unto God. The mind of man is often compared in the Bible to ground, and the word of God to seed sown in it, and the fruit represents the actions and affections of those who receive it. To break up the fallow ground, therefore, is to bring the mind into such a state, that it is fitted to receive the word of God. Sometimes your hearts get matted down hard and dry, and all run to waste, till there is no such thing as getting fruit from them till they are all broken up, and mellowed down, and fitted to receive the word of God. It is this softening of the heart, so as to make it feel the truth, which the prophet calls breaking up your fallow ground.

II. HOW IS THE FALLOW GROUND TO BE BROKEN UP?

It is not by any direct efforts to feel. People run into a mistake on this subject, from not making the laws of mind the object of thought. There are great errors on the subject of the laws which govern the mind. People talk about religious feeling, as if they thought they could, by direct effort, call forth religious affection. But this is not the way the mind acts. No man can make himself feel in this way, merely by trying to feel. . . . But they can be controlled indirectly. Otherwise there would be no moral character in our feelings, if there were not a way to control them. We cannot say, "Now I will feel so and so towards such an object." But we can command our attention to it, and look at it intently, till the involuntary affections arise. Let a man who is away from his family, bring them up before his mind, and will he not feel? But it is not by saying to himself, "Now I will feel deeply for my family." A man can direct his attention to any object, about which he ought to feel and wishes to feel, and in that way he will call into existence the proper emotions. Let a man call up his enemy before his mind, and his feelings of enmity will rise. So if a man thinks of God, and fastens his mind on any parts of God's character, he will feel—emotions will come up, by the very laws of mind. . . . It is just as easy to make your minds feel on the subject of religion as it is on any other subject. God has put these states of mind under your control. If people were as unphilosophical about moving their limbs, as they are about regulating their emotions, you would never have got here to the meeting to-night. . . .

You see I have only begun to lay open this subject to-night. I want to lay it out before you, in the course of these lectures, so that if you will begin and go on to do as I say, the results will be just as certain as they are when the farmer breaks up a fallow field, and mellows it, and sows his grain. It will be so, if you will only begin in this way, and hold on till all your hardened and callous hearts break up.

REMARKS.

1. It will do no good to preach to you while your hearts are in this hardened, and waste, and fallow state. . . .
2. See why so much preaching is wasted, and worse than wasted. It is because the church will not break up their fallow ground. . . .
3. Professors of religion should never satisfy themselves, or expect a revival, just by starting out of their slumbers, and blustering about, and making a noise, and talking to sinners. They must get their fallow ground broken up. It is utterly unphilosophical to think of getting engaged in religion in this way. If your fallow ground is broken up, then the way to get more feeling, is to go out and see sinners on the road to hell, and talk to them, and guide inquiring souls, and you will get more feeling. . . .
4. And now, finally, will you break up your fallow ground? Will you enter upon the course now pointed out, and persevere till you are thoroughly awake? If you fail here, if you do not do this, and get prepared, you can go no further with me in this course of lectures. . . .

Source: Charles G. Finney, *Lectures on Revivals of Religion* (Oberlin, Ohio: E. J. Goodrich, 1868).

Document 5
Angelina Grimke, "Why should not all this be done immediately?"

Angelina Grimke (1805–1879) and her sister Sarah (1792–1873) were two of the most influential women in the abolition movement. Together with Angelina's husband Theodore Dwight Weld (1803–1895) the Grimke sisters were part of a family threesome that argued against slavery in lectures, essays, and books. In the 1830s they attempted with varying success to persuade moderate or "gradualist" abolitionists to become more radical in their opposition to slavery. In the excerpt below, Grimke defends the immediate abolition of slavery. Notice the biblical and constitutional themes that Grimke relies on to make her case. In closing she mentions that she was born and raised in the South (South Carolina) and as such saw slavery firsthand.

The great fundamental principle of Abolitionists is that man cannot rightfully hold his fellow man as property. Therefore, we affirm that every slaveholder is a man-stealer; a man, is a man, and as a man he has inalienable rights and he cannot rightfully be reduced to slavery. Our principle is that no circumstances can ever justify a man in holding his fellow man as property.

We hold that all the slaveholding laws violate the fundamental principle of the Constitution of the United States. So far from thinking that a slaveholder is bound by the immoral and unconstitutional laws of the southern states, we hold that he is solemnly bound as a man, as an American, to break them, and that immediately and openly. Every slaveholder is bound to cease to do evil now, to emancipate his slaves now.

Dost thou ask what I mean by emancipation? I will explain myself in a few words. 1. It is to reject with indignation the wild and guilty fantasy that man can hold property in man. 2. To pay the laborer his hire, for he is worthy of it. 3. No longer to deny him the right of marriage, but to "let every man have his own wife, and let every woman have her own husband," as saith the apostle. 4. To let parents have their own children, for they are the gift of the Lord to them, and no one else has any right to them. 5. No longer to withhold the advantages of education and the privilege of reading the Bible. 6. To put the slave under the protection of equitable laws.

Now, why should not all this be done immediately! Which of these things is to be done next year, and which the year after! and so on. Our immediate emancipation means, doing justice and loving mercy to-day—and this is what we call upon every slaveholder to do. I have seen too much of slavery to be a gradualist. I say [the slaveholder] is able to let the oppressed go free. Oh, my very soul is grieved to find a northern woman thus "sewing pillows under all armholes," framing and fitting soft excuses for the slaveholder's conscience, while with the same pen she is professing to regard slavery as a sin.

With regard to the connection between the North and the South, I shall say but little. I deny the charge that abolitionists are endeavoring to convince their fellow citizens of the faults of another community.

Not at all. We are spreading out the horrors of slavery before Northerners, in order to show them their own sin in sustaining such a system of complicated wrong and suffering. It is because we are politically, commercially, and socially connected with our southern brethren, that we urge our doctrines upon those of the free states.

As soon as we rectify public opinion at the North, then I for one, will promise to go down into the midst of slaveholders themselves to promulgate our doctrines in the land of the slave. But how can we go now, when northern pulpits and meeting-houses are closed, and northern Governors are declaring that "the discussion of the subject of slavery ought to be made an offence indictable at common law," and northern women are writing books to paralyse the efforts of southern women, who have come up from the South to entreat their northern sisters to exert their influence in behalf of the slave. To my own mind, the exasperation of the North at the discussion of slavery is an undeniable proof of her guilt.

Thou asketh very gravely, why James C. Birney [an abolitionist] did not go quietly into the southern States, and collect facts? Indeed! Why should he go to the South to collect facts, when he had lived there forty years? Thou mayest with just as much propriety ask me, why I do not go to the South to collect facts. The answer to both questions is obvious: We have lived at the South, as integral parts of the system of slavery, and therefore we know from practical observation and sad experience, quite enough about it already.

Source: Angelina Grimké, *Letters to Catharine E. Beecher in reply to an Essay on Slavery and Abolitionism addressed to A. E. Grimké by the Author* (Boston, 1838).

Document 6
Theodore Dwight Weld, *Introduction to American Slavery As It Is: Testimony of a Thousand Witnesses* (1839)

With the help of his wife Angelina Grimke Weld (1805–1879) and her sister Sarah Grimke (1792–1873), Weld (1803–1895) gathered clippings from southern newspapers as well as personal testimonies and other sources documenting the ill treatment of slaves in the South. This was a shift of strategy in that before this book, Weld had emphasized freedom first, then the horrors of slavery.

Here he and the Grimke sisters turn that strategy around, exposing the brutality of slavery. The book sold over 100,000 copies the first year.

READER, you are empannelled as a juror to try a plain case and bring in an honest verdict. The question at issue is not one of law, but of fact—"What is the actual condition of the slaves in the United States?" A plainer case never went to a jury. Look at it. TWENTY-SEVEN HUNDRED THOUSAND PERSONS in this country, men, women, and children, are in SLAVERY. Is slavery, as a condition for human beings, good, bad, or indifferent? We submit the question without argument. You have common sense, and conscience, and a human heart;—pronounce upon it. You have a wife, or a husband, a child, a father, a mother, a brother or a sister—make the case your own, make it theirs, and bring in your verdict. The case of Human Rights against Slavery has been adjudicated in the court of conscience times innumerable. The same verdict has always been rendered—"Guilty;" the same sentence has always been pronounced, "Let it be accursed;" and human nature, with her million echoes, has rung it round the world in every language under heaven, "Let it be accursed. Let it be accursed." His heart is false to human nature, who will not say "Amen." There is not a man on earth who does not believe that slavery is a curse. Human beings may be inconsistent, but human *nature* is true to herself. She has uttered her testimony against slavery with a shriek ever since the monster was begotten. . . .

As slaveholders and their apologists are volunteer witnesses in their own cause, and are flooding the world with testimony that their slaves are kindly treated; that they are well fed, well clothed, well housed, well lodged, moderately worked, and bountifully provided with all things needful for their comfort, we propose—first, to disprove their assertions by the testimony of a multitude of impartial witnesses, and then to put slaveholders themselves through a course of cross-questioning which shall draw their condemnation out of their own mouths. We will prove that the slaves in the United States are treated with barbarous inhumanity; that they are overworked, underfed, wretchedly clad and lodged, and have insufficient sleep; that they are often made to wear round their necks iron collars armed with prongs, to drag heavy chains and weights at their feet while working in the field, and to wear yokes, and bells, and iron horns; that they are often kept confined in the stocks day and night for weeks together, made to wear gags in their mouths for hours or days, have some of their front teeth torn out or broken off, that they may be easily detected when they run away; that they are frequently flogged with terrible severity, have red pepper rubbed into their lacerated flesh, and hot brine, spirits of turpentine, &c., poured over the gashes to increase the torture; that they are often stripped naked, their backs and limbs cut with knives, bruised and mangled by scores and hundreds of blows with the paddle, and terribly torn by the claws of cats, drawn over them by their tormentors; that they are often hunted with blood hounds and shot down like beasts, or torn in pieces by dogs; that they are often suspended by the arms and whipped and beaten till they faint, and when revived by restoratives, beaten again till they faint, and sometimes till they die; that their ears are often cut off, their eyes knocked out, their bones broken, their flesh branded with red hot irons; that they are maimed, mutilated and burned to death over slow fires. All these things, and more, and worse, we shall *prove*.

Reader, we know whereof we affirm, we have weighed it well; *more and worse* WE WILL PROVE. Mark these words, and read on; we will establish all these facts by the testimony of scores and hundreds of eye witnesses, by the testimony of *slaveholders* in all parts of the slave states, by slaveholding members of Congress and of state legislatures, by ambassadors to foreign courts, by judges, by doctors of divinity, and clergymen of all denominations, by merchants, mechanies, lawyers and physicians, by presidents and professors in colleges and *professional* seminaries, by planters, overseers and drivers. We shall show, not merely that such deeds are committed, but that they are frequent; not done in corners, but before the sun; not in one of the slave states, but in all of them; not perpetrated by brutal overseers and drivers merely, but by magistrates, by legislators, by professors of religion, by preachers of the gospel, by governors of states, by "gentlemen of property and standing," and by delicate females moving in the "highest circles of society." . . .

The foregoing declarations touching the inflictions upon slaves, are not hap-hazard assertions, nor the exaggerations of fiction conjured up to carry a point; nor are they the rhapsodies of enthusiasm, nor crude conclusions, jumped at by hasty and imperfect investigation, nor the aimless outpourings either of sympathy or poetry; but they are proclamations of deliberate, well-weighed convictions, produced by accumulations of proof, by affirmations and affidavits, by written testimonies and statements of a cloud of witnesses who speak what they know and testify what they have seen, and all these impregnably fortified by proofs innumerable, in the relation of the slaveholder to his slave, the nature of arbitrary power, and the nature and history of man. . . .

Source: American Slavery As It Is: Testimony of a Thousand Witnesses (New York: American Anti-Slavery Society, 1839).

Document 7
Theodore Weld and Angelina Grimke, The "lesser work"

The excerpts below are from an 1837 exchange of letters between Weld (1803–1895) and the Grimke sisters, Angelina (1805–1879) and Sarah (1792–1873), concerning the place of woman's rights and abolition. While Weld supported full equality for women, he believed that issue was second to abolition. First free the slaves, he argued, then equality for women will follow naturally and easily. Grimke, writing for herself and her sister, would have none of this. For the sisters, as for most woman's rights advocates, the two reforms went hand-in-hand, neither more important than the other. The Pastoral Letter to which Grimke refers was a letter from the New England clergy opposing the Grimke sisters and other women because they spoke in public to mixed-gender audiences.

Note that Weld broaches the issue of marriage, even if only to say that he believes women as well as men should have the right to propose. He may have had an ulterior motive here, for partly as a result of this letter exchange, Weld and Angelina Grimke fell in love and were married. Sarah, then, lived with the Welds as they continued antislavery work, farmed, and raised children.

My dear sisters,

I had it in my heart to make a suggestion to you in my last letter about your course touching the "rights of women," but it was crowded out by other matters perhaps of less importance. Now as I have a small sheet (fool that I didn't take a larger) and much to say, I'll make points. 1. As to the rights and wrongs of women it is an old theme with me. It was the first subject I ever discussed. In a little debating society when a boy, I took the ground that sex neither qualified nor disqualified for the discharge of any functions mental, moral or spiritual; that there is no reason why woman should not make laws, administer justice, sit in the chair of state, plead at the bar or in the pulpit, if she has the qualifications, just as much as tho she belonged to the other sex. Further, that the proposition of marriage may with just the same propriety be made by the woman as the man, and that the existing usage on that subject, pronouncing it alone the province of the man, and indelicate and almost, if not quite immoral for woman to make the first advances, overlooks or rather perverts the sacred design of the institution and debases it. Now as I have never found man, woman or child who agreed with me in the "ultraism" of woman's rights, I take it for granted even you will cry out "oh shocking"!! at the courting part of the doctrine. Very well, let that pass. What I advocated in boyhood I advocate now, that woman in EVERY particular shares equally with man rights and responsibilities. Now I have made this statement of my creed on this point to show you that we fully agree in principle except that I probably go much farther than you do in a single particular.

Now notwithstanding this, I do most deeply regret that you have begun a series of articles in the Papers on the rights of woman. Why, my dear sisters, the best possible advocacy which you can make is just what you are making day by day. Thousands hear you every week who have all their lives held that woman must not speak in public. Such a practical refutation of the dogma as your speaking furnishes has already converted multitudes. Because you are Southerners, you can do more at convincing the north than twenty northern females, tho' they could speak as well as you. Now this peculiar advantage you lose the moment you take another subject. You come down from your vantage ground. Any women of your powers will produce as much effect as you on the north in advocating the rights of free women (I mean in contradistinction to slave women) Now you two are the ONLY FEMALES in the free states who combine all these facilities for anti-slavery effort: 1. Are southerners. 2. Have been slaveholders. 3. For a long time most widely known by the eminence of friends. 4. Speaking and writing power and practice. 5. Ultra Abolitionist. 6. Acquaintance with the whole subject, argumentative, historical, legal and biblical. Now what unspeakable responsibilities rest on you—on YOU! Oh my soul! . . .

Now can't you leave the lesser work to others and devote, conse-crate your whole bodies, souls and spirits to the greater work which you can do far better and to far better purpose than any body else. Let us all first wake up the nation to lift millions of slaves of both sexes from the dust, and turn them into MEN and then when we all have our hand in, it will be an easy matter to take millions of females from their knees and set them on their feet, or in other words transform them from babies into women. I pray our dear Lord to give you wisdom and grace and help and bless you forever.
Your brother T. D. Weld

Brookline [Mass.] 8th Mo 20—[1837]
To Theodore D. Weld and J. G. Whittier
Brethren beloved in the Lord,

As your letters came to hand at the same time and both are devoted mainly to the same subject we have concluded to answer them on one sheet and jointly. You seem greatly alarmed at the idea of our advocating the rights of woman. . . . These letters have not been the means of arousing the public attention to the subject of Woman's rights, it was the Pastoral Letter which did the mischief. . . . The ministers seemed panic struck at once and commenced a most violent attack upon us. . . . This letter then roused the attention of the whole country to enquire what right we had to open our mouths for the dumb; the people were continually told "it is a shame for a woman to speak in the churches." Paul suffered not a woman to teach but commanded her to be in silence. The pulpit is too sacred a place for woman's foot etc.
Now my dear brothers this invasion of our rights was just such an attack upon us, as that made upon Abolitionists generally when they were told a few years ago that they had no right to discuss the subject of Slavery. Did you take no notice of this assertion? Why no! With one heart and one voice you said, We will settle this right before we go one step further. The time to assert a right is the time when that right is denied. We must establish this right for if we do not, it will be impossi-ble for us to go on with the work of Emancipation. . . . And can you not see that women could do, and would do a hundred times more for the slave if she were not fettered? Why! We are gravely told that we are out of our sphere even when we circulate petitions; out of our "appropriate

sphere" when we speak to women only; and out of it when we sing in the churches. Silence is our province, submission our duty. If then we "give no reason for the hope that is in us", that we have equal rights with our brethren, how can we expect to be permitted much longer to exercise those rights? . . . If we are to do any good in the Anti Slavery cause, our right to labor in it must be firmly established. . . . O that you were here that we might have a good long, long talk over matters and things, then I could explain myself far better. And I think we could convince you that we cannot push Abolitionism forward with all our might until we take up the stumbling block out of the road. . . . How can we expect to be able to hold meetings much longer when people are so diligently taught to despise us for thus stepping out of the "sphere of woman!" . . .

With regard to brother Weld's ultraism on the subject of marriage, he is quite mistaken if he fancies he has got far ahead of us in the human rights reform. We do not think his doctrine at all shocking: it is altogether right. . . . By the bye it will be very important to establish this right for the men of Mass. stoutly declare that women who hold such sentiments of equality can never expect to be courted. They seem to hold out this as a kind of threat to deter us from asserting our rights.

Anti Slavery men are trying very hard to separate what God hath joined together. I fully believe that so far from keeping different moral reformations entirely distinct that no such attempt can ever be successful. They blend with each other like the colors of the rainbow. . . . As there were prophetesses as well as prophets, so there ought to be now female as well as male ministers. Just let this one principle be established and what will become of the power and sacredness of the pastoral office? Is brother Weld frightened at my ultraism? Please write to us soon and let us know what you think after reflecting on this letter. . . .

May the Lord bless you my dear brothers.
A. E. G.

[P.S.] We never mention women's rights in our lectures except so far as is necessary to urge them to meet their responsibilities. We speak of their responsibilities and leave them to infer their rights. We could cross this letter all over but must not encroach on your time.

I should not be at all surprised if the public demanded of us "by what authority doest thou this thing", and if we had to lecture on this subject specifically and call upon the men "to show cause if any they had" why women should not open their mouths for the dumb.

Source: The Letters of Theodore Weld, Angelina Grimké Weld and Sarah M. Grimké, ed. Gilbert Barnes and Dwight Dumond (New York: DaCapo Press, 1970).

Document 8
Ralph Waldo Emerson, "Self-Reliance"

By most accounts, Ralph Waldo Emerson (1803–1882) was the founder and intellectual leader of Transcendentalism. His book *Nature* was a veritable manifesto for the movement. Below is an excerpt from one of his many essays where he advocates individual freedom and, as the title says, "self-reliance." The original essay ran in excess of 10,000 words, so the excerpt below is less than one-tenth of the whole.

In Transcendentalist fashion, Emerson urges people to throw tradition aside and look within themselves for authority and truth. This position directly opposed the Protestant theology and republican political theory that reigned in his day. Protestant theology taught that truth was found in the Bible and that individuals should put themselves under its authority. Republican political theory emphasized the good society and the ways that individuals must submit to the common good, even as they exercise their freedom. Emerson's Transcendental notions of self-reliance were in keeping with the American spirit of individualism, which would grow much stronger throughout the nineteenth century and into the twentieth century. Transcendentalism contributed to the individualistic belief that human beings find their true selves by looking within, instead of conforming to an outward authority such as the Bible, God, or one's community.

I read the other day some verses written by an eminent painter which were original and not conventional. The soul always hears an admonition in such lines, let the subject be what it may. The sentiment they instill is of more value than any thought they may contain. To believe your own thought, to believe that what is true for you in your private heart is true for all men,—that is genius. Speak your latent conviction, and it shall be the universal sense; for the inmost in due time becomes the outmost,——and our first thought is rendered back to us by the trumpets of the Last Judgment. Familiar as the voice of the mind is to each, the highest merit we ascribe to Moses, Plato, and Milton is, that they set at naught books and traditions, and spoke not what men [thought] but what they thought. A man should learn to detect and watch that gleam of light which flashes across his mind from within, more than the lustre of the firmament of bards and sages. Yet he dismisses without notice his thought, because it is his. In every work of genius we recognize our own rejected thoughts: they come back to us with a certain alienated majesty. Great works of art have no more affecting lesson for us than this. They teach us to abide by our spontaneous impression with good-humored inflexibility then most when the whole cry of voices is on the other side. Else, to-morrow a stranger will say with masterly good sense precisely what we have thought and felt all the time, and we shall be forced to take with shame our own opinion from another.

There is a time in every man's education when he arrives at the conviction that envy is ignorance; that imitation is suicide; that he must take himself for better, for worse, as his portion; that though the wide universe is full of good, no kernel of nourishing corn can come to him but through his toil bestowed on that plot of ground which is given to him to till. The power which resides in him is new in nature, and none but he knows what that is which he can do, nor does he know until he has tried. Not for nothing one face, one character, one fact, makes much impression on him, and another none. This sculpture in the memory is not without preestablished harmony. The eye was placed where one ray should fall, that it might testify of that particular ray. We but half express ourselves, and are ashamed of that divine idea which each of us represents. It may be safely trusted as proportionate and of good issues, so it be faithfully imparted, but God will not have his work made manifest by cowards. A man is relieved and gay when he has put his heart into his work and done his best; but what he has said or done otherwise, shall give him no peace. It is a deliverance which does not deliver. In the attempt his genius deserts him; no muse befriends; no invention, no hope.

Trust thyself: every heart vibrates to that iron string. Accept the place the divine providence has found for you, the society of your contemporaries, the connection of events. Great men have always done so, and confided themselves childlike to the genius of their age, betraying their perception that the absolutely trustworthy was seated at their heart, working through their hands, predominating in all their being. And we are now men, and must accept in the highest mind the same transcendent destiny; and not minors and invalids in a protected corner, not cowards fleeing before a revolution, but guides, redeemers, and benefactors, obeying the Almighty effort, and advancing on Chaos and the Dark. . . .

So use all that is called Fortune. Most men gamble with her, and gain all, and lose all, as her wheel rolls. But do thou leave as unlawful these winnings, and deal with Cause and Effect, the chancellors of God. In the Will work and acquire, and thou hast chained the wheel of Chance, and shalt sit hereafter out of fear from her rotations. A political victory, a rise of rents, the recovery of your sick, or the return of your absent friend, or some other favorable event, raises your spirits, and you think good days are preparing for you. Do not believe it. Nothing can bring you peace but yourself. Nothing can bring you peace but the triumph of principles.

Source: Essays, First Series (Boston: James Munroe and Company, 1847).

Document 9
Ralph Waldo Emerson, "The Transcendentalist"

The excerpt below comes from a lecture Emerson gave at the Masonic Temple in Boston in 1842. In it he attempted to define Transcendentalism. Like many religious and philosophical groups in American history, the Transcendentalists never intended to found a movement, and it appears that they never consciously chose their name. Five years after their first meeting in 1837, however, because the group that formed around Emerson had become known as Transcendentalists, Emerson attempted to define the term. Notice that he viewed Transcendentalism as a form of idealism, as opposed to materialism, but that he did not believe there was such a thing as pure Transcendentalism.

The first thing we have to say respecting what are called new views here in New England, at the present time, is, that they are not new, but the very oldest of thoughts cast into the mould of these new times. The light is always identical in its composition, but it falls on a great variety of objects, and by so falling is first revealed to us, not in its own form, for it is formless, but in theirs; in like manner, thought only appears in the objects it classifies. What is popularly called Transcendentalism among us, is Idealism; Idealism as it appears in 1842. As thinkers, mankind have ever divided into two sects, Materialists and Idealists; the first class founding on experience, the second on consciousness; the first class beginning to think from the data of the senses, the second class perceive that the senses are not final, and say, the senses give us representations of things, but what are the things themselves, they cannot tell. The materialist insists on facts, on history, on the force of circumstances, and the animal wants of man; the idealist on the power of Thought and of Will, on inspiration, on miracle, on individual culture. These two modes of thinking are both natural, but the idealist contends that his way of thinking is in higher nature. He concedes all that the other affirms, admits the impressions of sense, admits their coherency, their use and beauty, and then asks the materialist for his grounds of assurance that things are as his senses represent them. But I, he says, affirm facts not affected by the illusions of sense, facts which are of the same nature as the faculty which reports them, and not liable to doubt; facts which in their first appearance to us assume a native superiority to material facts, degrading these into a language by which the first are to be spoken; facts which it only needs a retirement from the senses to discern. Every materialist will be an idealist; but an idealist can never go backward to be a materialist.

The idealist, in speaking of events, sees them as spirits. He does not deny the sensuous fact: by no means; but he will not see that alone. He does not deny the presence of this table, this chair, and the walls of this room, but he looks at these things as the reverse side of the tapestry, as the other end, each being a sequel or completion of a spiritual fact which nearly concerns him. This manner of looking at things, transfers every object in nature from an independent and anomalous position without there, into the consciousness. Even the materialist Condillac, perhaps the most logical expounder of materialism, was constrained to say, "Though we should soar into the heavens, though we should sink into the abyss, we never go out of ourselves; it is always our own thought that we perceive." What more could an idealist say? . . .

In the order of thought, the materialist takes his departure from the external world, and esteems a man as one product of that. The idealist takes his departure from his consciousness, and reckons the world an appearance. The materialist respects sensible masses, Society, Government, social art, and luxury, every establishment, every mass, whether majority of numbers, or extent of space, or amount of objects, every social action. The idealist has another measure, which is metaphysical, namely, the rank which things themselves take in his consciousness; not at all, the size or appearance. Mind is the only reality, of which men and all other natures are better or worse reflectors. Nature, literature, history, are only subjective phenomena. Although in his action overpowered by the laws of action, and so, warmly cooperating with men, even preferring them to himself, yet when he speaks scientifically, or after the order of thought, he is constrained to degrade persons into representatives of truths. He does not respect labor, or the products of labor, namely, property, otherwise than as a manifold symbol, illustrating with wonderful fidelity of details the laws of being; he does not respect government, except as far as it reiterates the law of his mind; nor the church; nor charities; nor arts, for themselves; but hears, as at a vast distance, what they say, as if his consciousness would speak to him through a pantomimic scene. His thought,—that is the Universe. His experience inclines him to behold the procession of facts you call the world, as flowing perpetually outward from an invisible, unsounded centre in himself, centre alike of him and of them, and necessitating him to regard all things as having a subjective or relative existence, relative to that aforesaid Unknown Centre of him. . . .

The Transcendentalist adopts the whole connection of spiritual doctrine. He believes in miracle, in the perpetual openness of the human mind to new influx of light and power; he believes in inspiration, and in ecstasy. He wishes that the spiritual principle should be suffered to demonstrate itself to the end, in all possible applications to the state of man, without the admission of anything unspiritual; that is, anything positive, dogmatic, personal. Thus, the spiritual measure of inspiration is the depth of the thought, and never, who said it? And so he resists all attempts to palm other rules and measures on the spirit than its own. . . .

Source: Nature; Addresses and Lectures (Boston: James Munroe and Company, 1849).

Document 10
Henry David Thoreau on the Art of Walking

More than any other, Thoreau (1817–1862) lived out the Transcendentalist creed that human beings were part of nature. His classic, *Walden,* is based on his attempt to live in solitary fashion in nature. In the essay from which the excerpt below is taken he extols the art of walking through fields and woods as a way of getting in touch with nature. This was not a matter of physical exercise, although that would certainly be a side benefit, but a matter of experiencing and intuiting the natural world, which for the Transcendentalist was none other than the World Spirit of which all are a part. It seems extraordinary that he claims to need four hours of walking per day in order to feel right with himself and the world. One might wonder, how would he have the time to walk that much? But, part of the Transcendentalist's ideal was to keep life simple enough to have time for the really important things, like walking and communing with nature. In the twenty-first century, when life is far more hectic and busy than it was in Thoreau's day, he has something to say to us about how we spend our time. He wants us to ask whether we are nurturing our minds and spirits and taking time for the most important endeavors.

I wish to speak a word for Nature, for absolute freedom and wildness, as contrasted with a freedom and culture merely civil—to regard man as an inhabitant, or a part and parcel of Nature, rather than a member of society. I wish to make an extreme statement, if so I may make an emphatic one, for there are enough champions of civilization: the minister and the school committee and every one of you will take care of that. I have met with but one or two persons in the course of my life who understood the art of Walking, that is, of taking walks—who had a genius, so to speak, for *sauntering,* which word is beautifully derived "from idle people who roved about the country, in the Middle Ages, and asked charity, under pretense of going *a la Sainte Terre,*" to the Holy Land, till the children exclaimed, "There goes a *Sainte-Terrer,*" a Saunterer, a Holy-Lander. . . .

I think that I cannot preserve my health and spirits, unless I spend four hours a day at least—and it is commonly more than that—sauntering through the woods and over the hills and fields, absolutely free from all worldly engagements. You may safely say, A penny for your thoughts, or a thousand pounds. When sometimes I am reminded that the mechanics and shopkeepers stay in their shops not only all the forenoon, but all the afternoon too, sitting with crossed legs, so many of them—as if the legs were made to sit upon, and not to stand or walk upon—I think that they deserve some credit for not having all committed suicide long ago. . . .

When we walk, we naturally go to the fields and woods: what would become of us, if we walked only in a garden or a mall? Even some sects of philosophers have felt the necessity of importing the woods to themselves, since they did not go to the woods. "They planted groves and walks of Platanes," where they took *subdiales ambulationes* in porticos open to the air. Of course it is of no use to direct our steps to the woods, if they do not carry us thither. I am alarmed when it happens that I have walked a mile into the woods bodily, without getting there in spirit. In my afternoon walk I would fain forget all my morning occupations and my obligations to Society. But it sometimes happens that I cannot easily shake off the village. The thought of some work will run in my head and I am not where my body is—I am out of my senses. In my walks I would fain return to my senses. What business have I in the woods, if I am thinking of something out of the woods? I suspect myself, and cannot help a shudder when I find myself so implicated even in what are called good works—for this may sometimes happen.

My vicinity affords many good walks; and though for so many years I have walked almost every day, and sometimes for several days together, I have not yet exhausted them. An absolutely new prospect is a great happiness, and I can still get this any afternoon. Two or three hours' walking will carry me to as strange a country as I expect ever to see. A single farmhouse which I had not seen before is sometimes as good as the dominions of the King of Dahomey. There is in fact a sort of harmony discoverable between the capabilities of the landscape within a circle of ten miles' radius, or the limits of an afternoon walk, and the threescore years and ten of human life. It will never become quite familiar to you. . . .

I took a walk on Spaulding's Farm the other afternoon. I saw the setting sun lighting up the opposite side of a stately pine wood. Its golden rays straggled into the aisles of the wood as into some noble hall. I was impressed as if some ancient and altogether admirable and shining family had settled there in that part of the land called Concord, unknown to me—to whom the sun was servant—who had not gone into society in the village—who had not been called on. I saw their park, their pleasure-ground, beyond through the wood, in Spaulding's cranberry-meadow. The pines furnished them with gables as they grew. Their house was not obvious to vision; the trees grew through it. I do not know whether I heard the sounds of a suppressed hilarity or not. They seemed to recline on the sunbeams. They have sons and daughters. They are quite well. The farmer's cart-path, which leads directly through their hall, does not in the least put them out, as the muddy bottom of a pool is sometimes seen through the reflected skies. They never heard of Spaulding, and do not know that he is their neighbor— notwithstanding I heard him whistle as he drove his team through the house. Nothing can equal the serenity of their lives. . . .

We had a remarkable sunset one day last November. I was walking in a meadow, the source of a small brook, when the sun at last, just before setting, after a cold, gray day, reached a clear stratum in the horizon, and the softest, brightest morning sunlight fell on the dry grass and on the stems of the trees in the opposite horizon and on the leaves of the shrub oaks on the hillside, while our shadows stretched long over the meadow east-ward, as if we were the only motes in its beams. It was such a light as we could not have imagined a moment before, and the air also was so warm and serene that nothing was wanting to make a paradise of that meadow. When we reflected that this was not a solitary phenomenon, never to happen again, but that it would happen forever and ever, an infinite number of evenings, and cheer and reassure the latest child that walked there, it was more glorious still. . . .

Source: Henry David Thoreau, *Excursions* (Boston: Houghton-Mifflin, 1899).

Document 11
Henry David Thoreau, "On Civil Disobedience"

Along with his book *Walden,* "Civil Disobedience" is the most famous and influential work authored by Thoreau (1817–1862). As an act of protest against the Mexican War (1846), Thoreau refused to pay his poll tax and was jailed briefly. He subsequently wrote "On Civil Disobedience," from which the excerpt below is taken, and delivered it as an address to the Concord Lyceum in January 1848. Thoreau believed, as did many abolitionists, that the Mexican War was being fought primarily to expand slave territory.

For this reason, he believed that any complicity with the war, even in paying taxes that might be used to support it, was evil.

In the essay, Thoreau lays out what he believes are the moral options when one's government is engaged in immoral acts that a citizen cannot support. His ideas contributed to the development of nonviolent civil disobedience, wherein one disobeys unjust laws but remains under the authority of the state by submitting to the state's punishment. The essay was an important influence on twentieth-century activists such as Mahatma Gandhi in India and Martin Luther King, Jr., in the United States.

I heartily accept the motto, "That government is best which governs least"; and I should like to see it acted up to more rapidly and systematically. Carried out, it finally amounts to this, which also I believe—"That government is best which governs not at all"; and when men are prepared for it, that will be the kind of government which they will have. Government is at best but an expedient; but most governments are usually, and all governments are sometimes, inexpedient. The objections which have been brought against a standing army, and they are many and weighty, and deserve to prevail, may also at last be brought against a standing government. The standing army is only an arm of the standing government. The government itself, which is only the mode which the people have chosen to execute their will, is equally liable to be abused and perverted before the people can act through it. Witness the present Mexican war, the work of comparatively a few individuals using the standing government as their tool; for in the outset, the people would not have consented to this measure. . . .

How does it become a man to behave toward the American government today? I answer, that he cannot without disgrace be associated with it. I cannot for an instant recognize that political organization as my government which is the slave's government also. . . .

I do not hesitate to say, that those who call themselves Abolitionists should at once effectually withdraw their support, both in person and property, from the government of Massachusetts, and not wait till they constitute a majority of one, before they suffer the right to prevail through them. I think that it is enough if they have God on their side, without waiting for that other one. Moreover, any man more right than his neighbors constitutes a majority of one already. . . .

Under a government which imprisons unjustly, the true place for a just man is also a prison. The proper place today, the only place which Massachusetts has provided for her freer and less despondent spirits, is in her prisons, to be put out and locked out of the State by her own act, as they have already put themselves out by their principles. . . .

I have paid no poll tax for six years. I was put into a jail once on this account, for one night; and, as I stood considering the walls of solid stone, two or three feet thick, the door of wood and iron, a foot thick, and the iron grating which strained the light, I could not help being struck with the foolishness of that institution which treated me as if I were mere flesh and blood and bones, to be locked up. I wondered that it should have concluded at length that this was the best use it could put me to, and had never thought to avail itself of my services in some way. I saw that, if there was a wall of stone between me and my townsmen, there was a still more difficult one to climb or break through before they could get to be as free as I was. I did not for a moment feel confined, and the walls seemed a great waste of stone and mortar. I felt as if I alone of all my townsmen had paid my tax. . . .

There will never be a really free and enlightened State until the State comes to recognize the individual as a higher and independent power, from which all its own power and authority are derived, and treats him accordingly. I please myself with imagining a State at last which can afford to be just to all men, and to treat the individual with respect as a neighbor; which even would not think it inconsistent with its own repose if a few were to live aloof from it, not meddling with it, nor embraced by it, who fulfilled all the duties of neighbors and fellow men. A State which bore this kind of fruit, and suffered it to drop off as fast as it ripened, would prepare the way for a still more perfect and glorious State, which I have also imagined, but not yet anywhere seen.

Source: The Writings of Henry David Thoreau (New York: Houghton, Mifflin, and Co., 1906).

Document 12
Margaret Fuller—"Summer on the Lakes" and "To a Friend"

Margaret Fuller (1810–1850) was perhaps the most influential woman in Transcendentalist circles. Below are two of her poems, written in 1843 and published the next year. She wrote them after spending a summer in the Great Lakes region of the Midwest.

Transcendentalists believed that truth and beauty could often be found or expressed more readily in poetry than in prose-style treatises or even scientific experiments. Like all romantic idealists, they believed that truth was experienced through intuition as opposed to being known through the intellect alone.

"Summer on the Lakes"

Summer days of busy leisure,
Long summer days of dear-bought pleasure,
You have done your teaching well;
Had the scholar means to tell
How grew the vine of bitter-sweet,
What made the path for truant feet,
Winter nights would quickly pass,
Gazing on the magic glass
O'er which the new-world shadows pass;
But, in fault of wizard spell,
Moderns their tale can only tell
In dull words, with a poor reed
Breaking at each time of need.
But those to whom a hint suffices
Mottoes find for all devices,
See the knights behind their shields,
Through dried grasses, blooming fields.

"To a Friend"

Some dried grass-tufts from the wide flowery plain,
A muscle shell from the lone fairy shore,
Some antlers from tall woods which never more
To the wild deer a safe retreat can yield,
An eagle's feather which adorned a Brave,
Well-nigh the last of his despairing band,
For such slight gifts wilt thou extend thy hand
When weary hours a brief refreshment crave?
I give you what I can, not what I would,
If my small drinking-cup would hold a flood,
As Scandinavia sung those must contain
With which the giants gods may entertain;
In our dwarf day we drain few drops, and soon must thirst again.

Source: Margaret Fuller, *Summer on the Lakes, in 1843* (1844).

GLOSSARY OF
SELECTED TERMS

Abolition: The reform movement aimed at abolishing slavery in the United States. Gradual abolitionists wanted to move slowly and end slavery gradually, often with compensation for slave owners. They hoped to avoid armed conflict over slavery. Immediatists called for the immediate end to slavery with no compensation for owners. Products of the revivals of the Second Great Awakening tended to be immediatists.

American Colonization Society: Founded in 1817, this organization advocated freedom for slaves along with their repatriation back to Africa. The colony, then nation, of Liberia was founded by freed American slaves. Before the founding of the American Anti-Slavery Society in 1833, the American Colonization Society was the first and only national organization seeking an end to slavery in the United States

Anxious bench: Invented by Charles Finney, this was a special section of seating at a revival meeting where those who were agonizing over the condition of their souls could sit during the preaching service. Others present would pray for those on the anxious bench.

Arminian: The theological position that emphasizes free will. In opposition to Calvinism, Arminians believe that anyone can be converted at any time by merely deciding to submit to God. Methodists were Arminians from their beginning, and during the Second Great Awakening many former Calvinists from the ranks of Presbyterians and Baptists began to lean toward an Arminian theology.

Brook Farm: A Transcendentalist commune started in 1841 by George and Sophia Ripley. Residents attempted to pool their labor and live communally in an effort to create more leisure time for literary pursuits and other aesthetic pleasures. These activities would help promote peace and harmony, leading to the ideal way of life. The community faltered after a few years and was abandoned in 1847.

Burned-over district: The region of western New York where revivals swept back and forth from the 1820s to the 1840s. Preachers often referred to "revival fires," hence the "burned-over" imagery. Several new religious movements and reform organizations developed there, including Mormonism.

Calvinism: Named for the sixteenth-century theologian John Calvin, this was the dominant theological position in American Protestantism until the Second Great Awakening. Calvinism emphasizes the sovereignty of God, original sin, the depravity of humankind, and the human need for God's unmerited saving grace. Calvinists believe that as a result of original sin all people are depraved and in need of salvation. God predestines some people to be saved and others to be damned, but salvation is God's choice, not that of individuals. Human beings do not choose God, but rather God chooses them. Revivalists of the Second Great Awakening moved away from Calvinism toward Arminian theology that stressed free will and the ability of all human beings to make their own decision to be converted.

Camp meeting: Believed to have occurred for the first time at Gaspar River, Kentucky, in 1800, the camp meeting became a staple of the early Second Great Awakening and continued in some American Protestant denominations well into the twentieth century and is still experienced by many evangelical Protestants even today. The camp meeting consists of many families gathered together in an encampment for a number of days for the purpose of religious worship, especially revivalist preaching. There were multiple services each day, and, if the encampment were large enough, many preachers conducted meetings simultaneously in different locations.

Circuit rider: A Methodist preacher who pastored several congregations simultaneously. He did this by "riding the circuit"—that is, riding on horseback from one congregation to the next, preaching and administering the sacraments. Many circuit riders literally wore themselves out and died young as a result of their efforts to meet the needs of their flocks. The circuit-rider method was ideally suited to the frontier and helped facilitate the revivals of the Second Great Awakening.

Deism: A theological/philosophical position emanating from the Enlightenment. Deists believed that God created the universe, instituted the laws of nature, then withdrew to allow the natural world to run according to those laws. God was like a watchmaker who builds a watch, winds it up, and lets it run naturally. Deists did not believe that God intervened supernaturally in creation. Deism became very significant among the intellectual elites during and after the American Revolution (1776–1783), and it looked as if this might become the dominant theological position in America. The Second Great Awakening, however, was the reassertion of the belief in God's supernatural influence in human affairs. Deism continued to be a significant, but minority, view held mostly by educated elites.

Enlightenment: The late seventeenth- and eighteenth-century intellectual movement built on the foundation of early modern science from the century before. While very diverse, Enlightenment thinkers emphasized the primacy of reason and nature. Essentially, they believed that all that could be known was already present in nature and that the way to knowledge was through the application of human reason to nature via the scientific method. This contrasted with the evangelical Protestant view that some things could be known through reason but that the most important truths were revealed by God in scripture.

Evangelical Protestantism: The belief that the Bible is the ultimate authority in spiritual matters and that human beings stand in need of a supernatural, life-transforming experience of salvation made possible by the death and resurrection of Christ. This was the dominant theological position of Presbyterians, Methodists, Baptists, many Congregationalists, and some Episcopalians. Evangelicals could be Calvinist or Arminian, and most were somewhere in between those two positions. The Second Great Awakening reasserted evangelical dominance in American theology that would continue into the twentieth century when evangelicalism was challenged by theological liberalism, which held that Protestant doctrine must be harmonized with modern ways of thinking in science and literary criticism.

Evangelism: The effort to spread the gospel message of Christianity through a variety of means including revivals, street witnessing, door-to-door canvassing, and handing out tracts.

Evangelist: One who preaches revivals. (see Itinerant and Evangelism)

Feminism: While there are many variations of feminism today, in the nineteenth century, during the period of the first woman's rights movement in American history, feminists desired and demanded basic equality with men in all areas. Many of the leaders of nineteenth-century feminism were products of the revivals of the Second Great Awakening. They believed that, properly interpreted, the Bible taught that men and women were equal before God.

Fruitlands: A Transcendentalist communal experiment started by Bronson Alcott. Believing that all living creatures were related, Alcott opposed the butchery of animals or even the use of animal products. The diet, therefore, consisted primarily of fruit and water, but fruit cultivation was difficult without animal fertilizer. Clothing was mostly linen and canvass, cotton being disallowed because it was produced with slave labor. The commune lasted only from June until December 1843 largely because residents were ill clothed and undernourished.

Holiness: A religious experience advocated first by Methodists then by others during the Second Great Awakening. People who had previously been converted had a second blessing whereby they laid themselves figuratively on the altar as a sacrifice to God. God's acceptance of the sacrifice resulted in the individual's being filled with the holy spirit, leading to spiritual perfection. While this did not mean that a person would never make a mistake again, it did mean that one could will perfectly. The terms "holiness," "second blessing," and "perfection" were used almost interchangeably during the Second Great Awakening and after.

Immediatism: (see Abolition)

Intuition: The Transcendentalist way of experiencing the truth. Whereas orthodox Protestants believed that God reveals truth in an act of divine revelation, and Enlightenment intellectuals believed that truth was discovered by reason applied to nature using the scientific method, Transcendentalists believed that the most important truths could be intuited—that is, felt and experienced. Literature, art, and the natural world should be experienced intuitively, Transcendentalists believed, and individuals were likely to get closer to the truth this way than in studying scripture or scientifically analyzing the natural world. This was a romantic concept that emphasized feeling rather than thinking.

Itinerant: A preacher who travels from one place to another preaching revivals.

Liberal Protestantism: A theological position that began with Unitarianism in the early nineteenth century. Liberalism sought to harmonize Protestant theology with modern ideas emanating from the Enlightenment. Ideas that could not be understood rationally were usually deemed nonessential and therefore dismissed. The concept of the trinity (God having three natures in one) was the first to go. Liberals tended to view many of the Bible's teachings as myths or stories from which timeless truths could be gleaned rather than as actual historical events or teachings that should be taken literally. In the second half of the nineteenth century, after Charles Darwin's work appeared, liberal Protestant theologians harmonized theology with evolution, eventually adopting the view that even the Christian faith had evolved over time. This stance pitted evangelicals, who believe that the faith taught in the Bible is the most pure and authoritative, against liberals, who believe the faith found in the Bible is Christianity in a rudimentary and undeveloped form.

New measures: Charles Finney's revivalistic methods. They consisted primarily of the protracted meeting, the anxious bench, daytime prayer meetings before nightly meetings, and canvassing the town to invite people to attend the evening revivals. Finney also named sinners by name from the pulpit as he preached and allowed women to pray in services. These and other innovations resulted in Finney being called the "father of modern revivalism."

Over soul: Ralph Waldo Emerson's term for the world spirit that connects all living things. This over soul was the all-encompassing divinity of which human beings were part. This Transcendentalist concept led to the desire to commune with nature because to do so was to partake of the divine.

Perfectionism: (see Holiness)

Populist religion: Religion that appeals directly to the common person in democratic form, meaning that the preachers and churches that flourish are the ones that can win the most converts. Before the Second Great Awakening, ministers often gained the mantle of authority as a result of their education and the elite status that ordination within a mainstream denomination afforded them. During the revivals of the Second Great Awakening, however, the preachers who became most influential and popular were those who appealed directly to the people in plain language anyone could understand. Often these preachers were not highly educated. This populist element in American Christianity can still be seen in the number of popular Protestant preachers who communicate primarily through television. With little theological education and in some cases no backing from a denominational authority, they nevertheless have thousands and sometimes millions of followers who support their ministry.

Protracted Meeting: Like camp meetings in rural areas, the protracted meetings in urban centers consisted of revival services nightly for a number of weeks. Charles Finney is often credited with popularizing them, but no one can be sure if he was the first urban evangelist to hold protracted meetings. (see New measures)

Restorationism: The Protestant attempt to restore pure, New Testament Christianity like that found in the book of Acts. While the restorationist urge started originally in the Protestant Reformation of the sixteenth century, it was renewed and energized by the revivals of the Second Great Awakening. Under the leadership of Alexander Campbell and Barton Stone, the restorationist impulse produced the Disciples of Christ. The Mormons, founded in the 1840s by Joseph Smith, have also been considered a restoration movement.

Second blessing: (see Holiness)

Social-control theory: The interpretation of the Second Great Awakening that views revivals as socially conservative because they tended to reduce misbehavior, sloth, and drunkenness among urban workers. Social-control interpreters believe capitalist business owners promoted revivals partly as a way of ensuring that their workers lived rightly and were maximally productive. In other words, revivals were a top-down phenomenon. After flourishing in the 1980s, social-control theory has been eclipsed by the view that revivals were a populist phenomenon that empowered common people by giving them a sense of equality and power to resist unjust working conditions. Viewed this way, revivals were for the most part a grassroots, or bottom-up, phenomenon.

Spiritual exercises: The name given to physical manifestations of the power of God during the early camp-meeting revivals of the Second Great Awakening. Exercises included the falling exercise, jerking exercise, dancing exercise, barking exercise, laughing exercise, running exercise, and singing exercise. These names are usually credited to Barton Stone's observations at the Cane Ridge revival that he planned and promoted. Highly controversial, some believed the exercises to be genuine, while others thought them excessive and without merit. The exercises are part of the reason that the revivals at Gaspar River and Cane Ridge have been hard to evaluate fairly.

Temperance: The reform movement that opposed consumption of alcohol launched in the 1820s and largely a result of the revivals of the Second Great Awakening. Early temperance advocates often opposed only excessive drinking and drunkenness, but over time most came to oppose all use of fermented or distilled spirits. In the late nineteenth century, temperance advocates began to call for legal measures against the production and consumption of all alcoholic beverages. This became known as prohibition and culminated in 1919 with the passage of the Eighteenth Amendment to the U.S. Constitution, which made alcohol illegal across the nation until the Twenty-first Amendment repealed the Eighteenth in 1833.

Transcendentalism: A romantic and idealistic movement started in the 1830s by Ralph Waldo Emerson and friends. Transcendentalism, like all romantic movements, was an attempt to experience, feel, and intuit the truth. While there were diverse views within the movement, most Transcendentalists followed Emerson in believing that the universe was part of a world soul or over soul that was divine. Individuals should seek harmony and unity with nature as the highest form of human existence. Such harmony could be achieved by communing with the natural world through long walks, by reading poetry that inspired one's soul, or by contemplating the meaning of life through meditative study. Transcendentalism was in many ways a revolt against Enlightenment science and its emphasis on rational study and against orthodox Protestantism with its notion of a God who was a being other than creation. (see Intuition)

Unitarianism: The first manifestation of liberal Protestantism, Unitarianism was an attempt to reconcile Congregational (Puritan) theology with Enlightenment rationalism. The result was the rejection of the Trinity because it could not be rationally explained. This position got its name originally from a unitarian view of God that had appeared as early as the sixteenth century with Michael Servetus who was burned at the stake in John Calvin's Geneva in 1553. Once Unitarians jettisoned the Trinity, other supernatural aspects of Protestant theology were soon called into question, including the deity of Christ and his physical resurrection, leaving only the moral program of the Christian faith intact. Most of the Transcendentalists were originally Unitarians, and a few attempted to remain so even after taking on the Transcendentalist mantle. (see Liberal Protestantism)

Voluntarism: The reform impulse engendered largely by the revivals of the Second Great Awakening that led to the formation of many voluntary societies such as the American Anti-Slavery Society, the American Temperance Society, and the American Education Society. The voluntaristic spirit remains intact as many Americans in the twenty-first century join a variety of private agencies and clubs to help improve American society.

ANNOTATED BIBLIOGRAPHY

Abzug, Robert H. *Passionate Liberator: Theodore Dwight Weld and the Dilemma of Reform*. New York: Oxford University Press, 1980. Definitive biography of Weld by prominent scholar of nineteenth- and twentieth-century American culture.

Albanese, Catherine L. *Corresponding Motion: Transcendental Religion and the New America*. Philadelphia: Temple University Press, 1977. An interpretation of Transcendentalism as a religious movement and its role in shaping nineteenth-century America.

Bellah, Robert, et. al. *Habits of the Heart: Individualism and Community in American Life*. Updated edition. Berkeley: University of California Press, 1985. An analysis of American individualism and its drawbacks by a prominent team of sociologists. While mostly covering late-twentieth-century America, the book's coverage of individualism provides important context for understanding both revivalism and Transcendentalism, especially the latter.

Boles, John. *The Great Revival: Beginnings of the Bible Belt*. Lexington: University Press of Kentucky, 1972. One of the most important scholarly treatments of the frontier revivals that launched the Second Great Awakening, paying particular attention to how they shaped the South.

Boller, Paul F., Jr., *American Transcendentalism, 1830–1860*. New York: G.P. Putman's Sons, 1974. Accessible general history of Transcendentalism by scholar of American culture.

Cameron, Kenneth Walter. *Young Emerson's Transcendental Vision: An Exposition of His World View with an Analysis of the Structure, Backgrounds, and Meaning of Nature* (1836). Hartford: Transcendental Books, 1971. An in-depth study of the formation of Emerson's thought as manifested in his ground-breaking work *Nature*.

Cross, Whitney. *The Burned-Over District*. New York: Harper and Row, 1950. Old, but still useful, interpretation of western New York during the Second Great Awakening. Shows how revivals swept back and forth across the region producing significant religious developments, some of which competed with the orthodox Protestantism that spawned the revivals in the first place.

Fish, Roy. *When Heaven Touched Earth: The Awakening of 1858 and Its Effects.* Azle, Tex.: Need of the Times Publishers, 1996. A popular and sympathetic rendition of the urban revivals of 1858.

Grodzins, Dean. *American Heretic: Theodore Parker and Transcendentalism.* Chapel Hill: The University of North Carolina Press, 2002. The first of a projected two volumes on Parker. Attempts to restore his reputation as a leading Transcendentalist and liberal preacher.

Hambrick-Stowe, Charles E. *Charles G. Finney and the Spirit of American Evangelicalism.* Grand Rapids, Mich.: Eerdmans Publishing Company, 1996. An accessible biography of the leading preacher of the Second Great Awakening. Written by a scholar, the book is for a popular audience.

Harding, Walter. *The Days of Henry David Thoreau: A Biography.* New York: Dover Publications, 1962. Standard biography of Thoreau.

Hardman, Keith J. *Charles Grandison Finney, 1792–1875: Revivalist and Reformer.* Syracuse, N.Y.: Syracuse University Press, 1987. Standard scholarly biography of Finney. Contains more footnote documentation than Hambrick-Stowe's biography listed above.

Hatch, Nathan. *The Democratization of American Christianity.* New Haven, Conn.: Yale University Press, 1989. Groundbreaking interpretation of religion in America during the period of the Second Great Awakening. Indispensable reading for anyone attempting to understand how revivalist religion shaped and was shaped by America's democratic culture.

Johnson, Paul. *A Shopkeeper's Millennium: Society and Revivals in Rochester, New York, 1815–1837.* New York: Hill and Wang, 1978. Provocative interpretation of the effects of revivals in Rochester, New York, during the Second Great Awakening. Part of the "social-control" school of interpretation, Johnson sees religion as a conservative, restraining influence on working-class people. Other interpretations challenge this view, arguing that religion empowered average Americans rather than suppressing their desires for justice.

Koster, Donald N. *Transcendentalism in America.* Boston: Twayne Publishers, 1975. A brief but instructive and interesting history of Transcendentalism.

Lincoln, C. Eric and Lawrence H. Mamiya. *The Black Church in the African American Experience.* Durham, N.C.: Duke University Press, 1998. An interpretation of African American religion by two prominent scholars.

Long, Kathryn. *The Revival of 1857–58: Interpreting an American Religious Awakening.* New York: Oxford University Press, 1998. The definitive interpretation of the urban revivals of 1857 and 1858.

Marsden, George. *Religion and American Culture.* New York: Oxford University Press, 1990. Readable textbook overview of religion in America. Argues that American culture has always been simultaneously religious and secular.

McLoughlin, William G. *Revivals, Awakenings, and Reform: An Essay on Religion and Social Change in America, 1606–1977.* Chicago: University of Chicago Press, 1978. Scholarly interpretation of the connection between religion and reform in American history. Interprets revivals as perhaps the most important agent of social change.

Raboteau, Albert J. *A Fire in the Bones: Reflections on African-American Religious History.* Boston: Beacon Press, 1995. Perhaps the most influential interpretation of African American religion to date. A standard work on the subject; the starting place for understanding African American religion.

——. *Slave Religion: The "Invisible Institution" in the Antebellum South.* New York: Oxford University Press, 1978. Raboteau's earliest work on African American religion. Raboteau documents extensively the importance of black churches among slaves. A wealth of data.

Richardson, Robert D., Jr. *Emerson: The Mind on Fire.* Berkeley: University of California Press, 1995. The standard and most influential biography of the founder of the Transcendentalist movement.

Rose, Anne C. *Transcendentalism as a Social Movement, 1830–1850.* New Haven, Conn.: Yale University Press, 1981. Analyzes how Transcendentalism affected society through reform efforts, literary endeavors, and alternative living arrangements such as Brook Farm. A standard work for understanding how the ideas of Transcendentalism were translated into social life.

Shepard, Odell. *Pedlar's Progress: The Life of Bronson Alcott.* Boston: Little, Brown, 1937. Old, but still useful biography of one of Transcendentalism's original members.

Smith, Timothy. *Revivalism and Social Reform: American Protestantism on the Eve of the Civil War.* Baltimore: Johns Hopkins Press, 1980. Originally appearing in the late 1950s, Smith documented the connection between revivalism and social reform movements such as abolition, temperance, and women's rights.

Sobel, Mechal. *Trabelin' On: The Slave Journey to an Afro-Baptist Faith.* Westport, Conn.: Greenwood Press, 1979. A provocative and highly interpretative account of African American religion.

Sutton, William R. *Journeymen for Jesus: Evangelical Artisans Confront Capitalism in Jacksonian Baltimore.* University Park.: Pennsylvania State University Press, 1998. An analysis of the effects of revivalist religion in Baltimore primarily during the 1830s and 1840s. Sutton's interpretation directly challenges the "social-control" school of Paul Johnson because he argues that religion radicalized working-class society.

Wilmore, Gayraud S. *Black Religion and Black Radicalism: An Interpretation of the Religious History of Afro-American People,* 3d ed., rev and enl. Maryknoll, N.Y.: Orbis Books, 1998. A sound and enduring interpretation of

African American religion that first appeared in the early 1970s. A great synthesis of scholarship on the subject.

Wyatt-Brown, Bertram. *Lewis Tappan and the Evangelical War Against Slavery*. Cleveland, Ohio: The Press of Case Western Reserve University, 1969. Standard scholarly biography of Lewis Tappan.

INDEX

About the Author

BARRY HANKINS is Associate Professor of History and Church-State Studies, Baylor University, Waco, TX. He is the author or co-editor of *New Religious Movements and Religious Liberty in America* (2002), *Uneasy in Babylon: Southern Baptist Conservatives and American Culture* (2002), *Welfare Reform and Faith-Based Organizations* (1999), and *God's Rascal: J. Frank Norris and the Beginnings of Southern Fundamentalism* (1996).